Stewart Riley

HELENA STAR

An Epic Adventure through the Murky Underworld of International Drug Smuggling

Robert D. Reed Publishers

Robert D. Reed Publishers • Bandon, OR

Robert D. Reed Publishers
P.O. Box 1992
Bandon, OR 97411
Phone: 541-347-9882; Fax: -9883
E-mail: 4bobreed@msn.com
Website: www.rdrpublishers.com

Editor: Cleone Reed
Cover Designer: Cleone Reed
Book Designer: Amy Cole

Cover Photo: Indian Ocean Island Sunset by Dmitri Laudin

Soft Cover: 978-1-944297-82-4
EBook: 978-1-944297-83-1

Library of Congress Control Number: 2020943992

Designed and Formatted in the United States of America

DEDICATION

To my loving and accepting wife, Laurie,
and our children, Jessica and Pete,
and in loving memory of my older brother, Pete,
whose extraordinary legacy
provided me with a lifetime of sustenance.

ACKNOWLEDGMENTS

To all those, who over the decades of my fascinating career, constantly asked why I had never written a book, you inspired me to finally sit down and give it a go.

I want to give special thanks to my long-time friend and distinguished author, Ron Clark, for his support, suggestions, encouragement, and editing expertise; and another long-time friend and lawyer, Doug Dunham, for his editorial assistance. I am grateful to esteemed attorneys Steve Schroeder, Bill Urich, and Rick Troberman for helping me fill in some blanks, particularly Steve, who was a fountain of information. The ever-patient Brita Merkel helped direct me to sources of information at the National Archives. Many thanks also to Cleone Reed for her brilliance and unforgettable assistance in putting the final touches on this endeavor and designing a sensational cover. I would also like to express my deepest appreciation to Amy Cole for making the interior pages of the book come alive and to the publisher, Bob Reed, for overseeing it all and taking a chance on a first-time author.

Above all, I am indebted to my family—my wife, Laurie, and our children, Jessica and Pete, who read early drafts of the book and provided invaluable advice and encouragement.

CONTENTS

CAST OF CHARACTERS

Aleman, Lola: Captain Rubies' wife

Arieta-Lineros, Pedro Jose: Colombian coconspirator

Azuero, Alvaro: Prominent Colombian attorney, who assisted the conspirators in laundering money

Bayley, Christopher: King County Prosecuting Attorney, who indicted his predecessor and All-American football player, Charles O. Carroll

Becker, Dr. Mark: Prospective witness, who died of an overdose in a seedy motel in Miami

Bowen, Dean: Coconspirator, who helped unload marijuana

Charles O. Carroll: King County Prosecuting Attorney and All-American football player, indicted by his successor

Cooke, Guillermo: Felon, who provided evidence linking former police captain to the conspiracy

Coughenour, John: U.S. District Court Judge

Del Valle, Angel "Tito": U.S. Marshal, who arrested Mike Lund

Emery, John: Felon, who surreptitiously taped a conversation for the government with flamboyant San Francisco attorney Robert Moran

Fisher, Ivan: Eric Hale's high-profile Manhattan Attorney

Friedman, Ron: Assistant U.S. Attorney

Gaitan, Jose: Assistant U.S. Attorney

Hale, Eric: David Victorson's partner and major coconspirator

Hodgman, William: Law student who Guillermno Cooke threatened to kill and who became heavily involved in prosecution of O.J. Simpson

Hogan, Bill: Assistant U.S. Attorney who assisted in the prosecution of Robert Moran and then transferred to the Chicago U.S. Attorney's office

Hughes, Samuel: Barry Wilson's banker at Allied Bank of Texas in Houston

John, Walter: Coast Guard Lt. Commander, who led the boarding party that seized the Helena Star

Jones, Charles: Gave access to Guillermo Cooke to take Moran's cash out of Jones' safe deposit box

Jones, Richard: Assistant U.S. Attorney

Karnik, Patricia: Mike Lund's girlfriend and coconspirator

Kennedy, Anthony: Judge, U.S. Court of Appeals for the Ninth Circuit and later Justice of the U.S. Supreme Court

Kessler, Susan: Prospective witness, who died of an overdose in a seedy motel in Miami

Kinzel, Bill: Chief Criminal Deputy, King County Prosecutor's Office

Larson, Stan: Fellow freestyle skier with Mike Lund

Lund, Mike: Former champion freestyle skier and coconspirator

Martinovich, Walter: Retired law enforcement agent who carried cash for Robert Moran to Grand Cayman for deposit in bank

McGovern, Water T.: U.S. District Court Judge

McGowen, Patricia: Robert Moran's housekeeper and former classmate of Hargreaves Rawstrom

Miller, Chet: An acquaintance of Mike Lund, who lived nearby on Sequim Bay

Moran, Robert: High-profile San Francisco attorney and coconspirator

Morgan, Charles O.: Attorney for Robert Moran

Morgan, Charles: Commander of Coast Guard Cutter Yocona that seized the Helena Star

Morton, Bob: Sold Knik Wind tug and Chignik barge to Mike Lund

Niemi, William: Owner of famous racing sailboat, Joli, and former President of Eddie Bauer

O'Brien, Bill: San Francisco attorney

O'Brien, Herb: Convicted of smuggling cocaine from Chile in hollowed out water skis

Osorio-Pacheco, Carlos: Colombian coconspirator

Ospina, Homero: Coconspirator, who purchased water pump for Helena Star

Perlaza, Pervi: Loaned money to Captain Rubies

Prange, Jim: DEA agent

Rawstrom, Hargreaves: Opened bank account in Grand Cayman at former classmate Patricia McGowen's request

Rubies, Domingo: Son of Captain Rubies

Rubies, Roman: Captain of the Helena Star

Savage, Tony: Attorney for Bill O'Brien

Sawicki, Lyle: Coconspirator involved in distribution of offloaded marijuana

Schroeder, Steve: Assistant U.S. Attorney

Schwartz, Irwin: Federal Public Defender

Shorett, Dave: Attorney for James Turner

Sim, Ron: Assistant U.S. Attorney

Smith, Dan: Attorney for First Mate Pedro Vera

Sweigert, Philip: U.S. Magistrate

Starcher, Wendy: Mike Lund's third wife

Troberman, Rick: Attorney for Mike Lund

Turner, James: Offloading expert

Ulibarri, Paul: Crewed on the Joli and helped William Niemi locate her in Sequim Bay

Vera, Pedro: First Mate of the Helena Star

Victorson, David: Major American coconspirator

Voorhees, Donald: U.S. District Court Judge

Weinberg, John: U.S. Magistrate

Wolover, Al: Towed the Chignik barge from Seattle to Port Angeles

INTRODUCTION

THIS IS THE EPIC TALE OF THE MOTOR VESSEL HELENA STAR. On April 17, 1978, the United States Coast Guard seized the aging freighter 140 miles off Washington State's coast with its cargo hold loaded with hundreds of bales of marijuana, the west coast's largest pot bust, worth an estimated street value at the time of $74 million. A couple weeks later, federal drug agents seized the sleek Joli, a 61-foot sailboat, for its suspected role in the case. A past winner of the prestigious Victoria to Maui sailboat race, the Joli had been purchased the previous summer from William Niemi, Jr., former president of Seattle based Eddie Bauer, by champion freestyle skier Mike Lund of Sequim, Washington. The attorney for the captain of the Helena Star provides an insider's unvarnished account of the case from the trenches. The freighter and the conspirators involved were in the news from its seizure in 1978 to its death by sinking in 2013. This drug bust and the ensuing events make up an unbelievable, but true saga with twists and turns about the inner workings of a Colombian-American drug cartel, smuggling on a massive scale, money laundering, the capture of fugitives in Bolivia, suspicious deaths, the lives of some high-profile individuals, and courtroom battles in Seattle and San Francisco. It also provides a unique and incisive look into the mind of a criminal defense attorney.

1

CAPTAIN RUBIES

IT WAS APRIL 19, 1978. I WAS IN THE LOCK-UP AREA OF THE United States Marshal's Office in the old United States Courthouse in Seattle, Washington. The lock-up area was usually populated with new arrestees or detainees waiting for their court appearances. I was meeting with a client of mine, who had been arrested going through U.S. Customs at Seattle-Tacoma International Airport. After attempting to smuggle valuable jewels from the Far East into the United States to avoid paying duty, my client had been charged with smuggling in the United States District Court for the Western District of Washington. While I was conferring with her in the lock-up, it came to my attention that the Customs agents had not seized all the jewels in her possession. I was astounded to find out that she had secreted some of them in her mouth—the most valuable ones I presume. In my work as a criminal defense attorney, I have found that surprises like this are commonplace.

After I finished conferring with her, I was hailed by a grizzled looking man, who was also in lock-up and had been arrested with eight others two days earlier by the United States Coast Guard on the high seas of the Pacific Ocean approximately 140 miles off the coast of Washington State. He was the captain of the motor vessel (MV) Helena Star, a small freighter with hundreds of bales of marijuana stashed in its cargo hold. His name was Roman Ferrer Rubies. He had just arrived in lock-up along with his eight other crew members. It had taken the Coast Guard and Drug Enforcement Agents two days to transport them and escort the Helena Star to Seattle. Captain Rubies was waiting for his initial court appearance that afternoon and was in desperate need of an attorney. He spoke excellent English with a Spanish accent. I conferred with him for over an hour, after which he provided me with a modest retainer—modest because his financial resources had been substantially depleted as the Helena Star tried to flee from the Coast Guard Cutter Yocona. Five thousand dollars in cash flew off the stern of the freighter into the Pacific Ocean so that the captain would not appear to the American authorities to be more than just a small cog in the wheel of a well-financed and sophisticated smuggling operation. He was just a courier, transporting a shipload of product from one place to another.

I gave Captain Rubies the usual spiel that I gave to all my clients. I can't perform miracles. All I can promise you is to provide my best professional ability. Speak with no one regarding the facts of the case except me. A closed mouth catches no flies. In other words, keep your mouth shut.

All our private conversations are covered by the attorney/client privilege. Anything that you tell me in private cannot be relayed to anyone else in the world without your consent. You could confess to a murder and I could not divulge this to anyone—not the authorities, not my wife, not a judge, not your friends or loved ones—no one. Any

WHEN YOU ARE IN DEEP TROUBLE, LOOK STRAIGHT AHEAD, KEEP YOUR MOUTH SHUT and

SAY NOTHING.

FOX HUNT

violation of this principle by me would be a violation of the ethics that I am bound by as a lawyer authorized to practice law. Because of the attorney/client privilege, it is extremely important that you be totally truthful with me. If there are incriminating circumstances or embarrassing incidents in your past, I want to know about them up front, so that I can be prepared to deal with them. Do not wait to spill your guts to me, because I don't like surprises down the road when I may have no time to prepare to deal with them. Not being truthful with me may jeopardize my commitment to represent you. I may withdraw from representing you if you are not candid with me. By the time that your case is over, I expect to know more about you than you know about yourself. In your situation as an alien with no legal status in the United States, you have the same Constitutional rights as a U.S. citizen, and rest assured that I will vigorously pursue these rights for you. What a great country! You must understand that I will make all strategic decisions regarding your case after consulting with you—— all except two decisions that are yours to make and yours only—the decision whether to plead guilty and, if you decide to go to trial, the decision whether to testify in your own behalf. Our system of justice in the United States is not an inquisitorial system as is prevalent in many other nations. In the United States, you have the right to remain silent and no one can force you to testify against yourself.

I was never known for having a great bedside manner when meeting with clients. I wasn't going to be their social worker. Some attorneys in my view get too close to their clients. I tried to avoid that. I was not their friend. I was their lawyer. Becoming good friends with one's clients eliminates perspective and may color one's objectivity. I was not about to invite a client home for dinner while his future was in my hands, even my white-collar clients.

I represented the captain at his initial appearance that afternoon, during which he and his eight crew members were advised of certain rights. Magistrate Philip Sweigert set his bail at $25,000 and that of the crew at $10,000 each. Assistant U.S. Attorney Ron Sim represented the government. Irwin Schwartz, the Federal Public Defender, represented one of the crew members. Together we questioned the sufficiency of the complaint against our clients, arguing that there was no evidence the vessel was headed for the United States because it was seized 140 miles from our coastline. The cargo could well have been going to Canada. It is not a crime in the United States to import marijuana from the high seas into Canada. The Magistrate rejected our argument. I was confirmed as Roman's attorney of record and a preliminary hearing on charges of conspiring to import a controlled substance into the United States was set for April 28.

Mr. Sim indicated to the magistrate that he had received inquiries from various members of the press for access to the defendants. Sim, Irwin Schwartz, and I then asked the magistrate to issue an order forbidding the marshal or jail officials from allowing anyone other than attorneys for the accused men to discuss the case with them. The magistrate then signed such an order limiting access to the prisoners.

The other crewmen identified at the hearing were Pedro Vera, 43, of Bogota, Colombia; Juan Elles, 43, of Cartagena, Colombia; Manuel De Oliveira, 32, of Belem, Brazil; Edinel Martinez, 29, of Bocachica, Colombia; Fernando Diaz, 26, of Tumaco, Colombia; Emeris Segura, 29, of Tumaco, Colombia; Jose Torres, of Arboletes, Antigua (with a Colombian passport); and Efren Garcia Landazuri, 31, of Tumaco, Colombia.

Roman assured me that more funds for his defense would be on their way. I told him that I would rather spend my time working on his case, than worrying about how or when I would be paid. As Al Capone was rumored to say, "A good mouthpiece is worth whatever he wants." I felt that he trusted me and that we had built a good rapport within a short period of time. I was not about to paint a rosy picture about his future. Unfortunately, a few lawyers in my opinion over promise and under deliver. I preferred to under promise and hopefully over deliver.

Roman was lean—6 feet and 160 pounds—polite and respectful, but quite taciturn. His visage was weathered from long stretches at sea. He was 46 years old, born on May 30, 1931, in Artesa de Segre,

Spain, the third son of a middle-class Spanish family. He was a citizen of Spain and, when I met him, a resident of Cartagena, Colombia. His father was killed in the Spanish Civil War. Roman completed high school in 1949. From 1952 to 1956 he went to nautical school in Barcelona. After graduation he spent two years as an apprentice seaman to qualify as a ship's officer. In 1959, Roman received his mate's license. Due to lack of employment and low wages in Spain, he took a job as a third mate for a Panamanian motor vessel flagship, the "Cali," owned by the Continental Shipping Company of Panama. This ship had a regular route of New York City to Barranquilla, Colombia, to Cristobal, Panama, through the Panama Canal to Buenaventura on the Pacific coast of Colombia, back through the Canal to Jacksonville, Florida, and on to New York.

By 1963, Roman had completed the necessary time at-sea requirements to allow him the opportunity to apply for a captain's license. He returned for another six months study at nautical school, after which he passed the examination required to become a licensed captain.

In 1965, Roman returned to work again for the Cali Corporation as a first mate until an opening for a captain came up. From May 1965 to April 1969, he was captain of the MV Cali with the same run as before. In 1969, the ship was sold and the company went out of business. That was the last year that Roman had put into the United States prior to his arrest on April 17, 1978. He had saved $40,000, which was parked in a savings account at a bank in New York.

Roman decided to leave Spain and relocate to the most beautiful city that he had seen during his travels up and down the Atlantic and Pacific Oceans and through the Caribbean. The decision was easy. He would make his new home in the Caribbean port city of Cartagena, Colombia, where winter does not exist. It was close to Barranquilla and the enticing Islas del Rosario, an archipelago of about 30 islands right off the coast from Cartagena.

After arriving in Cartagena in 1969, Roman decided to go into the fishing business. With $25,000 left from what he had saved and the assistance of a $60,000 loan from the Instituto de Fomento

Industrial, which was a Colombian governmental agency comparable to our Small Business Administration, he purchased a shrimp boat and started fishing off the north coast of Colombia. He married his wife, Lola, in 1974. They had one son, Domingo, born in 1976. Roman had been in the fishing business right up until the time that he went aboard the Helena Star in February of 1978.

The loan from the Instituto had been paid down to $27,000 but carried an interest rate of 15%. On October 15, 1972, the loan was refinanced, requiring it to be paid off by October 15, 1977. Unfortunately, Roman was not able to pay off the loan by the due date and the loan began accruing interest at the exorbitant rate of 26%. Fishing was poor and he had suffered other business reversals. He borrowed a total of $15,000 from someone by the name of Pervi Perlaza and paid off the loan from the Instituto. Shortly thereafter, Roman lost his shrimp boat. He had chartered it to some guys who apparently were going to use it to smuggle coffee into Panama. Unfortunately, during the voyage between Cartagena and Panama, the shrimp boat sank. During the middle of February 1978, Perlaza demanded repayment of the $15,000 loan and advised Roman that the money loaned to him had come from two of Perlaza's friends. Roman could not pay back the loan, so Perlaza asked him to meet with his friends at Estrella Del Mar, a cantina in Cartagena.

Perlaza introduced him to Senor Osorio from Barranquilla, believed by the Drug Enforcement Administration to be Carlos Osorio-Pacheco, and Senor Arieta-Lineros from Medellin, Colombia, believed by the DEA to be Pedro Jose Arieta-Lineros—"described as a Latin male with a cocked eye." Ramon advised these gentlemen that he could not repay the loan. They offered to forgive the loan, if he would act as the captain of one of their vessels and transport a large quantity of marijuana to the Pacific Northwest. If the trip was successful, they would pay him $20,000 as a bonus. Roman was in a tough spot. After much reflection, he agreed to this proposal.

At the time of this meeting at the cantina, Roman observed an Anglo male in his late twenties that Osorio pointed out as the purchaser of the marijuana to be transported up the coasts of Central and North America. This man was probably an American named David Victorson. I later reviewed Victorson's passport, which indicated that he had been in Colombia in February 1978. Victorson and his best friend, Eric Hale, had transported large sums of money from the United States to Colombia, which were used to purchase a huge amount of marijuana. Within a few days, the two Colombian "businessmen," Osorio and Arieta-Lineros, took Roman to a bay not far from Cartagena, where the Helena Star was anchored.

The Helena Star was built in Westerbroek, Holland, in 1947 and was formerly named "Fraternite." The 161-foot, small freighter packed an eight-cylinder turbo-charged Lister diesel engine rated at 600 horsepower, installed in 1974. The current owners had purchased the vessel at Tortola Island, one of the British Virgin Islands, on December 22, 1976. She sailed to Bonaire in the Netherlands Antilles, also in the Caribbean and on January 30, 1978, obtained a Deratting Certificate issued by the Chief Health Inspector, indicating that it was a British vessel. Apparently, there were no rats cavorting on board the ship. Shortly thereafter, Captain Rubies boarded the vessel and took over the steering wheel. It was a large, elegant wheel, polished by the hands of many helmsman.

Roman first sailed the vessel to Aruba, also in the Netherlands Antilles, where on February 24 she took on 14,800 gallons of fuel oil. She cleared Aruba and proceeded to Barahona in the Dominican Republic, where on February 28, 1978, she was loaded with 400 tons of gypsum for ballast and a means of raising the bottom of the cargo hold to more easily offload its expected cargo of marijuana on the high seas of the North Pacific. The consignee of the gypsum was Pedro Jose Arietta, one of the two Colombian businessmen. A letter of clearance was issued by the vessel's agent to the port captain indicating that the Helena Star was bound for the port of Esmeraldas, Ecuador, on the west coast of South America, just south of Colombia. The vessel next sailed to Cartagena.

Roman hired Pedro Vera to be his first mate on the Helena Star's ill-fated run with the same rank as the chief engineer. Roman had met

Pedro a few years earlier while trawling for shrimp. He had recently resurfaced, was broke and in need of a job. He viewed Captain Rubies as a schooled mariner and cultured European. Pedro was 43 years old, originally from Bogota, Colombia, and supposedly had no criminal record. He said he had only smoked marijuana once—that the experience paled in comparison to the sweet intoxications brought on by French cognac or Colombian rum. He was expecting to be paid $15,000 if the venture was successful. Success should have been relatively easy to determine. If the mothership offloaded the product and the product was distributed, the run would be a success. On the other hand, if the product was seized by the Coast Guard or Drug Enforcement Administration, prison in the United States, Canada, or even Colombia was a very real possibility, if not a probability. If the run was not successful, the buyers of the marijuana would be out a bundle of cash and payment of $15,000 to Pedro Vera would turn out to be a pipedream.

On March 1, the Helena Star dropped anchor in Bahia de Cartagena, several miles offshore from Cartagena, Colombia, the only walled city in South America. Colombia borders both the Pacific Ocean and the Caribbean Sea, with Panama intersecting it in the Northwest. The Caribbean side of Colombia has an extensive shoreline facing north toward Jamaica and Cuba, running almost 1,000 miles from its border with Panama to the west to its border with Venezuela to the east.

Cartagena is located on the Caribbean Sea and was founded in 1533. It was named after Cartagena, Spain, and is now the fifth largest city in Colombia. During the colonial era, Cartagena was a key port for the import of enslaved Africans. It was raided many times by marauding pirates trying to steal Peruvian silver headed for Spain. Most notably, Sir Francis Drake attacked the city in 1586 with 23 ships and 3,000 men. Drake burned it to the ground—some 200 houses and the cathedral. The current walled city and its imposing fortress were the result of the carnage perpetrated by Sir Francis. From then on, Cartagena would be able to defend itself. The construction of the fortress and massive walls around the old city lasted nearly two centuries, with construction ending in 1796. The walls are eleven kilometers long and up to twenty meters thick—thick enough that today you can go to the Café del Mar on top of the wall to eat and drink mojito's or caipirinhas while flying kites or watching the sun set over the Caribbean.

The main fortress, the Castillo de San Felipe de Barajas, was the greatest fortress built by the Spaniards in their colonies. Tunnels inside the fortress led to cubicles where the defenders of the city would live and protect. Like a rabbit warren, the tunnels were built in such a way as to make it possible to hear footsteps of an approaching army. The port, fortresses, and monuments of Cartagena were selected in 1984 by UNESCO to be a World Heritage site. Outside the walled city are the skyscrapers of Bocagrande, many of which are rumored to have been built with illegal drug profits resulting from America's insatiable appetite for marijuana and cocaine. Colombia had become the largest supplier of marijuana in the world.

First Mate Pedro Vera was summoned to a motor launch in the harbor by a call from Captain Rubies. It was occupied by a pilot and one other passenger. It shoved off from the Muelle de Pescadores (Fisherman's Wharf), passed the beachfront, two-story Hotel Caribe amidst a plethora of high rises on the Bocagrande (Big Mouth) Peninsula, and headed toward the discreet freighter about three miles in the distance. At the time, Roman lived in one of those high rises with his wife and child. The Caribe, a very historic and famous hotel, became infamous in 2012 when President Obama visited Cartagena and several of his Secret Service protectors got into hot water fraternizing with a bevy of beautiful Colombian prostitutes at the hotel. No wonder! Colombian women are known for their beauty and voluptuousness. Even the mannequins in the shop windows there are stacked.

It was about 2:30 in the afternoon on March 1, 1978. Cartagena glistened under a brilliant sun. Pedro Vera boarded the shabby old hulk and Captain Rubies welcomed him aboard as his first mate. The aging freighter was probably too small to be economically viable, unless, of course, it was used to smuggle tons of marijuana in its cargo hold. There were seven other crew members aboard the vessel. Three helmsmen reported to Vera. Two assistant engineers reported to the chief engineer. There was also a cook. Six were Colombian and the other was from Brazil. Roman and Pedro may have been the only ones on board without previous smuggling experience. The stern of the freighter showed its name in white letters as the "Helena Star" and its home port as "Road Harbour." Road Harbour is the harbor for Road Town on Tortola Island in the British Virgin Islands, where the vessel was purchased in 1976.

The first mate, after having spent a great deal of time on the bridge of the Helena Star, described the area of the bridge as follows:

Opposite the wheel, atop an old cylindrical platform, also of polished wood, rested a venerable compass on brilliant bronze supports. Gauges that indicated fuel, oil pressure, and engine temperature were behind the helm; some functioned, but others had been out of use for many years. The small radio room was overrun with anomalously ultra-sophisticated gadgets: one radio locator in use and another in reserve; two short-wave sets for maritime frequencies; one small short-wave transceiver with which we would be able to communicate with Colombia from almost anywhere at sea; two barometers; the fuse box of a complicated electrical installation; attached to the ceiling, was the apparatus that interested me the most at that moment: a gorgeous, exciting, resplendent Loran (a sophisticated system of long-range navigation). This was my first chance to work with one of those fascinating contraptions. I was eager to try it out and test its efficiency. Had this middle-aged, much-battered, merchant woman, the Helena Star, been chosen specifically to disguise this preposterous concentration of space-age communications technology?

2

THE VOYAGE NORTH

EADING UP TO THE RUN OF THE HELENA STAR, THERE HAD
BEEN a number of seizures of vessels by the Coast Guard in
the Caribbean—vessels carrying tons of marijuana on their
way to offload their contraband off the coast of Florida or the Eastern
Seaboard. It was only natural that, at some point, drug runners emanating from Colombia would begin to shift tactics and head up the
west coast of North America, rather than deal with the increased
attention and surveillance by the Coast Guard in the Caribbean.

The eventual seizure of the Helena Star was not the first multi-ton
seizure of marijuana off the west coast of North America, nor would it
be the last. About eight tons were seized New Year's Day, 1978, when
Coast Guard and Customs agents interrupted the offloading of a trawler,
the Cigale, off the coast of Bandon, Oregon. Seventeen people were
arrested. They had been using amphibious vehicles to offload the product. The marijuana seized was valued then at $16.8 million. Later in the
year on October 22, DEA agents arrested six men in a smuggling
attempt in the San Juan Islands in Washington State, close to the
Canadian border. Agents seized two boats after watching bales of marijuana being loaded onto one of the vessels at Barnes Island, about twenty
miles north of Anacortes, Washington. The six arrested were from the
East Coast, Nevada, and California. About two tons were seized, though

apparently more had already been moved from the island. Then on May 22, 1979, the Royal Canadian Mounted Police aborted the offloading of 35 tons of marijuana from the 168-foot freighter Samarkand onto the 55-foot cabin cruiser Whitecap in Sydney Inlet on the west coast of Vancouver Island. Sydney Inlet is located near the town of Tofino, which is nearly 150 miles north of Victoria, British Columbia, where the suspects were brought by plane to be arraigned. Twenty people were arrested, four of whom were Americans.

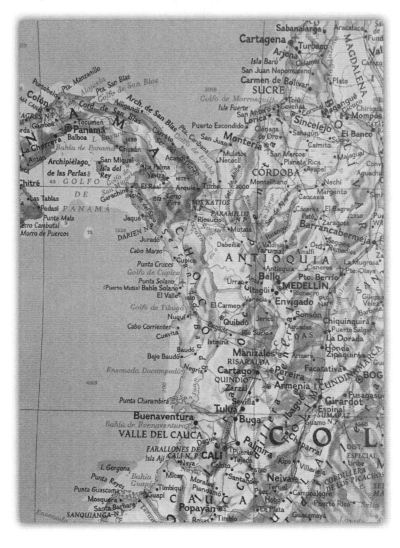

On March 1, 1978, Captain Rubies weighed anchor and set the Helena Star on a course toward the Panama Canal. France began work on the canal in 1881 but stopped due to engineering problems and a high worker mortality rate. The United States, under the watchful eye of President Theodore Roosevelt, took over in 1904 following U.S. involvement in Panama's successful quest for independence. Roosevelt had unexpectedly become the 26th President of the United States in 1901 after the assassination of William McKinley. He brought a new energy to the White House and overwhelmingly won a second term on his own merits in 1904, spearheading construction of the Canal. Those on board the Helena Star were able to enjoy an experience nearly unmatchable in its drama and engineering prowess. The Canal opened new channels of international trade, which the owners of the freighter were trying to take advantage of. The ingenious Canal is considered one of the Seven Wonders of the Industrial World by the American Society of Civil Engineers. It has been called "the greatest liberty man has ever taken with nature."

One of the largest and most difficult engineering projects ever undertaken, the Panama Canal shortcut through the Continental Divide greatly reduced the time for ships to travel between the Atlantic and Pacific Oceans, enabling them to avoid the lengthy, hazardous Cape Horn route around the southernmost tip of South America via the Drake Passage or the Strait of Magellan. To find the Strait of Magellan on a world globe, one must practically turn it upside down and look toward the bottom of the world. Colombia, France, and later the United States controlled the territory surrounding the canal during construction. The United States continued to control the canal and surrounding Panama Canal Zone until the 1977 Torrijos-Carter Treaties provided for handover to Panama after a period of joint American-Panamanian control.

Upon its completion in 1914, the Panama Canal was the most expensive undertaking in history, taking 33 years and 100,000 laborers to complete and costing approximately $400 million. Many of the workmen had left their homes in the Caribbean to dig the canal with nothing more than picks and shovels. As many as 40 men died each day, victims of malaria, yellow fever, or predatory jaguars. The Canal is 51 miles long; the locks in 1978 were 110 feet wide. They raise and lower ocean-going vessels 85 feet, employing the force of gravity to accomplish the transit in mere hours. This sliver of water connecting two massive oceans made the world a smaller place.

If drug smugglers were planning to transport a large amount of marijuana up the Pacific coast of North America, they would probably not want to load the dope before going through the Canal, for fear of discovery during transit. They would avoid that potential problem by going through the Canal from the Caribbean side to the Pacific coast side and loading the contraband after departing the Canal.

On March 3, Roman anchored the vessel in Panamanian waters outside the city of Colon, Panama, on the Caribbean side of the Canal. Senor Arieta-Lineros, one of the two Colombian businessmen who hired the captain, arranged a deposit of $6,000 to clear the vessel for Canal transit. On March 4, the Helena Star was cleared for transit.

While waiting for clearance, Captain Rubies had left the vessel to meet Senor Osorio, the other Colombian businessman, in front of the Hotel Washington in Colon. During this meeting Roman received instructions that he wrote on stationery from a Holiday Inn in Panama City, located on the Pacific side of the Canal. He was advised to keep in contact via the ship's radio each evening at 9:00 p.m. on a pre-set radio frequency. The call name for his contact in Colombia would be "Taboga," after an island off the coast of Panama City, Panama. The call names he was to use as he sailed north from Colombia were "Panama," "Salvador," "La Paz," and "Vancouver," corresponding to countries (Panama and El Salvador) and cities (La Paz, Mexico, and Vancouver, Canada) that he would pass on his way north. On this page of stationery was also a crude drawing of a sailboat, with the words "AZUL JOLLY" just beneath the drawing. Because the Helena Star was expected to be a mothership which would eventually offload a large amount of marijuana to a smaller vessel, Roman believed that the smaller vessel would be blue in color and named the "Jolly." This information and drawing on Holiday Inn stationery would provide law enforcement with a crucial clue in the later investigation.

Captain Rubies returned to his vessel and, on March 4, the Helena Star, after undergoing some minor repairs, journeyed through the Panama Canal from the Caribbean to the Pacific Ocean. Edinel Martinez, one of the first mate's helmsmen at his side, was awestruck as the freighter began its journey through the locks. First, it passed through a set of massive iron doors into the Gatun Locks, the first of the canal's twelve locks. Once the ship was inside the locks, they were flooded, causing the Helena Star to rise 85 feet above sea level. A pair of locomotive engines pulled the freighter into Lago Gatun, south of Colon. Created between 1907 and 1913 by the damming of the Chagres River, the huge man-made lake makes up nearly half of the Canal's length. During the day-long traverse of the Canal, the crew experienced the sight of massive cargo freighters, much larger than their vessel, passing them yards away.

The Helena Star proceeded south along the coast of Panama and then along the west coast of Colombia. The destination was apparently the Golfo de Tortugas, approximately twenty miles south of the city of Buenaventura. Pedro Vera, however, insisted that the destination was further south past the Colombian prison island of Gorgona near the delta of the Mira River, which forms the border between Colombia and Ecuador—an area of dense jungle. It was also near the town of Tumaco, Colombia, where three of the crewmen came from. On March 11, Captain Rubies contacted the shore-side loading party by walkie-talkie. Eventually, men from the shore party, with the help of the crew of the Helena Star, offloaded the cargo of marijuana from an armada of eight, 50-foot motorized vessels onto the Helena Star. Each vessel carried a crew of three or four men and carried about 150 bales of marijuana. Many hundreds of bales of "petroleum verde" (green oil—a reference to its value as a commercial product) ended up in the cargo hold of the Helena Star.

An operation of this magnitude in Colombia is not apt to be successful without the cooperation of some government officials and probably the military. The farmers would harvest the marijuana and fill burlap bags with about 60 pounds of the final product. They were happy to grow a crop they would be well paid for. The usual procedure was for the farmers to load the bales on old dugout canoes, which would be rowed down a river to meet a freighter anchored in a secluded bay.

In the United States at this time, government officials started to become very adept at arresting drug traffickers and turning them against their coconspirators to reap the benefit of a reduced sentence. This would not happen in Colombia. Colombians were not apt to snitch on their coconspirators. If an arrested smuggler cooperated with the authorities and he managed to make it out of his jail cell alive, he would probably end up as shark bait—a truly unfortunate experience. The biggest threat in Colombia was the increasing number of DEA and CIA surveillance planes flying over areas suspected of growing marijuana or harboring drug labs for processing coca leaves from Bolivia into cocaine. The so-called "war on drugs" had begun around 1970 and is still being fought today—50 years later. In 2019, agents from U.S. Customs and Border Protection Air and Marine Operations seized or disrupted almost 285,000 pounds of cocaine, 102,000 pounds of marijuana, 51,000 pounds of methamphetamine, 935 weapons, and $34.1 million. They also made 1,575 arrests according to their press release.

On March 12, 1978, Captain Rubies upped anchor and headed back up the west coast of Colombia laden with "Colombian Gold" worth many millions of dollars. He was embarking on a much longer and more arduous run north than most of those before him who only journeyed from northern Colombia across the Caribbean to Florida or the Eastern Seaboard. He had been given a set of coordinates on the high seas of the North Pacific Ocean some 70 miles off the coastal border between Washington State and British Columbia, Canada, where he was to offload his cargo to another vessel. The location was far from the territorial waters of the United States that extend only three miles seaward from its coast and far from the contiguous zone of the United States that extends another nine miles beyond its territorial waters. The captain had been promised that the Helena Star would do ten knots, but that turned out to be a bit optimistic.

After leaving Colombia behind, the Helena Star continued north, going past the entrance to the Panama Canal, from which it had come. It continued along the coast of Central America, passing in succession Panama, Costa Rica, Nicaragua, Honduras, El Salvador, Guatemala, and Mexico. The vessel was even with the border between Mexico and the United States on March 29 and was just off the American coast of San Francisco, California, on March 31. Next came Oregon and Washington. After leaving the warmth of the tropics, the crew was not prepared for the much colder climate of the Pacific Northwest. Except for the captain, none had ventured outside of South America or the Caribbean Sea. They had lived and worked not far from the equator. Cartagena, for example, is only about 500 miles north of the equator. Though the equator runs through Colombia, there are peaks in the Colombian Andes Mountains that are covered with snow all year round. Keeping warm on the North Pacific was a challenge for the crew, but that was not the only problem. Unfortunately, the Helena Star began having engine problems causing its speed to be substantially decreased, the further north it proceeded. In addition, its supply of food and fresh water was depleted.

The Helena Star finally arrived at the predetermined location on the high seas of the North Pacific around April 5, well out of sight of any land and many miles from the coasts of Washington and British Columbia. Captain Rubies contacted Senor Osorio in Colombia via the ship's single-sideband radio, advising him that they must have fresh water and food to maintain their current location. Prior to leaving Panamanian waters, Rubies had made some estimates as to the number of days the voyage north would take assuming a distance of 4,500 miles from loading to their destination and speed of somewhere between 9 and 10.5 knots. He came up with an estimated duration of 17 to 21 days if the seas were not too stormy. Because of the mechanical problems with the vessel, the voyage had taken a bit longer. Now that the Helena Star had reached the area of the predetermined coordinates given to the captain, he was expecting that contact with the offloading party would be made by radio, that the offloading would occur under cover of darkness and that the offloading would require one trip only. Captain Rubies knew it was certainly not prudent to stay in one place for long.

3
THE AMERICANS

AT THE TOP OF THE HELENA STAR DRUG CONSPIRACY IN North America was David Victorson, a self-described international financier, consultant, antique and securities dealer, and seller of collectible Ferarris. Eric Hale was his best friend and chief subordinate. Both lived in San Anselmo in Marin County, California. Victorson had established a Colombian drug connection in the mid-1970s. He oversaw and accepted deliveries in Miami; Hale was responsible for getting the product to San Francisco, and Lyle Sawicki was responsible for its distribution in the Bay Area.

Marijuana and cocaine smugglers during this time period thought of themselves as modern-day rum runners. They would not think of smuggling heroin or other extremely addictive drugs. They felt that marijuana should be legalized and that what they were doing was not all that bad. William F. Buckley, the preeminent voice of American conservatism at the time, advocated for the legalization of marijuana when he ran for mayor of New York City in 1965. I remember it vividly as I was working in New York then, taking a break from my college education. Buckley did not expect to win; when asked what he would do if he won the race for mayor, he famously responded, "Demand a recount." The quest to legalize marijuana—by its many users and Bill Buckley—would be realized in due time.

David Victorson was born in 1950 and grew up in a rough neighborhood in South Boston. He got his start in the marijuana business by selling lids of pot in the Boston Common. As time went on, he became an ambitious businessman but felt discarded by his family. He decided to travel to Amsterdam and buy hashish, thereby cutting out his regular suppliers. By his own account, Victorson and a partner at the time bought a few pounds of Lebanese red hash with $2,000 in cash. Next, they purchased ten, five-pound Edam cheese wheels, hollowed them out and filled them with hash, sealing the bottoms with the same wax they were already coated with. For effect, he wrapped the Dutch cheese wheels in red crate netting and made a special seal making them look like they had come from the cheese factory. The following day, he mailed the wheels to his Boston address. Upon his return to Boston, he sold the product and made so much money that he continued this routine until his partner bought two pounds of hash from an undercover agent and ended up spending two years in jail in Amsterdam.

Eric Hale had become one of Victorson's distributors in Boston. While staying at Eric's place in Boston, Victorson decided to step up his act and travel to Kathmandu, Nepal, the source of the best hashish in the world. According to him, beginning at age nineteen, over a two-year period he made about $200,000 buying and reselling pot and hashish from Amsterdam and Nepal.

One night, Victorson met a young woman named Susan at a jazz club on Harvard Square. They exchanged stories of his travel adventures in Nepal and India and hers in Colombia, South America. Susan invited him to join her on a trip to Bogota, which she visited frequently and where she had many friends. He decided to take this "wild and crazy tomato" up on her offer. They flew to Bogota and checked into the luxurious Hotel de la Opera located in the Candelaria (historic district) area of the city, just a short walk to the enormous and impressive Plaza de Bolivar. That evening they met her friends at a nightclub downtown. That was the last time that Victorson saw Susan. Victorson and one of her friends, Alfredo, began to realize that they had something in common. Alfredo invited him to go to Cartagena the next day. They took the short flight from Bogota to Cartagena, where Alfredo owned an apartment in a modern high-rise on one of the Bocagrande beaches. Alfredo introduced Victorson to members of a Colombian cartel that smuggled cocaine into Miami and marijuana into Florida and the Eastern Seaboard.

According to Victorson, he was hired to pick up a kilo of cocaine in Miami, have his boys distribute it, as they had done with hashish, and return the money to his contact in the cartel. After all expenses, he had made $30,000 on one kilo of cocaine. Eric Hale left Boston for Miami and rented an apartment at the Brickell Bay Club. Victorson rented an apartment on Cartagena Bay. Within the next six months, they had picked up and sold more than sixty kilos of cocaine. After a year, the total exceeded 200 keys. Eric Hale was holding Victorson's money, which had grown to more than $2,000,000.

David Victorson had gained substantial respect within the cartel. The head of the family wanted to meet him and make him a proposal. Victorson walked five blocks from his apartment along Cartagena Bay to a private casino in the Hotel Caribe, where he was summoned to meet with the patriarch of the cartel. The family wanted to change gears and shift their marijuana smuggling from the east coast to the west coast of the United States. Victorson agreed to handle the American side of the enterprise and decided that Marin County, just across the bay from San Francisco, would be a good base of operations. According to him, they started smuggling tons of marijuana from Colombia all the way to the Pacific Coast using freighters and smaller vessels to offload the product on remote beaches north of Long Beach, California.

The other aspect of such an operation, Victorson said, "was moving millions of dollars in cash out of the U.S. One of the methods was to meet a freighter with the cash as it travelled south to Colombia. Jim, one of my guys, and I would rent a nondescript fishing boat, a fifty-two-foot Egg Harbor, at a local marina for the weekend. We would dress in brand new L.L. Bean slacks and shirts, and, of course, the mandatory Top-Sider brown loafers, dark sunglasses, and caps with fishing logos." They would pack the cash in suitcases and duffel bags and transfer them at a prearranged set of latitude and longitude coordinates to the southbound freighter returning to Colombia.

Victorson bought a home in San Anselmo in the heart of Marin. He also hired a high-profile San Francisco attorney, Robert Moran, who became, as Victorson put it, "the conduit between my world, the black market, and the legitimate business world." Eric Hale joined Victorson in Marin County and rented a house overlooking San Francisco Bay. Eric became Victorson's high-priced gofer, a job description that included counting cash, loading bales of marijuana onto trucks, and chauffeuring Victorson. According to Victorson, by the time he was twenty-five, his net worth topped $20,000,000. He owned a multimillion-dollar estate, a stable of exotic cars, and an Arabian stallion. To help launder money, he opened a pre-Colombian jewelry store on the main street of Sausalito. At the suggestion of his San Francisco attorney, Robert Moran, Victorson also bought distressed properties and paid for the improvements in cash. When Victorson bought the abandoned estate on the hilltop in San Anselmo where he lived, he gave his contractor a suitcase filled with $600,000 to spend on the renovation.

Victorson flew to Cartagena in early 1978 to discuss logistics and finalize preparations for the importation of fifty tons of "Santa Marta Gold" into the United States. This was not his first rodeo, but it would be unlike any deal he had done before due to the extraordinary amount of marijuana to be purchased, imported, and distributed to middlemen. It would be the largest shipment the cartel had ever put together and was to be headed toward Washington State. Captain Rubies was present at the meeting of the cartel with Victorson in Cartagena. At this time, the best marijuana came from Mexico, Colombia, and Asia, principally Thailand. Pot from Colombia was particularly prized. The quality far surpassed anything grown outdoors in the States. Indoor marijuana growing operations did not become well established for quite a few years.

At this point, a high-profile American free style skier—Michael Lund—and a famous, racing sailboat—the Joli—became part of the drug smuggling venture. Victorson had hired James Turner to be their "offloading" expert after the run of the

Helena Star up the west coast of North America. In turn, Turner hired Michael Lund for his expertise with boats and experience as an ocean sailor. Lund and his girlfriend, Patricia Karnik of La Jolla, California, were both professional freestyle skiers. The sport of free-style skiing originated in the early 1970s in the United States. Early devotees were known as "hot doggers." The sport became divided into three basic events—aerials, moguls (skiing the bumps) and ballet. Mike did well in all three disciplines and was highly respected among his peers, most of whom were a decade or more younger. He would thrill rabid, hot-dogdom spectators with his high long layouts and 360s.

The Seattle Times described Lund as follows: "In 1978, Lund was a 42-year old darling of the Northwest and national skiing community, a 'hot dogger' who helped give birth to the sport of freestyle skiing. He won prizes, got his picture in the papers, and had a lot of fun." In 1975 before 35,000 people in Sun Valley, Idaho, Lund won a world championship in the fledgling ballet category of freestyle skiing with a dance down Baldy to the tune of Johann Strauss's "Blue Danube." He became the driving force behind creation of a professional freestyle skiers association. A competitor in the "hot dog" skiing arena, Stan Larsen, said that the association "got us right out of the bumps and into the big money." Lund and Larsen often appeared on ABC's popular program at the time, *Wide World of Sports*, while Lund also taught ski instructors at Sun Valley and was also an expert sailor. He had started out as a ski instructor in the 60s at Ski Acres on Snoqualmie Pass not far from Seattle.

Sports Illustrated reporter Kostya Kennedy wrote about Lund and the emerging sport of freestyle skiing:

> By the time freestyling really took hold, Lund was in his mid-30s and two decades removed from the day in 1952 when, at age 16, he bought a one-way ticket to Sun Valley and left his parents' home in San Diego to pursue a life on the slopes. Rooted in a tradition of acrobatics, freestyle skiing began to catch fire in the early 1970s when filmmakers such as Dick Barrymore and Warren Miller organized events for their cameras. The competitions were raucous affairs, and the term freestyle was apt: Apart from the requirement that you had to finish the run to get a score, competitors could ski, jump, and flip however they pleased. "If you wanted to ski down on one ski, the judges scored you for it," says Lund. "If you could do a flip and land in the chairlift, they scored that. It was all a form of expression." No one expressed himself as powerfully as Lund. The old films show him with a rare combination of elegance and guts. When he performed his signature "Moebius Flip" (a reverse somersault with a 360-degree twist), his midair fluidity resembled a bird's. Lund excelled in each of the sport's three disciplines—aerial, mogul, and ballet.

In the mid-1970s, Lund, Stan Larsen, and two other skiers put on a ski show that they performed throughout Europe, a show that featured spectacular aerial acrobatics and drew enormous crowds. Larsen recounted that, after the Shah of Iran saw them perform in Gstaad, Switzerland, he invited them to demonstrate their prowess for him on a mountain north of Teheran. They made great money performing their shows, flew on private jets, and stayed at extraordinary hotels. Larsen said that Mike "had a connection with the slope that no one else seemed to have."

Mike Lund's girlfriend, Patricia Karnik, was a sensational free-style skier in her own right—one of the first women to compete on the pro circuit and, in the early days, competed against men. Mike rented a two-story storage facility on Shilshole Bay in Seattle that housed a trampoline. He and Patricia would practice aerials on the trampoline. Mike taught her how to do a back flip on skis, and she became the first woman to do a back flip in a freestyle skiing event. She was also one of the first women to perform a reverse somersault in aerial competition. It was the only sport at the time in which a woman could make more money competing than a man. In 1976, during her fifth season of competition when she was 30 years old, she was featured on the cover of Ski magazine doing a back flip in her last competition at Alta, Utah. Patricia said at the time, "I concentrate on taking it up, going for height, reaching for the sky. It's really exciting, like stepping out past your limits—like flying free in the air with thousands watching." Besides competing, she performed in ski shows around the United States and in Germany and Italy. Freestyle skiing for her was "like doing a half-gainer into the mountainside."

By 1977, Lund was 41 and his freestyle career was over. A little earlier at a ski show in San Francisco, he had gone down a portable ski ramp, caught an edge, crashed, and broken his hip. His calling card referred to himself as a "Yacht Broker" for Lund Marine Investments (Yacht, Ship & Waterfront—Discovery & Management). The phone number listed on his card was a Seattle number for an answering service. His listed address was a post office box in Seattle. Lund, however, had no apparent wealth before being hired by Jim Turner, David Victorson's "offloading expert." He frequently had to borrow money from friends to meet living expenses. However, after Turner brought Lund on board, Lund displayed a seemingly inexhaustible supply of money.

During the lead up to the planned marijuana smuggling caper, Mike Lund and Patricia Karnik visited David Victorson a couple times at his estate in Marin County. The home was a bit stark inside with not much furniture. Cocaine was always prevalent, being snorted primarily by Victorson and his friends. Victorson had an air of malevolence. He would frequently wield a semi-automatic pistol and play with it which Patricia thought was strange. Her father was an avid sportsman and amateur gunsmith, who always had a lot of rifles in their home. He even built hunting rifles and used them for duck hunting. Though she was around rifles during her youth and was enamored with David Victorson, it was frightening for Patricia to be around someone who was so intense and frequently had a firearm in his hand. It was obvious to her that Victorson had major experience smuggling illegal drugs, but she never saw any cash transferred between Victorson and her boyfriend. Mike may have wanted to keep her from seeing too much.

In the summer of 1977, Mr. Lund went to work. He contacted William Niemi, who at the time was President of Reinell Boats, based in Marysville, Washington. He had previously been president of the well-known, outdoor outfitter, Eddie Bauer. Bauer had started the company in 1920 as a tennis store, where he built, sold, and strung tennis rackets. From a rented work bench inside another man's gun shop, Eddie Bauer grew to become an international brand, outfitting mountaineering, scientific, and exploratory expeditions all around the world. The company also supplied the United States Army Air Corps with over 50,000 flight jackets for the Aleutian Campaign during World War II. Bill Niemi first met Eddie Bauer in the 1940s. They frequently hunted and fished together. Niemi became Bauer's partner in 1947. In 1953, they supplied the down parkas for the American expedition attempting the first ascent of K2, the world's second highest peak, and in 1963 the first American ascent of Mount Everest by Jim Whittaker. In 1968, Mr. Niemi and his son bought out the Bauer family and began expanding the company's retail business. In 1971, Niemi sold Eddie Bauer to General Mills.

Mike Lund indicated to Mr. Niemi his desire to lease or purchase the sailing vessel Joli, which Niemi had purchased in 1974 and now had had for sale for over a year. Niemi had no interest in leasing it.

The Joli was the fourth C&C 61 launched. She was sloop rigged with a single 90-foot mast (the height of a seven-story building). She had a cobalt-blue hull and white deck, was 61 feet in length with a beam of 15 feet, 2 inches. When not under sail, she was propelled by a six-cylinder, 120-horse Volvo diesel engine. She could carry 110 gallons of diesel fuel, which would give her a range of about 650 nautical miles. She could do nine knots under power in a calm sea. The Joli was custom built for Niemi by Cuthbertson and Cassian Yachts in Bronte, Ontario, Canada, at a price of $390,000. This gem was designed for speed and ocean racing and normally carried a crew of twelve. She had a sewing machine for repairing sails, a full work bench, and long strips of copper bonded into her hull to provide a perfect grounding system for radio communications.

Niemi raced the Joli in local races and twice in the prestigious Victoria to Maui International Yacht Race (Vic-Maui), the longest offshore sailing race off the west coast of North America. Vic-Maui was the pinnacle of Pacific Northwest ocean racing. The first official race was in 1968 and sponsored by the Royal Vancouver Yacht Club and the Lahaina Yacht Club. Fourteen boats entered with Porpoise III sweeping the fleet, first to finish and first on corrected time. Her elapsed time was 17 days, 6 hours, and 50 minutes. The Vic-Maui race runs in even-numbered years, starting in June or July off Victoria, British Columbia, Canada, and finishes near Lahaina, Maui, United States—a distance of 2,308 nautical miles. The number of entrants has ranged from 4 to 37 boats. The crew in a typical race would face westerlies in the Strait of Juan de Fuca between the State of Washington and Vancouver Island, take a left turn down the coast to about the latitude of San Francisco followed by a right turn with the northeasterly trade winds filling spinnakers for the downhill sun run to Maui for Mai Tais.

In 1974, the Joli and Bill Niemi, representing the Seattle Yacht Club, were first to finish the Victoria to Maui race, setting a new elapsed time record of 12 days, 17 hours, 53 minutes and 26 seconds. Strangely enough, during that race, Niemi became aware that a small amount of marijuana had been smuggled aboard the Joli by one of its crew members and used in the middle of the Pacific Ocean. Later that year, she won the Los Angeles to Mazatlán, Mexico, race. Paul Ulibarri, owner of Hobie Cats Northwest at Shilshole Bay in Seattle, often crewed on the Joli. Once, during a race, he clocked her at 19 knots under sail, which a Coast Guard official told him was faster than the top speed of the Coast Guard cutter Yocona that would play a significant role in the unfolding drama of the Helena Star. There was no question—the Joli was fast. Niemi also raced the boat in the 1976 Victoria to Maui race. At one point he had a lead of 250 miles, but got becalmed and Ragtime, a 65-footer from Los Angeles, beat the Joli by an hour.

Mr. Niemi had become a motivated seller. Mike Lund told Niemi that he was interested in purchasing the Joli as an agent for a group of Swiss people. Later, he indicated that it was for a wealthy Swiss gentleman, who wanted to purchase it as a birthday present for his son. Originally, Lund was going to form a corporation for the Swiss and purchase the boat through that mechanism. However, a couple weeks later, Lund indicated to Niemi that the deal was going to be too complicated. Because the Swiss did not want to be identified, Lund decided to purchase the boat himself as an intermediary.

Lund intended to purchase all the shares of the Delaware Corporation that Niemi had formed two years earlier to own the Joli. She was the sole asset of the corporation and Niemi was the sole share-holder. The purchase price was $255,000 with a down payment of $55,000 required. Niemi agreed to assist Lund in getting a $200,000 first-preferred marine mortgage on the boat. Niemi did this through Old National Bank in Seattle, where he did his personal banking business, and surprisingly agreed to be a guarantor on the loan. Prior to signing the purchase and sale agreement, Lund had provided $2,500 in earnest money to Niemi in the form of a cashier's check. The remaining $52,500 of the down payment was to be paid as soon as Lund was satisfied that the boat met his specifications. Niemi, his sailing buddy and their two girlfriends flew from Seattle to San Diego, where the boat was moored, to meet Lund and inspect the boat.

Lund, Niemi, and Niemi's buddy went through the Joli to inventory its gear and the following day took her out for sea trials, spending the day sailing off the coast of California. Lund was given the opportunity to operate the boat and put up several different sails. Niemi was extremely impressed with Lund's competence as a sailor. He knew that Lund was an experienced ocean sailor and that he had delivered boats from Asia to the United States. The three of them returned in the evening and tied up at the Joli's slip just across from the San Diego Yacht Club. Niemi asked Lund if he was satisfied with the boat and was ready to complete the sale. Lund indicated he was ready.

They went below into the luxurious master stateroom of the Joli to execute the purchase and sale agreement that Niemi's attorney had prepared and that both he and Lund had previously approved. After signing the agreement, Niemi indicated to Lund that it was time for Lund to pay the balance owed on the agreed down payment of $55,000. Since Lund had already made an earnest money payment of $2,500, the balance owed on the down payment was $52,500.

Niemi, of course, expected Lund to present a cashier's check, but instead he pulled out a green, cloth knapsack and proceeded to give Niemi the balance in $20 bills—2,640 $20 bills, to be exact. The cash filled Niemi's briefcase. He had never seen so much cash in one place. Observing Niemi's amazement, Lund explained that he had just returned from Zurich with Swiss francs and had spent a couple days converting them to dollars. The sale of the Joli was consummated. It was August 14, 1977.

Niemi kept the brief case close to his vest through the rest of the weekend. On Monday morning, after returning to Seattle, he went into the Old National Bank carrying a boat load of $20 bills. It took the bank all morning to count the money and deposit it into Niemi's account. It also turned out that Lund had overpaid Niemi by $300. Niemi's yacht broker in San Diego, Murray Lawson, told him that after the sale was finalized, Lund and his friends had one hell of a party aboard the Joli.

Before sailing the Joli to Seattle, Mike Lund and Patricia sailed it from San Diego to San Francisco. Much of the time, they sailed at night, which Patricia thought was a bit odd. In retrospect, she realized that he was probably training her to assist him with the Joli's future rendezvous with the Helena Star, which in all probability would occur at night.

After closing the sale, Niemi had three or four conversations with Lund between November of 1977 and late March of 1978. Lund told him that he had sailed the Joli alone all the way from San Diego to Seattle and had also sailed the boat to Victoria, B.C., and to the nearby American San Juan Islands. Lund was such a good sailor that he frequently sailed alone. To be able to sail a 61-foot yacht alone was extraordinary. He had, however, bought a brand new, high quality VHF radio. Lund owed Niemi an additional amount of approximately $2,000 for accrued interest on the contract balance of $200,000 from the time of the signing of their agreement until the time that the marine mortgage was approved by the bank. Lund had made two payments to Niemi on the interest due of $650 each but had one remaining payment. Niemi contacted Lund around the end of February and Lund apologized for forgetting about making the last interest payment and indicated that he would send it to Niemi.

During the last two conversations that he had with Niemi regarding the delinquent last interest payment, Lund said he would not be making the payment, because around April 15 he expected to pay off the entire remaining principal of the mortgage and the remaining accrued interest. This was because, according to Lund, the Swiss buyers were in town, had been sailing the Joli and were preparing to complete their purchase of the boat through Lund as their intermediary. He went on to tell Niemi that the Swiss loved the boat, were having a great time, but were poor sailors, having already damaged the bow pulpit. He did not say how it was damaged. Lund invited Mr. Niemi to participate in skippering the Joli on any of the return legs to her eventual berth in the Mediterranean, via the Panama Canal and across the Atlantic Ocean. Niemi told him that he would take her from the east side of the Panama Canal through the Caribbean Sea.

In the meantime, in October of 1977, Lund was looking to buy property on Sequim Bay, located on the Olympic Peninsula in Washington State, halfway between the cities of Port Angeles and Port Townsend and just off the Strait of Juan de Fuca, which separates Washington from Vancouver Island, British Columbia. The Strait allows access from the Pacific Ocean to Puget Sound and Seattle to the south and Vancouver, Canada, to the north. On October 31, Lund purchased a modest, secluded house for $80,000 on the east side of Sequim Bay and moved in just before the end of the year. Lund paid $23,500 down and was to pay off the balance over ten years. The seller was Dr. Lincoln Ries, a physician from Eastern Washington. Lund was prompt with his payments. Dr. Ries never met Lund in person but did not care so long as Lund continued to pay off the mortgage. Chet Miller, a retired marine park planner for Washington State Parks, lived about a quarter of a mile south of Lund's house. Mr. Miller could not actually see Lund's house from his own house but could see the waterfront in front of Lund's property. There were no houses between Miller's house and Lund's. Miller described the Lund property as being mostly wooded with 150 feet of high bank waterfront, probably about 90 to 100 feet high.

Mr. Miller and his wife became quite well acquainted with Lund and would invite him over to their house. Lund seemed to be out of town quite often. Miller said that sometimes Lund would tell him that he was going to Seattle or San Diego or Switzerland or some other place–skiing in Utah or Canada. "Sometimes I'm here and sometimes I'm gone." Lund told Mr. Miller that he had purchased a boat that he wanted to moor in front of his residence and asked Miller to design a moorage for it. They bought a chain and buoys, filled a small skow with scrap iron to anchor the moorage, and installed everything in late December. In due time, a boat arrived and became moored in front of Lund's property. The stern of the boat identified her as the Joli with a home port of Wilmington, Delaware. Pursuant to Lund's request, Miller also rebuilt an old decayed log bulkhead in January of 1978 and built stairs up the bank from the water in March. Lund had a mobile home on his property that he wanted to get rid of, so Miller took the mobile home as payment for the work he had done.

Lund had acquired a powerful electric winch and asked Mr. Miller in late March or early April 1978, to help him unload it from his truck. Lund had had a concrete foundation poured to support the winch and Miller had a truck with a cherry picker. They unloaded the winch from Lund's truck and set it on the foundation. Lund said he wanted to set up a track like a marine railway down to the beach and use the winch to pull a skiff loaded with his sails up the high bank from the beach. Two log skids were laid down the high bank. Around the same time, Lund also bought another boat, a Raider, purchased at Bryant's Marina in Anacortes, Washington. Miller described it as a "big open boat, just like a gigantic skiff, about 26 feet long, I believe, and probably eight-foot beam. There's about a four-foot drop section in the front which would let down and you could roll a small vehicle off it and up on the beach." Lund told Miller that he wanted the

Raider to play around with and thought it would be adequate to haul sails on and off the Joli.

Another neighbor of Lund's, Truman Welch, spoke with Lund on March 30, 1978. Lund said he planned to have the Joli's bottom cleaned of marine growth on April 1. In the meantime, Homero Ospina had purchased a new water pump in Los Angeles for the Helena Star. It was purchased under a phony business name and delivered to Ospina's business, the Smarter Brothers Lounge, on March 30. The pump was flown to Seattle and delivered by a chartered seaplane on April 2 to Lund's home on Sequim Bay.

On March 31, Lund walked into Northwyn Sails in Seattle on Shilshole Bay not far from Shilshole Marina and the Hiram Chittenden Locks, which allow boats and vessels to go from Puget Sound all the way to Lake Washington in Seattle. The President of Northwyn, Mervin Abrams, had been the owner of Northwyn since 1947. The company made sails for sailboats. Mr. Abrams had known Lund, a man of many talents, as a sailmaker since the mid-1960s. There was a time when Lund built a temporary ski jump next to Northwyn Sails. It was intended to be used in sports shows. Lund would ski down the jump, turn a somersault in the air and land in some big air mattresses. He tested it for about a week, disassembled it and took it away.

Lund was at Northwyn on March 31 to buy sail bags. Mr. Abrams sold him fourteen No. 7 sail bags and twenty-one No. 6 sail bags. The No. 7 bags were 5 feet, 9 inches high and 24 inches in diameter. The No. 6 bags were about 4 ½ feet high with the same diameter as the No. 7s. All the bags had the signature Northwyn red stripe and label on them. Mr. Abrams asked Lund what he was going to do with the sail bags, and Lund responded that he was going to Europe the next morning, as he had a deal for some large sailboats there and none of the sails had bags, so he needed a lot of sail bags. This was an unusual sale according to Mr. Abrams, because sails usually come with their own sail bags and the bags last as long as the sails. Unless someone loses a bag, there would be no necessity for them. The bill for the bags came to $499.80, which Lund, of course, paid in twenty-dollar bills.

Back in Sequim, neighbors of Lund noticed that the Joli was gone from her moorings for three days in early April. But it was back in front of Lund's house on the morning of April 6. On April 7 Eric Hale rented a U-Haul truck. Around the same time, David Victorson was also at work in the background. He leased a fleet of trucks and on April 8 rented part of a barn owned by Allen Hall, a retired air traffic controller and Episcopal priest. The barn was located on the southwest side of the town of Sequim, approximately five miles from Mike Lund's property on Sequim Bay. Victorson indicated to Mr. Hall that he was interested in buying land in the Sequim area and had some equipment that he wanted to store in the barn until he found a place to buy. He said that the equipment would include tack for horses and some horse feed.

Victorson rented a portion of the barn for an indefinite time, paying Hall for two month's rent at $75 per month. Victorson returned the following day, April 9, in a U-Haul truck with a couple of other people and unloaded some sail bags with red stripes on them—Northwyn sail bags. The following day, Victorson returned in the U-Haul truck with other people and another vehicle. He told Mr. Hall that they were going to leave the truck there. Hall responded that they could park it out behind the barn. Victorson, however, said they wanted to park the truck inside the barn to make sure that everything that was in it stayed dry. The truck remained in the barn until April 18. Then the truck disappeared and Hall never saw it again.

4

THE RENDEZVOUS

"THAT MUST BE IT," CAPTAIN RUBIES SAID. FIRST MATE Pedro Vera responded, "You knew a sailboat would be coming?" Roman said, "Si." They told me it was a blue yacht; a racing yacht, very swift; and they said it was one of the very largest kinds. The advantage is that around here it does not attract attention. There are hundreds of sailboats in this area. They said it is a ninety-footer. If they took everything out of it and all that comes is the hull, it might carry a good amount. Let's wait till it approaches." Roman had sent out a coded signal that he was approaching the prearranged coordinates. It was April 4, 1978.

The captain must have confused the length of the Joli with the height of its mast, which was 90 feet tall. According to Vera, the sleek boat bore toward the Helena Star rapidly—very rapidly for a sailboat. About twenty minutes later, it was a quarter of a mile away, off starboard. The first mate expressed his regrets and described the scene:

In other circumstances, I would have described it as a beautiful vessel. Of fine lines, elegant and graceful, it was a priceless instrument for running with the wind. It was painted a brilliant, almost electric blue. Someone had put love into the construction of this luxurious, slender boat. The sail was

46

let go cleanly and rapidly, which showed that those who were manning that sailboat were not beginners. Then the yacht turned sharply toward us, using the auxiliary motor. It drew near and sailed by our side. On the bow, small and elegant, it sported the French-reminiscent name "Joli." And she truly fit the adjective, although I was cursing the person who came up with the bright idea of using her for this odious and complicated purpose.

Roman would have preferred a filthy lighter—a flat-bottomed boat—that could handle all the marijuana in the hold. There was a crew of three aboard the Joli in yellow rain gear. From the bridge Roman signaled to them to use their radio. Both vessels were equipped with a high-frequency crystal on their radios. The Joli asked to change channels. They said the water was too rough for their boat and wanted to look for calmer waters. Mike Lund had not anticipated such a large vessel. It was obvious to him that the boats were not at all compatible with each other for purposes of unloading such a huge cargo on the high seas. The seas along the Washington coast were wildly unpredictable. The bow pulpit of the Joli had already been damaged by the two vessels coming together in high swells. A transfer in the open sea was foolhardy. The skipper of the Joli said he knew of a safe place where the water was better. He said to follow them at a distance, but to not lose sight of them.

Roman was not happy with the change in plans. He did have a marine chart that covered the southern part of Vancouver Island, the Strait of Juan de Fuca, and the coast of the state of Washington. The situation seemed perilous. They followed the Joli into Canadian waters near the entrance to the Strait of Juan de Fuca. They were about to enter the natural route of vessel traffic entering or leaving the Strait, not a good place to conduct their business. Higher vessel traffic probably meant a greater likelihood of Coast Guard attention. Freighters from Canadian and Washington ports ply the Strait on their way to and from Asia, Alaska, and the west coast of North America. Its width

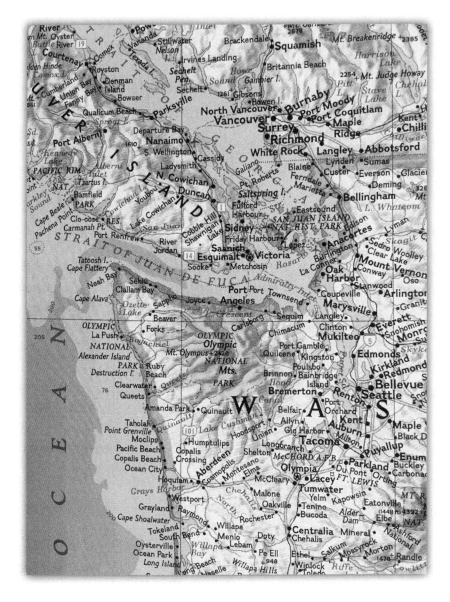

averages around ten miles. The Strait serves the big cities of Seattle and Vancouver, Canada, as well as the port of Tacoma, Washington.

The night was unusually dark as both vessels entered the Strait in a southeasterly direction, passing Port Renfrew, Vancouver Island, on the North and Neah Bay, Washington, on the south. Caution was thrown to the wind. The Joli kept going, seemingly with no intention of stopping. The Helena Star reluctantly followed. The Joli led them deeper and deeper into this long arm of water separating the United States from Canada. If they went much further, they would be opposite the much larger cities of Victoria, Canada, and Port Angeles, Washington. The Helena Star was without a cargo manifest and its British registration had expired. It was very vulnerable and, of course, was loaded with enough weed to bring high times to virtually every human being in the region.

The captain called for one of the crewmen, Emilio. He told Emilio that they would be stopping very soon and that the Joli would approach on their starboard side. "Tie it down very securely. If something bad occurs, there will be no chance to get out of here, so there is no point in tying it loosely. Tie the lines so the two vessels become one. Load on our vessel what they have brought us. Then cram as much weed into the Joli as she will take. One lantern in the hold and work as fast as you can." Finally, the Joli began to slow and Roman followed course. The Joli drew up and stopped just opposite of the Helena Star's engine room. Lines were thrown over and the Joli was secured to the rusty freighter. Mike Lund was at the helm. Also on board were David Victorson and Eric Hale. James Turner had started out with them from Sequim Bay, but he had gotten seasick due to the choppy seas and disembarked from the sailboat at Neah Bay, at the west end of the Strait of Juan de Fuca, where the Strait meets the Pacific Ocean. He took a float plane back to Sequim Bay to recuperate.

Crewmen from the Helena Star loaded a bunch of large light-colored bundles from the Joli—food, water, engine parts, and ski sweaters for the crew of the freighter who were from equatorial South America and not prepared for the much colder weather in the North Pacific. Lund had gotten the ski sweaters from one of his freestyle skiing sponsors. Then three crewmen in the cargo hold of the freighter lifted the bales of marijuana; two others took them from the deck and flung them toward the yacht, where two of the three crew on the Joli loaded the bales into the sailboat with the help of two other crewman from the mothership. Part of the problem loading and unloading was caused by the substantial height differential between the deck of the Helena Star and the deck of the Joli from the surface of the sea. The deck of the freighter was much higher off the water and the much smaller Joli was rocking and rolling. According to the first mate, "The muffled fall of the many bales acquired a certain rhythm and the men's silhouettes added to the eerie, grotesque atmosphere."

The last possible bale was crammed into the Joli. As a result, there was barely a crevice that had not been filled with "petroleum verde." There was little room left for the crew of the Joli to operate this famous sailboat. The last bales were secured around 3 a.m. They had pulled off an improbable, if not impossible, offloading in the middle of the Strait of Juan de Fuca, within sight of at least two cities. The Joli, laden with over 200 bales of "Colombian Gold," untied her lines, tilted with the wind, and rapidly disappeared into the night. The sailboat was filled to the brim, if not overloaded, but with a small amount of marijuana compared to over a thousand bales still residing in the hold of the Helena Star.

According to Lund, Victorson had wanted Lund to rip out all the Joli's interior cabins and interior bulkheads in order to increase its capacity, but Lund had refused to destroy the classic racing sloop.

The Joli returned to Sequim Bay arriving in front of Michael Lund's house under a full moon. The sailboat was anchored and the much smaller, flat-bottomed Raider boat pulled alongside and tied up. The haul was offloaded as quickly as possible, requiring quite a few trips from the Joli to shore. About 200 yards from Lund's house was a dirt back road that went straight to the water's edge. The Raider would head to shore and three men would transfer the bales from the Raider to a waiting truck. Two trucks full of marijuana were ready to roll east.

Sometime later, the Joli returned to the Helena Star for a second load of almost 200 more bales. The seas were unusually rough. Lund's girlfriend, Patricia Karnik, was on board the Joli this time with him and at least one other crew member. Karnik and Lund had been a pair on the freestyle skiing circuit's two-person ballet routine. She was dressed to look like a man but spent most of the unloading time hidden away. She was terrified by the rough seas and huge swells at night with no lights and the Joli constantly rolling and crashing into the side of the Helena Star. The second load was transferred to two more waiting trucks and by daybreak those two U-Haul trucks driven by James Turner and Eric Hale were on the road to a farm in Illinois, not far from Chicago. According to Victorson, "Each bale would be opened and the pot dumped into a silo, the seeds and stems would be sorted out, and the smokable pot would be repackaged into one-pound bags to be sold to wholesalers."

Before separating from the Joli the second time, Captain Rubies had one more task to accomplish. He was furious. He wrote a note to the skipper of the Joli, which stated in no uncertain terms: "Charter another boat because I will only come back to the sea buoy one more time. Wait for me there. Please try to discharge everything this day. If you can bring us fresh water in plastic cans, about 200 gallons, lube oil No. 40, about 100 gallons, fresh food. Thanks." The skipper of the Joli indicated that he would return in about three days to accomplish the offloading of the remaining bales to another vessel. Chet Miller, Lund's nearby neighbor, saw Lund, David Victorson, Eric Hale, and James Turner after the first trip to the Helena Star was completed. He said that Lund told him they had sailed up the west coast of Vancouver Island to Port Alberni, Canada. Lund said that the trip had been rough and they were tired. Miller had no clue that they had rendezvoused with a mothership to transfer many tons of marijuana.

The Helena Star vanished back out to the high seas of the North Pacific Ocean—the world's largest. Ernest Shackleton, the famous polar explorer, who led three expeditions to Antarctica, referred to oceans as "the void spaces of the world." A sense of urgency came over the Americans. They had to deal with an experienced sea captain, who was none too happy. If they followed the captain's instructions, they would have to come up very quickly with another vessel that could take the remainder of the load still wandering about the high seas.

Roman was faced with the unenviable proposition of having to get the hell out of the Strait of Juan de Fuca and disappear for who knows how long without attracting the attention of the Coast Guard or the Royal Canadian Mounted Police. His goal was to avoid entering the three-mile territorial waters of either the United States or Canada. That meant returning to the high seas, which are certainly vast, but virtually empty and not particularly suitable for hiding out. Who knew how long it would take for Mike Lund to come up with an alternative offloading vessel. They were to rendezvous again in the same place in three days.

The freighter arrived at the appointed place at the appointed time. Lund was a no-show. Victorson had directed Lund to find another vessel that was more suitable for offloading the remaining huge amount of marijuana. Lund looked for a fishing boat, but his efforts were unsuccessful.

Captain Rubies contacted the Colombian entrepreneur, Senor Osorio, the following morning via the ship's radio and advised Osorio that he had had no further contact with the purchasers of the load. Roman told Osorio:

Yesterday, no one showed up for the lumber. We waited much longer than we were supposed to and then, thinking they might have broken down on the way, we went looking for them on the highway, almost to the next town. But there was not the slightest indication that they had left. This has created a difficult situation. Our time was up four days ago. We have been waiting for our relief so we can go, and this just cannot keep going on and on. Over!

Osorio indicated he would get back to the captain at the usual hour. He would presumably be calling from somewhere in South America and I do not mean South Texas. At 8 p.m., Captain Rubies waited in the radio room for the call from Taboga, the code name for their radio contact. "Taboga calling." "Go ahead, Taboga. I read you.

Over." Taboga indicated that their relief was having difficulty mobilizing equipment and cannot meet the Helena Star till next Sunday, in five days. Taboga went on to say that if the captain could not wait that long, he could leave and go home. "The head office says that you have done your part. They leave the decision in your hands. You are the ones who know what the situation is out there." Roman decided to wait and sailed the freighter south for a couple days before heading back for hopefully the last rendezvous. On Saturday night, he set a course from a little further north with the intention of reaching the offloading spot coming from a point less likely to raise suspicions. The Helena Star would appear to be coming from Asia or Alaska. Her course was due east—just another vessel heading for the Strait.

Meanwhile, at about 1:00 p.m. on Sunday, April 16, Bob Morton, who bought and sold marine equipment, was in his office on the south side of the Duwamish River in Seattle. He received a phone call from a man identifying himself as Mike Lund. Lund inquired about an 82-foot tugboat, the Knik Wind that he had seen tied up at a dock on Lake Union that Morton had for sale for one of his customers. Lake Union is located in Seattle between Lake Washington and the Hiram Chittenden Locks, which provide access to Puget Sound, which leads to the Strait of Juan de Fuca and the Pacific Ocean. Lund indicated that he wanted to buy the tug and asked Morton if he had a barge for sale as well. Morton responded that he owned a barge, the Chignik 105, which was also for sale and advised Lund of its nearby location on Lake Union. Lund went and looked at the barge tied up next to Ivar's Salmon House restaurant and a few minutes later called Morton back and asked to meet with him. The barge was 82.5 feet long, 34 feet wide with an 11-foot draft. They agreed to meet that afternoon at the dock on Lake Union where the tug was tied up.

Patricia Karnik, Lund's girlfriend, accompanied him in a car to the dock. Lund and Morton agreed on a price of $42,500 for the Chignik barge. Lund said he had some salvage work to do out near Port Angeles near the confluence of Puget Sound and the Strait of Juan de Fuca. He gave Morton a down payment of $10,000 in cash with the balance to be paid off the next day, at which time he also wanted to buy the tug. Lund seemed to be in a hurry and wanted to take the barge out that night to the Port Angeles area. He told Morton that he had to have it there by 5:00 p.m. Monday afternoon, April 17, or he would lose the salvage job. Morton told Lund that he could take the barge out if it was towed by a tug skippered by someone Morton trusted.

Al Wolover, an independent tugboat operator, was selected as Morton's trusted skipper. Lund paid Wolover $750 to tow the barge, and Wolover towed it to Port Angeles arriving on Monday, April 17, before Lund's designated deadline. Upon his arrival in Port Angeles, Wolover received an agreed-upon additional $750 cash from a young man, who was later identified as Dean Bowen, who sped out to Wolover's tug in a small, new orange skiff powered by a new Mercury outboard. Bowen advised Wolover where to moor the barge—alongside a log boom 4,000 feet from the nearest landfall. According to Wolover, "This young man indicated that he was from California, that he was up here to do a job, and that he would be glad when it was over." The young man did not appear to be knowledgeable about boats, said he was on vacation, and that the barge would be used for a salvage job in Alaska. Lund had told Bob Morton that somebody from San Francisco (Eric Hale) would be flying up with more money that night to pay for the barge and that on Monday the Bank of California in San Francisco would be transferring even more money up to the Bank of California in Seattle to pay off Morton in full.

Lund called the owner of the tug in Anchorage, Alaska, around 6:30 Sunday night, April 16. They agreed on a price of $160,000 for the Knik Wind tug. It is doubtful that Lund, when deciding to buy the Knik Wind, knew that on May 12, 1974 (four years earlier), it had been lost at sea while being transported as cargo aboard the barge Anna Lee. The barge sank in the Kennedy Entrance on the south-central coast of Alaska below Cook Inlet during a storm. The Knik Wind was later salvaged and put up for sale by its Alaskan owner. Ironically, Knik Wind is a local name for a strong southeast wind in the vicinity of Palmer, Alaska, which is located at the head of Knik Arm, which flows into Cook Inlet.

Morton and Lund agreed to meet at 7:00 a.m. the next morning, Monday, April 17. Eric Hale had flown a substantial amount of money to Seattle the night before to close Lund's deal with Morton for the barge. After both arrived at the dock, Morton fired up the engines for Lund. One of the hydraulic valves on the tow hitch needed some work. After that was accomplished, Lund handed Morton $70,000 in small bills, nothing larger than a $50, from a green paper sack toward the outstanding balances owed for the tug and barge as well as another $5,000 or $6,000 in cash for Morton's commission for the sale of the tug. That left a remaining balance owed by Lund of $122,500. After delivering the cash to Morton, Lund wanted to run the tug with Morton down to the nearest fuel dock to fill the tank. After the tank was filled, Lund wanted to take the Knik Wind through the locks out to Shilshole Bay Marina to load some supplies on the tug—supplies he said he had bought from two different marine supply businesses located on Shilshole Bay. Morton authorized Lund to take the tug out to Shilshole, but not to depart the marina there until he was paid in full.

Morton and Lund parted ways. Morton drove under the Aurora Bridge, parked his vehicle and counted the cash. He expected the remaining $122,500 to be wired from California by 5:00 p.m. that afternoon. Lund had told Morton that he was staying at the University Towers Hotel near the University of Washington in Seattle. About 3:00 p.m. Lund called Morton asking him if he had heard from the Bank of California confirming that the remaining balance had been wired from its bank in San Francisco. Morton had not heard from the bank, so Lund asked him to call the bank to assure himself that the appropriate arrangements had been made. About 4:30 p.m. Lund called Morton again to see if he had heard from the bank. Morton finally called the bank and was told that Lund had been in and advised the bank to provide Morton with a cashier's check in the amount of $122,500 once the wire transfer was complete. Lund indicated at the time that the Knik Wind was tied up at the end of Pier G at the Shilshole Bay Marina.

Despite the fact that Morton had told Lund not to move the Knik Wind from Shilshole Bay until he was paid in full, Lund knew he needed to get the tug up to Port Angeles, if he was going to use it to tow the barge out through the Strait of Juan de Fuca to finish the offloading of the Helena Star. Captain Rubies was lingering somewhere in the ocean, not knowing when or if Lund would get his act together. Lund was concerned that he was taking too much time and that Rubies would give up on him and start to slither away down the coast and back to warmer climes in the South Pacific or the idyllic Caribbean. The captain knew that the more time that went by, the greater the risk would be for him and his crew. He had followed through on his part of the bargain and would have unloaded all the freighter's cargo had the Americans been prepared. Given the lack of capacity of the Joli to take the entire contents of the cargo hold, Rubies still had successfully offloaded thirteen tons of marijuana.

At 10:30 p.m. Bob Morton received a call from an attorney in San Francisco, Robert L. Moran. He was a well-known divorce and criminal defense lawyer, whose expensive home in Corte Madera had a sweeping view of San Francisco Bay and had been featured in San Francisco Magazine earlier in the year. Moran had a collection of luxury cars and would host formal dress dinners on his 50-foot yacht. Aside from his law practice, Moran dabbled in silver trading, oil wells, and cattle breeding. He had all the accoutrements of substantial wealth. He had graduated from the University of Maryland Law School, began his law practice in 1964 taking on personal injury accident cases, pursued business aggressively, and won some well-publicized trials. By all appearances he had made it big and was living the high life. One of his best clients was, of course, David Victorson.

Moran apologized to Morton for not getting the money wired up to Seattle that day; he had been in court all day and had not had time to do it. He assured Morton that the wire would be sent before noon the next day, Tuesday, April 18. Moran went on to say that the firm he was representing had money in five or six different banks in San Francisco and that the $122,500 owed by his client was just a drop in the bucket. About the same time as this phone call, the Knik Wind tug, with Mike Lund at the helm, left Pier G in the dead of night, leaving Shilshole Bay behind, and headed north up Puget Sound to hook up with the Chignik 105 barge in Port Angeles.

During the early morning hours of Tuesday, April 18, the tug and barge, with Lund at the helm and Patricia Karnick and Dean Bowen on board, left Port Angeles and headed westbound in the Strait of Juan de Fuca to rendezvous with the Helena Star and unload the remaining 37 tons of marijuana from the Helena Star on to the barge. Lund spotted his mothership in the distance, but it was being escorted towards him by the U.S. Coast Guard Cutter Yocona. Karnick was

asleep below. She was aroused by a commotion in the wheelhouse of the tug, got up, and ran up to see the Helena Star in the middle of a fleet of Coast Guard cutters. While the Cutter Yocona was escorting the Helena Star, other Cutters were stopping fishing boats and other vessels they thought might be connected to the mothership. Lund maintained his course so he would not arouse suspicion. Patricia Karnik's most vivid recollection of her time with Lund and the other conspirators was being on board the 82-foot Knik Wind towing the equally long Chignik barge right through the middle of all this commotion occurring in the Strait like they were invisible. Eventually the conspirators veered off and headed north for Canada and Port Alberni Inlet on the west coast of Vancouver Island, where Lund, Karnik, and Bowen abandoned the tug and barge and fled.

A diary seized by the DEA on May 3 from the pickup that Patricia Karnik was driving was very revealing. It was the only diary that she kept during her life. An entry dated April 24 stated:

> A week ago we see the "mystery ship" being ushered in—freak-out—we maintained course and headed for Canada—Alaska—no charts so pulled into Barkley Sound up to Bamfield parked barge a little further up—scammed a chart at Bamfield and went up the canal to Port Alberni—amazing journey indeed—parked—slept a bit—and split at 5:00 a.m.—breakfast—yuk—cab to airstrip—too cloudy—cab to Nanaimo, Air West to Vancouver—I went on to Seattle—ah—easing of the day-long adrenalin flash—almost intercepted M.D. at airport and flew to Port Angeles—passing right over Star coming in—rushed and busted.

Lund, Karnik, and Bowen tied the barge to a dock near Bamfield, in Barkley Sound on the west coast of Vancouver Island, leaving a note indicating that they had had an emergency and had to tie the barge up temporarily. They proceeded up the fjord-like Alberni Inlet and tied the Knik Wind to a dock in Port Alberni, leaving a similar emergency note. They "slept a bit," left the tug at 5:00 a.m., had breakfast, and took a cab to a nearby airstrip. They could not get a flight out due to bad weather, so took another cab across Vancouver Island to the Nanaimo Airport on the east coast of the Island. Lund and Karnik separated at the airport. Lund flew to Edmonton, Canada, and Karnik flew to Vancouver, where she bought an international ticket from Vancouver to Seattle. The authorities at the Vancouver Airport went through her luggage prior to boarding and found a loose bullet, which was confiscated. She had no idea where the unspent cartridge had come from. She was detained for a couple hours, missed her flight, but finally allowed to catch another flight to Seattle.

5

HIGH NOON

CAPTAIN CHARLES MORGAN HAD BEEN COMMANDING OFFICER of the U.S. Coast Guard Cutter Yocona for one year. Based in Astoria, Oregon, its mission was general law enforcement including drug enforcement. It was 213 feet long. The first night at sea after leaving Astoria on April 15, 1978, the vessel was heading in a northerly direction twelve to fifteen miles off the coast of Grays Harbor, Washington, when a nineteen-year-old seaman spotted the flashing lights of a low flying aircraft to the west. It was moving relatively slowly from what the lookout reported, so was probably either a small plane or a helicopter. It occurred to Captain Morgan that it might possibly have been an aircraft looking for a vessel, since small aircraft do not normally fly that far out to sea. As a result, Morgan decided to go farther offshore.

Though Captain Morgan apparently did not consider this, a low-flying aircraft off the coast of Grays Harbor might cause a savvy law enforcement agent to think of the Copalis Beach Airport, located on a remote beach between the mouth of the Copalis River to the south and the mouth of Boone Creek only three miles north of Grays Harbor. It is the only known beach airport in the contiguous United States and the only stretch of beach in Washington State where it is legal to land an airplane. It was named one of the eighteen most unusual airports in the world by Popular Mechanics Magazine. Established in 1976 and open year around, this airport has some unusual characteristics. On the upside, the razor clam digging can be crazy good and the views of the Pacific Ocean are extraordinary. On the downside, the runway and airplane parking lot are underwater during high tide, making it the only airport in the United States to be submerged every single day by the incoming tide. There are no buildings or facilities associated with the airport except airport end markers and a windsock. Anchored at the north end of the airport and across from Boone Creek is the historic and iconic Iron Springs Resort with its cabins etched into the cliffs of the seashore—today, still a sensational, thriving destination.

Is it possible that the American smugglers were using a low-flying aircraft out of this new, unusual, little publicized and remote airport to scout for the Helena Star or to somehow assist in the importation of contraband into the United States? What were the tide conditions on the night of April 15 when the seaman on the Cutter Yocona spotted the flashing lights of the low-flying aircraft off the coast of Grays Harbor heading slowly over the ocean to the west—high or low tide?

Around noon the following day, a Sunday, Captain Morgan was called to the bridge. The Yocona had picked up a radar contact. Shortly afterward the contact came into visual view. The vessel was headed in an easterly direction toward the Strait of Juan de Fuca. She was proceeding at about seven to eight knots. The Coast Guard passed its stern from a distance of a quarter mile identifying it as the Helena Star by the use of binoculars. The Yocona adjusted her speed to that of the freighter and followed her at a distance of 200 meters. She was flying no flag.

The captain of the Helena Star was horrified. He turned on the radio and tuned in the international channel and waited for the inevitable call. Captain Morgan called on the radio and asked what her nationality was. She replied that she was British. He then asked her where she was bound. She responded that her destination was Victoria, B.C. The person responding spoke English with what appeared to be a Spanish accent. Morgan said, "Thank you. Have a good trip." Morgan described her as a small, older freighter of a sort that he had never seen in these waters. She had a green hull, superstructure aft, two cargo hatches in her forward deck area, and two masts. He had seen similar vessels in waters off the coast of Florida. What appeared to be a previous name for the Helena Star, Fraternite, had been painted over with green paint matching the green hull.

Captain Morgan was suspicious of the vessel because it was flying no flag. In addition, he was aware that this was the type of vessel that had been seized several times on the east coast of the United States in connection with drug smuggling. He turned east and took up a position seven or eight miles astern of the Helena Star and followed her easterly heading from 2:00 to 4:00 in the afternoon. Morgan then sent a message to the Thirteenth Coast Guard District Headquarters in Seattle and to the Coast Guard communication station in Kodiak, Alaska. At around 4:00 p.m. he decided to stop following the freighter and headed north for two reasons. Morgan had sighted some fishing vessels within the 200-mile fisheries zone of the United States and Canada that he wanted to investigate. He also wanted to position himself north of the Helena Star in case his suspicions about the vessel proved to be accurate. It was cat-and-mouse time.

First Mate, Pedro Vera, felt a surge of hope as the Cutter Yocona veered off to the north. After an hour passed, he and the captain could no longer see the Cutter and were just a few miles from the buoy at the entrance to the Strait of Juan de Fuca. One of the crew members approached the captain and said the crew was prepared to sink the vessel—a not uncommon practice in the Caribbean in the event nothing can be done to elude capture. Sink the ship, jump in her lifeboats and head for shore. The incriminating evidence ends up on the bottom of the sea—a sort of irretrievable treasure chest. Captain Rubies was reluctant to sink the Helena Star. Around 6:00 p.m. he turned the vessel around and headed southwest. Soon a plane flew ominously low overhead. Was it the Coast Guard or a plane sent by the American coconspirators to locate her? Another crewman suggested to the captain that they slit the bales and throw them into the high seas. If slit, presumably the bags full of marijuana would sink to the bottom.

Lt. Commander Walter John, executive officer on the Yocona, thought the Helena Star was too big to be a fishing trawler and too small to make an honest living hauling freight. She was out of place on this coast.

At 5:30 p.m. Captain Morgan directed the officer of the deck to regain contact with the freighter. Heading east, the Yocona picked her up at about 6:45 p.m., while the captain of the Helena Star was pondering his limited options. She had reversed course and was now heading outbound in a generally westerly direction when he spotted the Yocona coming in her direction. The freighter's maximum speed at this point was only about seven knots. She was no match for the much speedier Yocona. The reversal of direction by the suspect vessel made Captain Morgan even more suspicious. The District Commander sent a message directing the Yocona to continue surveillance. The freighter had said she was headed to Victoria, B.C., but the next time she was spotted, she was headed toward China, some 12,000 miles across the North Pacific. She was now located about 18 miles off the coast of Cape Flattery, Washington, and after nightfall proceeded into the darkness without navigation lights due to generator problems. The Cutter Yocona maintained surveillance throughout the night about 12 miles astern as the Helena Star proceeded seaward.

Late that night, plans began to take shape if the Yocona was given the go ahead to board the Helena Star—plans that took into consideration the worst possible scenarios. Lt. Commander John, who graduated from the Coast Guard Academy in 1966, had been designated to lead the boarding party. He described the boarding party's meeting that night in a later interview with the *Seattle Times*:

What if she refused to let us board or opened fire on us? We decided which Yocona crew members would be in the boarding party and in which order we would board. We decided what weapons we would carry. A backup team on the Yocona would be ready with .50-caliber machine guns mounted on the ship, but only one person had authority to open fire. That fire, if necessary, would be only to disable the freighter, not to wound her crew. We had gotten close enough to draw a rough diagram of the Helena Star and we assigned each of our people a place to go once on board.

On Monday morning, April 17, two volunteers took turns in the crow's nest atop the Yocona's forward mast. From this perch 70 feet above the water, they maintained an excellent view of the freighter, twelve miles away. The remainder of the morning was generally consumed by the Coast Guard and U.S. State Department attempting to determine whether the Helena Star was a British registered vessel or registered anywhere at all. During this process, the Yocona continued to follow the freighter. If a vessel is legally registered by a country other than the United States, it cannot be boarded without authorization from the country of registration. If the vessel is registered in the United States, it can legally be boarded, even on the high seas. Communications with the British government were by message traffic from the Commandant of the Coast Guard, Washington, D.C., and State Department in Washington, D.C., to the American Embassy in London, with some of the messages copying the U.S. Department of Transportation and the Situation Room at the White House.

The situation had reached a level of extreme importance and sensitivity with the decision-making authority reaching the highest levels of the United States government. The last thing the United States wanted to do was displease one of its closest allies. In short, the British government determined that the Helena Star was not a British registered vessel, even though its home port was Road Harbour, Tortola Island, British Virgin Islands in the Caribbean.

In the meantime, other government officials were checking other sources of possible information regarding this suspicious, out-of-place freighter heading west on the high seas. A check with the El Paso Intelligence Center (EPIC) came back negative with respect to any intelligence regarding the vessel. The DEA uses EPIC on a regular basis to run names of individuals or vessels to see if they have been previously involved or suspected of being involved in illegal drug trafficking. Canadian authorities could find no evidence that the vessel was expected at any port in British Columbia. Canada had previously authorized the Yocona to surveil the Helena Star in Canadian waters with the understanding that the Coast Guard could not board the freighter in Canadian territorial waters without their authorization. The entire time that the Helena Star was under surveillance by the Yocona, she never sailed within the territorial waters or customs zone of either Canada or the United States. She sailed only within the 200-mile fishery zone of Canada, which only has to do with fishing and is otherwise considered international waters.

Having found no evidence that the Helena Star was properly registered in any country, the vessel was determined to be "stateless," requiring no authorization from a foreign state to board her. A message went out saying: "Department of State concurs with Coast Guard proposal to board and inspect M/V Helena Star as a stateless vessel and to seize her if contraband found aboard." As a result, around 1:00 p.m. eastern standard time (10:00 a.m. in Seattle), the Commandant of the Coast Guard in Washington, D.C., sent a message to the Thirteenth Coast Guard District in Seattle, indicating it had no objection to a boarding of the Helena Star. This message was then communicated to Captain Morgan by the Thirteenth with a directive to board the vessel to determine her nationality if any, identity and recent activity.

Any attempt by Captain Rubies to flee the scene with his unconventional cargo was dead in the water about 140 miles from land fall. The Helena Star was having engine trouble. The mothership was doomed. The asthmatic gasp of its engines signaled that the chase was over, but the case in which I was to be embroiled for several years was just beginning.

The Coast Guard already had several vessels on standby status. One of them, the 213-foot Coast Guard Cutter Campbell, had been directed to get underway and proceed toward the location of the Yocona and Helena Star. She was armed with a five-inch cannon, as well as several machine guns and small arms. One aircraft had already been deployed the previous evening. Two aircraft were deployed the morning of the intended seizure, including a helicopter launched around 10:00 a.m. from Astoria, Oregon, and a C-130 from San Francisco. Both flew low back and forth over the Helena Star, so low that those on board the freighter could see photographers taking front-page pictures of the ship from all angles. The Cutter Yocona was still hanging back several miles, but the air show seemed to suggest that the moment of truth was quite near. The large aircraft with the Coast Guard red tail made the crew of the Yocona feel more secure. She approached rapidly and one of the aircraft, flying so low that it almost clipped the Helena Star's mast, dropped a flare in front of its bow and a message to the freighter to heave to. The Coast Guard Cutter White Bush was also hovering nearby. The mothership's voyage had ended 140 miles west of the coast of North America.

Planning for the boarding was completed. The Yocona pulled alongside of the doomed ship. At high noon on the high seas of the North Pacific, the Yocona raised a signal for the freighter to heave to and that it was going to board the vessel. Commander Morgan also used an electronic megaphone to convey the same instructions. The Helena Star hove to with the Yocona off its starboard. Commander Morgan advised her to have its crew gather on the deck and rig a ladder for the boarding party to come aboard. A salvage team stood by in case anyone on board tried to scuttle the freighter. The boarding party of six came aboard the freighter from a 26-foot boat. They carried two twelve-gauge shot guns and each member was armed with a .45 caliber pistol. Remaining on the Yocona were two 50-caliber machine guns and two M16 rifles.

Assignments had been worked out earlier as to who would go where once the boarding was complete. Lt. Commander John was the first to board. The assembled crew members were standing together on the main deck. Captain Rubies was standing back underneath the bridge wing. Two members of the Coast Guard guarded the Helena Star crew and two members made a cursory sweep of the vessel. John and the other member of the boarding party approached Captain Rubies, who identified himself as Captain of the Helena Star and shook Lt. Commander John's hand. John advised the captain that they boarded his vessel to determine its identity, nationality, and recent activities. He asked for Roman's captain's license which he promptly produced. Lt. Commander John had never boarded a merchant vessel on the high seas before. Because John had only seen the Helena Star on the high seas, never even within the 200-mile fishing zone of the United States, and because she was at all times closer to Canada than the United States, he had no reason to believe that she was headed toward the United States. The Helena Star's destination was unknown.

Captain Rubies escorted John up the port side ladder to the bridge. One of the Coast Guardsmen guarding the crew had a shotgun and the Coast Guardsman accompanying John had the other shotgun. All sidearms were holstered. John asked to see the vessel's registration documentation and any other documents that would help him identify the vessel. The captain took John down to his cabin on the main deck. The door to his cabin was inscribed, "Kapitan." Rubies took a large sheaf of papers from a desk drawer. Lt. Commander John noticed an empty case of Olympia beer, brewed in Washington, on the floor. They took the papers back up to the bridge and John began looking through them. John found a Provisional Certificate of British Registry, which had expired on June 22, 1977, approximately ten months earlier. Captain Rubies responded that he was not aware of any other pertinent registration documents on board.

The Provisional Certificate was signed by the Britannic Majesty's Vice Consul at the Port of Gothenburg, Sweden, on December 22, 1976. It indicated that the Helena Star was purchased at Tortola by Starboard, Box 53, Tortola, BVI, on the same day and that the owner intended to effect permanent registry at Road Harbour, BVI. Road Harbour is the port for Road Town located on Tortola Island in the British Virgin Islands. In other words, a representative of the British Majesty had given the new owners of the Helena Star six months to accomplish full British Registry. That apparently never came to pass. In addition, the freighter had no vessel logs or cargo manifest.

Lt. Commander John sent one or two of his men along with a member of the Helena Star's crew down into the engineering spaces to make sure that no valves had been opened—to confirm that the vessel was not taking on water and being intentionally sunk. If the vessel sunk, it would take with it all the evidence of a sophisticated marijuana smuggling operation and tons of marijuana would be locked like a treasure chest on the bottom of the ocean. Their inspection revealed that no nefarious activity had occurred in the engine room. John then told Captain Rubies that they were going to have to continue their inspection to check the hold to see if there was a main beam number. The main beam number can be useful in determining the identity and registration of a vessel. Rubies responded that the Helena Star had no main beam number. John told the captain that they would have to verify that there was no main beam number. John asked the captain to direct members of his crew to remove a hatch cover so they could go down in the hold and check for such a number.

Captain Rubies said something to his crew in what John assumed was Spanish. He then turned back to John and said: "They refuse to work." After several more attempts to get the crew's assistance, the hatch covers were finally opened. John sent Ensign Wheatley and Petty Officer Bowling into the hold to look for the main beam number. Clearly, the boarding party was more interested in finding illegal cargo than looking for a main beam number but used that excuse as a pretext to get into the hold. Sure enough, within seconds, the two Coast Guardsmen in the cargo hold asked for a drug test kit. A kit was sent down into the hold. About five minutes later, Wheatley emerged triumphantly from below with a positive test for marijuana. It was stacked nine feet high. The positive test result was radioed back to the Yocona, which responded that the Helena Star was to be seized and all persons on board the freighter were to be arrested. Audible jubilation rang out across the water from the Yocona. Its first marijuana bust had been consummated and what a bust it was.

Lt. Commander John took Captain Rubies down to the main deck and assembled the entire crew. Rubies was advised that his vessel had been seized and he and his crew were under arrest. He was asked to convey that to his crew in Spanish. John then advised Rubies of his Miranda rights and asked him to translate those rights to his crew. Rubies willingly complied. All, except the captain, were transferred to the Yocona, strip searched and locked up. The strip search resulted in the detection of the possibility that one of the Helena Star's crew was infected with syphilis, causing U.S. Immigration to be notified to examine for possible communicable disease on the ship's arrival in Seattle. Two more Coastguardsmen were airlifted by helicopter from the Coast Guard Air Station in Astoria, Oregon, to supplement the custodial crew on board the Yocona.

Lt. Commander John asked Captain Rubies some questions about the operation of the vessel and then confined him to his stateroom with an armed guard outside. The capture of the Helena Star was a smooth operation, in large part because all hands-on board the Yocona were prepared. Places were found for the boarding party to sleep and then the Helena Star, under the control of the U.S. Coast Guard, headed back toward the Strait of Juan de Fuca. No firearms or other obvious weapons were found on board. The following day, April 18, while en route to Seattle, a member of the Coast Guard found a case breaking clue—a page of stationery from the Holiday Inn in Panama City in a desk drawer in the captain's cabin. It was the same piece of paper that was given to the captain in Colon, Panama, which contained a crude drawing of a sailboat and the words, "AZUL JOLLY."

It had taken David Victorson, Michael Lund, and their crew several days to get their act together and get the Knik Wind and the Chignik 105 on their way to complete the offloading of the Helena Star. As night fell on April 17, the day of its seizure, Victorson and his crew, who were not involved with getting the tugboat and barge out to sea to meet the freighter, were sitting in Lund's house awaiting news of the offloading. A news flash came across their television stating that the Coast Guard had seized a freighter with a multi-ton load of marijuana and were escorting it to Seattle. It was obvious that their offloading efforts were dead in the water. During the early morning hours of April 18, the tug and barge left Port Angeles and headed westbound in the Strait of Juan de Fuca to rendezvous with the Helena Star. Mike Lund, Patricia Karnik, and Dean Bowen, aboard the Knik Wind tug, were astonished to see in the distance the Helena Star being escorted by the Cutter Yocona heading in their direction. Once they realized their quest had come to an end, they continued in the same direction to avoid any suspicion and then veered up the west coast of Vancouver Island. They ditched the barge in Barkley Sound near Bamfield, British Columbia, and the tug in Port Alberni. According to Victorson, the crew was supposed to have scuttled the Joli after its part in the operation was finished because, no matter how thoroughly a boat was cleaned after carrying pot, residue was always left over. Michael Lund, however, had a different idea, believing that he had a vested interest in the great racing sailboat.

Victorson's crew vanished. He and Eric Hale returned to Marin. According to Patricia Karnik, she and Mike Lund eventually reconnected in Seattle. They went on a shopping spree, spending money like it was going out of style. They hopped into a big, black pickup registered to Lund and headed south. Karnik wanted out of their relationship. She dropped Lund off like a hot potato at the Sun River resort in central Oregon. She said, "Bye, bye," and kept going south to her home in La Jolla, California. "I never saw him again." She compared Mike Lund's and her lives to the back flips they did on skis. Their lives had been turned "upside down."

While the Yocona and Helena Star worked their way through the Strait of Juan de Fuca on the day after the seizure, DEA Agents flew from Seattle to Port Angeles, boarded a Coast Guard vessel, and made their way to the Yocona to begin conducting their investigation. They had obtained a search warrant for the Helena Star earlier in the day. They interviewed the First Mate, Pedro Vera, at approximately 1:00

a.m. on the morning of April 19 and then transferred to the Helena Star to interview Captain Rubies.

Roman was amazingly candid with the agents. He admitted to being at the helm of the Helena Star when it went through the Panama Canal and took on the cargo of marijuana on the west coast of Colombia. He told them that he sailed north to a set of coordinates on the high seas of the North Pacific. He even admitted to meeting a blue sailboat to take on "twenty boxes of supplies, water, and necessary engine parts." He said, "The individuals aboard the sailing vessel stated that they would return in approximately two days to accomplish the transfer of the marijuana to another vessel." Rubies also gave the DEA agents the names of the two Colombians that he had been dealing with since he joined the team. He left out the part about having already transferred a substantial quantity of marijuana to the Joli. Little did the DEA know at that time that they had already been had—that thirteen tons was either on its way to the Midwest or had already arrived to the satisfaction of its voracious consumers.

Meanwhile, plans were made for guarding the freighter and its valuable load once it docked in Seattle. Twelve petty officers with three loaded .45 caliber pistols and two riot shot guns were ordered to meet the Yocona and the Helena Star. The intent was to conduct shore-side surveillance with a three-station watch force—one petty officer stationed at the freighter's bow armed with a .45 caliber pistol and two petty officers, one armed with a .45 caliber pistol and one with a riot shotgun, stationed at each of the two access points to the pier. Water surveillance was to be conducted by a 41-foot boat with one mounted M-60 machine gun and a coxswain armed with a .45 caliber pistol.

The Helena Star sailed under its own power until it got to Admiralty Straits where it slowed to less than one knot. It was beginning to approach a state of paralysis. By the time it passed Marrowstone Island in northern Puget Sound, it was going about as slow as a drunken cockroach. The Coast Guard then decided to have the Cutter Yocona tow the freighter the last thirty to forty miles due to its mechanical problems. The engines were overheating to the point that the vessel had to frequently slow down. It would have taken at least another day to get to Seattle if she had not been towed. Who wouldn't want to get to Seattle with great haste to receive the adulation of their superiors and the attentive public? What a bust! It would turn out to be the largest seizure of marijuana on the west coast of the United States, if not the largest such seizure in the northern hemisphere. As the vessel proceeded to Seattle, Captain Rubies was very cooperative with the Coast Guard any time they had questions about the operation of the freighter.

Early in the afternoon of April 19, 1978, after traveling a couple hundred miles over two days, the Yocona towing the Helena Star arrived at Pier 36 in Seattle. The freighter had entered Elliot Bay flying a flag the size of a bedsheet with a greenish marijuana leaf. There was some dispute as to who was responsible for this. Commander Morgan thought it had been made by the jubilant boarding party of the United States Coast Guard Cutter Yocona under his command. However, Lt. Commander John, head of the boarding party, said he thought the pennant was compliments of the DEA agents who came aboard after his boarding party. The Helena Star was also flying an American flag fluttering proudly and the Coast Guard ensign. In addition, the Cutter's crew had stenciled a small silhouette of a marijuana leaf on the Yocona's bridge to signify the ship's first seizure of an illegal drug-laden vessel.

Droves of spectators lined up along the docks; some wept. "This bust is going to drive the price of pot out of sight," someone said. "If," someone else said, "they burn it." Another said, "Or they ought to store it until it's legalized.

They are not criminals. They are just entrepreneurs." Reporter Rick Anderson wrote: "They did not have to telegraph the Helena Star's arrival, as they did on this same waterfront in July 1897, when the steamship Portland arrived from Alaska. Aboard the Portland was a ton of Klondike gold." Willard Hatch, a prominent Seattle attorney, said he was down at the waterfront when the ship pulled in and saw hundreds of sea birds circling overhead. "By the end of the day, there was no tern unstoned." George Burke at Bethlehem Steel said that, if the ship operators had any class at all, they would have named the ship the "Joint Venture."

The *Seattle Times* described the grand entrance of the freighter:

"Dozens of radio, newspaper and television reporters and photographers watched from the helicopter deck of the ice-breaker Polar Sea at Pier 36 as the Helena Star and then the Yocona were maneuvered to their berths. Smaller 40-foot Coast Guard vessels armed with machine guns patrolled the waterfront as the ships docked, and dozens of security officers armed with shotguns and handguns patrolled near the ships."

Even so, a few intrepid workers on the pier found a way to extract a bit of the cargo for their personal use. They secreted a small amount of the bounty within the cuffs of their pants legs before they finished their shifts.

While the marijuana, along with a few scorpions in the hold, was under armed guard, the Helena Star's crew was transferred from the Yocona to the Polar Sea and then into waiting Customs Service cars. The nine men were driven to the United States Courthouse and appeared before Magistrate Swiegert at 5:05 p.m., all wearing Mike Lund's ski sweaters.

6

THE BIG BURN

THE DINGY, GREEN HELENA STAR LAID AT REST IN ITS BERTH at Pier 36 under the watch of armed guards. The day after its arrival, Assistant United States Attorney Ron Sim wanted to get rid of the load of pot in its cargo hold as soon as possible. He was worried about the high cost of guarding the marijuana and "organized criminals" trying to steal it. Customs agents had advised him that this had been tried two times recently on the East Coast. Sim had a "serious security problem" on his hands. The *Seattle Post-Intelligencer* reported: "Blue uniformed customs officers, who were pacing the dock next to the captured ship yesterday, were growing weary of guarding the prize. A U.S. Coast Guard patrol boat floated constantly at the mouth of the ship's berth. No one was allowed near the ship, or even out on the pier where newsmen had been permitted Wednesday." No one had stepped forward to claim ownership of the beleaguered vessel. It was also discovered that some Colombian scorpions were hiding in the cargo hold, having hitched a ride to the great Pacific Northwest. Fortunately, there are only two varieties of Colombian scorpions that are potentially deadly. According to Sim, scorpions will multiply the longer the marijuana is stored.

On Friday, April 21, Mr. Sim obtained a court order signed by United States District Court Judge Morell Sharp allowing the destruction of the boat load of weed—1,239 bales wrapped in burlap with an average weight of 60 pounds each. Sim said, "I've never had my phone ring so many times no matter what I'd done." The order had been hammered out and agreed to by Federal Public Defender Irwin Schwartz, the lawyer for one of the Helena Star's crew. Sim said that Schwartz, concerned about pretrial publicity, agreed to the order only if it limited press coverage. Schwartz said he wanted to "tone down" a "circus atmosphere" that had surrounded the Helena Star since its capture.

Instead of keeping things quiet, all hell broke loose. The *Seattle Times* reported:

> Coast Guardsmen presented reporter after reporter with the court order, which said "press coverage" of the unloading of the Helena Star was prohibited. Politely, the guards said reporters had to leave Coast Guard facilities or face possible arrest. Attorneys representing both *The Times* and *The Seattle Post-Intelligencer* questioned the order in court. While the newspapers argued over the order, which they said was "overly broad," plain-clothes federal agents began unloading the marijuana. Reporters waited outside the fenced pier. Meanwhile, 300 yards away the marijuana, contained in gunny sacks, was hoisted out of the ship's hold and into waiting trucks. Shortly after 4:00 p.m. the first truck, tightly guarded by federal agents who feared a possible hijacking of the exotic cargo, rolled through the gate.

Over the next three hours there was a flurry of phone calls between reporters, editors, newspaper attorneys, the United States Attorney's Office, and the DEA.

The marijuana was weighed at a truck stop in South Seattle—an astounding 37 tons of "Colombian Gold" worth an estimated street value of $74 million. Thirty-seven tons works out to well over a million one-ounce bags of weed. After refueling, the trucks, accompanied by marked Customs vehicles, snaked their way through rush-hour traffic and onto the freeway heading north. After about thirty miles on the road, the trucks arrived at 5:20 p.m. at the gate to the Scott Paper Co. plant on the city of Everett's waterfront followed by a cast of reporters. A DEA agent waved the trucks through but ordered reporters, despite their protests, to stop. He said there was a court order banning the press from being present when the marijuana was destroyed. It was here at the Scott Paper Co. mill, behind closed doors, that the humongous load of weed would be burned. All that would be kept were two whole bales and core samples from every twenty bales of the 1,239 bales of marijuana seized, samples that would be kept as evidence in the case. Presumably 37 tons (or to be slightly more precise, 74,180 pounds) went up in smoke. One person from Seattle, referring to the city of Everett, commented, "It was the first time in history that anyone ever enjoyed the air of the city to the north of us."

Government officials refused to let the public see how much marijuana was taken off the Helena Star or see it burned. As a result, skepticism around Seattle and its environs ran rampant. One story in the *Seattle Post-Intelligencer* referred to the pot as "supposedly" burned. Bob Tuengel, 53, a steam plant fireman at the Scott Paper mill, worked the boilers "the night they burned the pot." He had worked at Scott Paper for twenty-four years. He wanted to clear up any misunderstanding about the fate of the 37 tons. "It was burned; I was there. When I got to the plant to start my shift at 11:00 p.m. Friday, I could not believe it. I thought something blew up; everybody was running around. They had been burning it since about 6:00 p.m. The federal people broke up the bales, some of them with fire axes; they would not let anyone else touch it. We burned it in the hogged fuel boilers that make steam to run paper-making machines, and that night it was taking the place of other fuel. The boiler around the chutes off the conveyor belts got so hot that some of the pot caught fire before it went in the furnace. I was the only one there besides the federal agents, who put it in the furnaces. I was walking in the stuff six to eight inches deep." Tuengel said the job was not wrapped up till about 4 a.m. It had taken almost ten hours to burn. Law enforcement officials there came from the Coast Guard, U.S. Customs, DEA, and the Washington State Drug Control Assistance Unit.

A huge amount of media interest in this gigantic drug bust continued. It became part of Seattle folklore. One day I was sitting in my office when I received a call from a vendor who decided to cash in on the publicity. His day job entailed being the chief purser aboard the Alaska State Ferries' MV Malespina. He was selling yellow t-shirts with a silk-screened image of the freighter, with the words, "CREW, HELENA STAR," emblazoned on the front. The freighter had a flag hanging over its stern bearing a marijuana leaf. According to the *Seattle Post-Intelligencer*, he told how he "climbed over a lot of old dead ships" at the south end of Lake Union so he could get a broadside photograph of the Helena Star. "I then brought the pictures to a staff artist at Edmonds Athletic Supply. He drew up the sketch of the ship, did the lettering, and printed it up." Within several weeks, he had sold several hundred t-shirts. County Cork Clothiers reported brisk sales of the t-shirts. I ended up buying several dozen shirts and giving them away or selling them at cost, in particular to several assistant U.S. Attorneys and other staff in their office. It was a big seller. I joked to people that I had the t-shirt concession for the Helena Star.

7

INVESTIGATION AND INDICTMENT

O N APRIL 25, 1978, A FEDERAL GRAND JURY IN SEATTLE formally indicted my client, Captain Rubies, and his First Mate, Pedro Vera. The grand jury accused the two men of "importing and attempting to import marijuana" into the United States. At that time, the alleged crime was punishable by a maximum sentence of five years in prison. According to the Indictment, between March 1 and April 17, 1978, "within the Western District of Washington and within the special maritime and territorial jurisdiction of the United States," the men "did conspire with each other and with others who at this time are unknown" to import marijuana. The exact date that the conspiracy began was also unknown.

The United States Immigration and Naturalization Service had placed holds on the other seven crew members because they were not citizens of the United States and had no legal basis for being in the United States. On the same day, the Helena Star was moved from the Coast Guard's Pier 36 through the Hiram Chittenden Locks to the U.S. Naval Reserve base at the south end of Lake Union. Within a few days the unindicted crew members were deported back to the countries of their citizenship, six to Colombia and one to Brazil.

Once the freighter had been seized on the high seas, the Drug Enforcement Administration took over the continuing investigation. They had boarded first the Yocona and then the Helena Star during the vessels' two-day trip to Seattle. They interviewed all the captives and, pursuant to a search warrant, seized miscellaneous papers, documents, navigational charts, a water pump, and $1,113.65 in U.S. currency. The water pump was the one purchased by Homero Ospina in Los Angeles, which was flown to Seattle and on to Sequim Bay by float plane. Fortunately, the DEA in their search had not found the modest retainer that Roman provided to me at our first meeting at the Marshal's lockup in the United States Courthouse. As evidence that the destination of the freighter's load of contraband was the United States, they seized a wrapper for a sirloin tip dated April 6, 1978, distributed by a company in Gig Harbor, Washington; a wrapper for 22.7 kilograms of onions from Salem, Oregon; a Sure-Fresh bread wrapper; a wrapper used for 25 pounds of carrots packaged in California; a Darigold butter carton from Seattle; a cheese wrapper from Tillamook, Oregon; an empty gallon container for water from Seattle; the empty Olympia beer carton for 24 cans of beer observed earlier in Captain Rubies quarters; and a February, 1978, *Playboy* magazine, a critical piece of evidence.

Among the most interesting papers and documents found on board the Helena Star were the following: (1) the Provisional Certificate of British Registry which expired about ten months earlier on June 22, 1977, which indicated that the owner of the freighter was Starboard, Box 53, Tortola, British Virgin Islands, (2) one share certificate of Starboard LTD for Carlos Osorio-Pacheco, (3) one share certificate of Starboard LTD for Pedro Jose Arieta-Lineros, (4) a document charging the Helena Star with violation of the Water Pollution Control Act as the vessel entered the Panama Canal Zone on March 4, 1978, and (5) three receipts bearing the name of Pedro Jose Arrieta-Lineros. These two individuals, Osorio-Pacheco and Arieta-Lineros, were the two Colombian businessmen who talked Roman Rubies into captaining the Helena Star on its ill-fated trip from Cartagena, Colombia, to a set of coordinates on the high seas of the North Pacific Ocean.

The night of the seizure of the freighter, April 17, 1978, Bob Morton, who had sold the Knik Wind tug and Chignik 105 barge to Michael Lund earlier in the day, had just gotten off the phone around 10:30 p.m. Robert Moran, David Victorson's San Francisco attorney, had called to apologize to Morton that he had not had time to wire the remaining amount owed on the tug and barge that day, but would get it done the next day. Morton said, "My wife had been out that evening to one of her dealies and about 11:30 she came in and told me that she had heard on the news where a boat had been picked up with marijuana on it. And I got to thinking, My God, I wonder if that is what they wanted the tug and the barge for. I was getting a little concerned then. On Tuesday morning I called over to the Shilshole Marina to see if the boat was tied up there." The Knik Wind tug was no longer tied up at Pier G and had apparently disappeared in the darkness of night.

Morton had agreed with Lund the day before to allow the Chignik 105 barge to be towed to Port Angeles by his trusted friend, Al Wolover. Morton got Wolover on the radio and Wolover told him where he had left the barge in Port Angeles. Morton then called a tug company there and determined that the Chignik barge was no longer where Wolover had left it. Morton got a phone number from the telephone company operator for Lund in Sequim, but there was no answer at Lund's house. He called the University Towers Hotel several times, where Lund was supposedly staying, with no success. He finally reached attorney Moran in San Francisco, who advised him that he had not wired the money to Morton yet, because he hadn't been able to reach Lund to obtain authorization to wire the funds. Morton became very agitated. He was selling the missing tug for someone else and the missing barge for himself.

The next day, April 19, Morton chartered a plane and went all the way out one side of Puget Sound looking in all the bays. That afternoon he chartered another plane and went up the other side of the Sound all the way to Point Roberts and came back over the San Juan Islands but did not see the tug or barge anywhere. Thursday morning, April 20, Morton sent another plane up and told those onboard to look on the west side of Vancouver Island in British Columbia. The Chignik barge was located anchored in the second little bay north of the village of Bamfield on Barkley Sound on the west coast of Vancouver Island. The Knik Wind tug was found about fifteen miles away at the head of Alberni Inlet, which is essentially a fjord that connects Barkley Sound to Port Alberni. The tug was tied up to a float at the boat harbor in Port Alberni.

Years later, Patricia Karnik, Mike Lund's girlfriend, who had moved to Jackson Hole, Wyoming, had a date with a guy who said he was instrumental in locating the Chignik barge in Barkley Sound. She spilled red wine on the white carpet in his house. The gentleman never called her again.

During the same day that the tug and barge were located in Canada on April 20, Morton had his first conversation with Patricia Karnik. Morton reached her at the University Towers Hotel where she was supposedly staying with Lund. She said the Knik Wind tug was on its way to a boat harbor in either Anacortes or Edmonds in Puget Sound, she was not sure which, and would be there within about an hour. She wanted copies of the Certificates of Registry for the tug and barge. Morton told her she would get nothing until he was paid in full. As Karnik had indicated earlier in the day, the Knik Wind did end up traveling south from Port Alberni back through the Strait of Juan de Fuca, around the tip of Vancouver Island, past the American San Juan Islands, and docking at the end of a pier at Sky Marina in Anacortes, Washington. Narcotics agents seized the errant tug there on May 4. It was searched, but nothing of significance found.

Mr. Morton then called Robert Moran in San Francisco and told his secretary that he now knew where the tug and barge were located. If he wasn't paid by five o'clock he had a man standing by with a crew to fly up there and get the equipment and bring it back, and that he would turn the matter over to the Coast Guard. The secretary said:

"Don't do that. We'll make sure that you get your money there." For the next hour, the phones were busy. A gentleman from the Bank of California in San Francisco called Morton and said that someone from Moran's office had brought some stocks and bonds to the bank to put up for collateral to get the rest of the money and that he had just called the Bank of California in Seattle requesting the bank to issue a cashier's check to Morton. Morton got a call from the bank in Seattle at about 4:20 p.m. indicating that they had a check for him. Morton went downtown and picked up the check. The balance owed to Morton was $122,500, but the check was for $125,000 because Morton demanded an additional $2,500 for the time and expenses required by him to locate the tug and barge. The check was paid on behalf of Diversified Investment Portfolios, Inc., a Panamanian corporation, at the direction of David Victorson, the firm's United States agent.

The same day, April 20, Morton had received three or four calls from Patricia Karnik about obtaining the documentation for the tug and barge. He told her to meet him around 5:00 p.m. at an office in the Smith Tower in Pioneer Square, which did the documentation work on marine equipment for him. Because he had just been paid off, Morton provided her with the necessary documentation for the Knik Wind and the Chignik.

Karnik seemed to be quite shook up when they met. Morton told her to tell Mike Lund that he was not mad at him, that if he wanted to do some more business to come on back. Karnik's response was that Lund had gone south to buy another boat. Several days later, DEA agents contacted the University Towers Hotel, where Lund had supposedly been staying when he was in Seattle. A check of phone records at the hotel determined that Lund had made several calls from his room to a room at the Red Lion Bayshore Hotel in Port Angeles. That room had been registered to David Victorson.

On April 27, U.S. Magistrate John Weinberg issued two Federal search warrants to search the 61-foot Joli and the two-story house of Michael J. Lund on East Sequim Bay Road. These warrants were not executed till four days later on May 1 at 1:15 p.m. That morning, Bill Niemi, former president of Eddie Bauer who had sold the Joli to Lund, received a phone call from Cliff Goudie, an employee at his bank, the Old National Bank in Seattle. Cliff said that the bank had received a phone call from a woman in San Francisco on April 29 asking about the amount remaining due on the sale of the Joli. Cliff also told Niemi that Mike Lund had missed the April 15 payment on the sailboat's mortgage. Niemi was not particularly surprised because he had had several conversations with Lund, who told him that the Swiss people were here sailing the boat and preparing to pay off the boat mortgage in full around April 15. Lund, however, had made no such arrangement with the bank. So Niemi gave Cliff the phone number that he had for Lund's home on Sequim Bay. Twenty minutes later, Cliff called Niemi back and said that Lund's phone had been disconnected for nonpayment of his bill. This delinquency by Lund was quite an embarrassment for Niemi with the bank, given his role as guarantor of the loan.

Niemi said, "These facts raised an enormous doubt in my mind. I just simply could not understand what was going on here. I knew that Mike did a lot of travelling because he had related to me that during the previous few months he had been to Hawaii several times during the winter, spent a good deal of time helicopter skiing in the Bugaboos, and had been to Europe a number of times. And I could see him being late on a bill, but you've got to go a long time before the phone company cancels your service."

Niemi called around to some of the sailboat people he knew to see if anybody had talked with Lund recently. Nobody had seen him for a couple weeks. Niemi was left in an uncomfortable situation because he had no way of contacting Lund. Niemi called a friend of his, Paul Ulibarri, who had sailed a lot with him. Niemi believed that Ulibarri knew where Lund's house was on Sequim Bay.

Niemi owned a Cessna 180 float plane, but his pilot's license was not current. On May 1 he got a pilot to fly Ulibarri and him from Seattle's Kenmore Air Harbor up to Sequim Bay. Unbeknownst to them, the DEA had already arrived at Lund's house and had just executed the two search warrants issued four days earlier for the Joli and Lund's house. It was 1:15 in the afternoon. There was a small orange skiff in the yard. It matched the description of the skiff, which Dean Bowen from California had used to meet and pay Al Wolover the second half of the $1,500 that Lund agreed to pay Wolover to tow the Chignik barge to Port Angeles. As there was no one at Lund's residence, the DEA forced entry through the bathroom window. In the house, Agent Prange seized approximately 40 grams of marijuana, a rather paltry amount given the nature of the investigation.

The magnificent Joli was moored below the high bank in the bay in front of Lund's house. The DEA searched the Joli and found marijuana residue throughout the vessel in every cabin and storage area, some outside on the deck and later in a vacuum cleaner inside a storage locker in Federal Way, Washington. Miscellaneous papers, documents, and receipts were seized from both the Joli and the house. Among the papers seized was a damp and crumpled piece of paper found in the garbage can behind Lund's house. It was the same piece of paper that Captain Rubies gave to Lund during the second partial offloading from the Helena Star to the Joli. In the note Rubies had told Lund: "Charter another boat. Please try to discharge everything" when he returned and to bring some more water, oil and food.

Also found in Lund's residence was a receipt for a stay at the Chateau Lacombe, a Canadian Pacific Hotel in Edmonton, Alberta, Canada, for the night of April 19, a photograph of the historic Empress Hotel in Victoria on Vancouver Island, and a receipt for a stay at the beautiful Bayshore Inn in Vancouver, Canada, for the period of time between April 22 through April 24 in the name of Mr. and Mrs. Karnik. Lund had remained in Canada for a few days before calling Karnik in Seattle, who informed him that he was a prime suspect. April 20 was the day that the Knik Wind tug and Chignik barge were spotted in Canada by a plane sent to search for them by Bob Morton.

Chet Miller, Lund's neighbor, contacted DEA Agent Moriarty outside of Lund's residence at the time that the search warrants were being executed and provided him with information about a skiff tied to a buoy out in the water in front of Miller's property. Miller said it was metal and about a 25-foot-long landing craft type boat—a flat-bottom boat with a front end that dropped down. Miller also said there appeared to be marijuana residue in the boat. The last conversation Miller had had with Lund was around April 19, probably just after news broke of the seizure of the freighter when Lund called and asked Miller if the Joli was okay. Lund told Miller that a couple of fellows were coming by his house to get an anchor and some other gear off the Joli and wondered if they could unload at Miller's dock and if Miller cared if they tied the skiff to Miller's buoy. On April 20, one day after the Helena Star was towed into Seattle, two guys showed up at Mike's house, went out to the Joli, took some things off the sailboat, and transported them in the skiff over to Miller's dock. Miller helped them tie up, unload, and carry the gear up to the beach, where they loaded the gear into a white van and left. The skiff was still there. Miller pointed it out to Agent Moriarty on May 1.

About this time, Niemi and Ulibarri came circling down out of the sky over the cliff on the east side of Sequim Bay. The Joli was tied to her mooring buoy. They landed on the water, and there were three gentlemen standing on the deck of the Joli. According to Niemi, "Since it was obvious that none of them were Mike—he's quite a slim fellow, slight build; these were some pretty good-sized, husky guys—I figured it was the Swiss guys he told me were out sailing this boat. So we taxied up to the boat, and I stepped out on the float and asked the gentlemen if Mike was around, and they indicated no, and every other question was in the negative, and one of them showed me his badge, and they were members of the DEA and members of the narcotics group, and they had seized the boat about an hour before." They asked Niemi and his friend, Ulibarri, to come aboard the Joli and identify themselves. The agents threw them a line and the float plane was tied up to the stern of Niemi's former sailboat. Niemi and Ulibarri came aboard and identified themselves. Niemi quickly realized that he had some explaining to do—that his interest in the Joli was purely financial.

Niemi said later, "I got the surprise of my life when I went on board and they told me they were federal narcotics agents. I was stunned. It was a bolt out of the blue. It is mind-boggling. I am going to be fascinated to see how it goes together. It's like something out of James Bond." The agents said the vessel was seized because it was involved in the commission of a crime, but they would not even say what crime. Imagine Niemi's amazement when he found out later that the Joli had been used to offload thirteen tons of Colombian Gold. Niemi hastened to explain his interest in the Joli to the agents. The DEA agents planned to tow the sailboat to Seattle.

After inquiring of the agents whether they planned to move the Joli, Niemi indicated, "I would be willing to assist them in moving it because it is a complicated ship to operate and difficult to move in those waters, and so they then waited to check, I believe, into the Seattle headquarters as to the plans and whether that was appropriate." While waiting for a response, Niemi took the opportunity to walk around the deck and examine the condition of the vessel, particularly the hull. The hull had severe abrasions on the port side along with a considerable amount of green paint on the edge of the toe rail, the rail that joins the deck with the hull. Unbeknownst to Niemi at that time, the paint appeared to match the color of the Helena Star's hull. An aluminum turning block in the same area, used to turn the direction of a line and that has two aluminum handles protruding from it, had been crushed. Obviously the Joli had been pushed up against something. The bow pulpit had also received a very severe blow and had been crushed down.

Niemi then went below deck in order to show the agents about the operation of the Joli. Niemi said, "Below she was in a very neat and orderly manner. The boat was in beautiful condition. However, it certainly surprised me to see that she had been virtually cleaned out below. The forward third of the boat is the sail locker and it was completely empty except for a few small empty sail bags. Even the main anchor had been removed. He had taken all the cushions out, left cushions only on the port side in the crew's quarters, took everything out, so the boat was really stripped out in that regard." A lot of miscellaneous gear was gone. Only two or three sails for the Joli were still on board. When Niemi sold the sailboat to Lund, she had thirty sails. The small empty sail bags were Northwyn sail bags that were not intended to be used for the Joli's sails, which were too large for the Northwyn bags found on board. Niemi, however, did not see obvious evidence that the sailboat had been used to transport contraband.

The DEA agents finally accepted Niemi's offer to help sail the boat to Seattle's Lake Union via the Hiram Chittenden locks, which carry more boat traffic than any other locks in the United States. Hiram Chittenden was the Seattle District Commander of the Army Corps of Engineers when construction of the locks began in the early 1900s. Outside of the Pacific Northwest, he was better known as a noted historian of the American West, especially the fur trade—documented in his two-volume treatise, *The American Fur Trade of the Far West*, published in 1902. The original plan was to have a single lock made of wood. Chittenden convinced the decision makers that there should be one small lock and one large lock for ships and that they be made of concrete. The locks would be constructed at the Narrows between saltwater Puget Sound and freshwater Salmon Bay. Chittenden retired as Brigadier General from the Army Corps and became President of the Seattle Port Commission. The locks were named for him in honor of the gigantic role he played in the completion of this mammoth project. The first ship passed through the locks in 1916. The official opening occurred on July 4, 1917. Leading the parade was the 184-foot *Roosevelt*, named after the former President who championed the construction of the Panama Canal.

Niemi, two crew members and two DEA agents took the Joli through the locks, Salmon Bay, and the Freemont Cut before arriving in Lake Union on May 3. They docked the boat at Cadranell's Marina. Bob Cadranell, one of the crew members helping to move the boat, was the Joli's former sailing master for Niemi on such races as the Victoria to Maui open ocean races.

On the same day that the Joli was seized, DEA agents seized from Mike Lund's house a receipt for the purchase of 35 sail bags from Northwyn sails and used airline tickets. Seized from the Joli were two Chevron gas receipts from Neah Bay, one dated April 4 and one dated April 9, 1978. Neah Bay is located at the head of the Strait of Juan de Fuca, the last gas dock available to gas up before meeting a mothership on the high seas of the North Pacific or the first place to refuel upon returning to the Strait from the high seas. Lund's house looked to the agents like someone had cleaned it out and moved on. Furniture and stereo gear were still there, but clothing and toiletries appeared to be missing.

Around the same period of time, DEA agents had contacted Seattle Air Charter Services at Boeing Field and learned that in April several individuals and a female matching the description of Lund's girlfriend, Patricia Karnik, had been making frequent and rather unusual trips back and forth between Seattle and Sequim Bay or Port Angeles. They would pay using hundred-dollar bills and not ask for any change back. They were always in a big rush. They would fly up wearing suits or nice clothes and a day later they would come back looking very dirty and sweaty.

Seattle Air Charter flew David Victorson to Port Angeles on April 13, around the time that part of the thirteen tons was offloaded onto the Joli. Four days later on April 17, Seattle Air Charter Services flew Victorson and two other people to Port Angeles. All three seemed happy and excited. On that day the Chignik barge had been towed to Port Angeles for Lund by Bob Morton's friend, Al Wolover, and that night the Knik Wind tug had surreptitiously left Shilshole Bay Marina presumably for Port Angeles so the tug and barge could connect and rendezvous with the Helena Star the next day.

The Coast Guard announced the seizure of the Helena Star late in the day on April 17 and news of the seizure was widely circulated by the media. Not having heard yet about the seizure, Mike Lund,

Patricia Karnik, and Dean Bowen on board the Knik Wind with barge in tow left Port Angeles the next morning, April 18, to rendezvous with the Helena Star. Lund spotted the Helena Star in the distance being escorted by a white vessel with a dominant red diagonal stripe—the Coast Guard Cutter Yocona—and quickly steered for Canadian waters and the shelter of Port Alberni, British Columbia, to hide. The next day, April 19, the two people flown to Port Angeles two days earlier with Victorson were flown back to Seattle. At that time, they were depressed and dejected. They had good reason to be.

On May 3, Patricia Karnik was observed leaving Lund's residence on Sequim Bay, driving very erratically and at high speeds. This was two days after the DEA seized the Joli and moved it to Seattle's Lake Union. Karnik had gone to Lund's house to retrieve some things. She was surveilled driving all the way from Sequim to Seattle by DEA agents, who eventually contacted her after she pulled into a parking lot at Ray's Boathouse, a well-known and popular restaurant located on Shilshole Bay. She was driving a 1978 black Chevrolet pickup with a silver canopy registered to Mike Lund, Sequim, Washington. At that time, the agents had an arrest warrant for Lund and were actively looking for him. He was considered a fugitive.

Karnik told the agents that she knew about the Helena Star and Joli, but she was not involved in the operation, that her knowledge was gained in conversation with Lund, David Victorson, Eric Hale, Jim Turner, and Dean Bowen. She said that Lund had little money and that Victorson was the source of all the money Lund used to buy the Joli, the Knik Wind, and the Chignik. She indicated that those guys had assisted in the offloading of marijuana from the mothership to the Joli and from the Joli to shore and that the tug and barge were purchased to remove the rest of the marijuana from the Helena Star.

The agents searched the new pickup she was driving, seized her diary and, among other things, a room registration receipt from the Bayshore Inn in Vancouver, British Columbia, a receipt from Seattle Air Charter Services, and a rental agreement for storage at Jonathan's Self-Service Storage. After being confronted with entries in her diary, she admitted to being on board the Joli with Mr. Lund for the second rendezvous with the Helena Star to provide fresh water, food, and other provisions. She said the storage unit in Federal Way, south of Seattle, contained parts from the Knik Wind tug. Finally, she said that on April 19, while returning by air from Vancouver, Canada, to Seattle, she had flown over the M/V Helena Star as it was being towed into Puget Sound by the Coast Guard.

On May 3, Chesterene Cwiklik, not a tugboat or barge, but a very accomplished Supervising Criminalist for the Washington State Crime Laboratory, took paint samples from both the Helena Star and Joli while they were moored in Lake Union. She determined that scratches and paint on both vessels were consistent with the Joli having scraped up against the Helena Star on the high seas of the North Pacific.

On May 8, David Victorson was arrested at his home in San Anselmo, California. On May 10 Patricia Karnik went to the United States Courthouse in Seattle in response to being served with a subpoena to testify before a federal grand jury investigating the conspiracy. The subpoena was quashed as the grand jury decided to indict her instead, and she surrendered to federal authorities at that time. Earlier in the day, the grand jury had returned a four-count indictment charging Michael Lund, David Victorson, and Karnik with (1) conspiring to import marijuana into the United States, (2) conspiring to possess marijuana, and (3) actual importation and possession of a large quantity of marijuana. Captain Rubies and First Mate Pedro Vera, having already been charged, were added to the new indictment.

Victorson posted a $50,000 bail bond, requiring nothing out of pocket except a ten% fee to a bail bondsman ($5,000). Karnik hired a San Diego lawyer, Joe Giovanazzi, the boyfriend of one of her freestyle skiing chums. He tried to get her bail reduced saying that her connection was peripheral. Assistant United States Attorney Ron Sim responded claiming his "evidence will show that she was up to her neck in it. I do believe there will be tremendous pressure from other people on her to disappear, to not show up for trial." Michael Lund had not been arrested and was considered a fugitive from justice.

The last communication that Niemi had with Lund was a note and cashier's check for the remaining interest owed by Lund on the Joli's mortgage in the amount of $650. The check was purchased on May 1 at the Bank of America Airport Branch in Sacramento, California, and postmarked at the airport. In the note, Lund apologized for the delay and looked forward to paying off the boat mortgage. The note was dated May 1, the same day that the Joli was seized by the DEA in front of Lund's house on Sequim Bay. In an effort to find the remaining sails and equipment from the Joli, Niemi tried to reach Patricia Karnik. He never reached her personally, but Karnik had told a "gal friend" of Niemi's that she had no idea of Lund's whereabouts and made the sinister comment that she "felt that perhaps, you know, he was no longer living."

In the meantime, Bill Niemi was getting more concerned about the lack of sails found belonging to the Joli. He had guaranteed the loan on the boat. Its real value was as a package and the boat had been stripped for its use in offloading product from its mothership. Most of the cushions had been removed to provide space for the marijuana. Only two out of thirty sails were still on board—a cruising main, which is a small mainsail, and a number five jib top. All the rest were missing. Niemi had paid $62,000 for the Joli's sails four years earlier. To replace them would cost significantly more. As the Joli sat in Lake Union after its seizure, it had depreciated in value greatly. The search warrants executed by the DEA for Lund's house, the barn that Victorson rented from Allen Hall near Sequim, and the storage locker in Federal Way had all expired.

Niemi's own search was on. To get back into these storage places, Niemi's bank, Old National, filed a civil suit resulting in a court order allowing for a warrant of arrest for sailing gear, rigging, and equipment taken from the Joli. On May 16 accompanied by a U.S. Marshall and a Clallam County Deputy and armed with the court order, Niemi went to all three places. In Lund's house they found all the missing cushions taken out of the Joli and two or three sails. In the barn they found six to eight sails for the Joli and about 40 small, empty sailbags with red stripes—too small for the Joli. They were some of the Northwyn sail bags purchased by Mr. Lund in April. These bags contained a small amount of marijuana debris. A strong odor of marijuana emanated from them. The Joli's sails were all Watch sails made in California.

A search of the storage locker in Federal Way revealed one of the self-inflating life rafts for the Joli, her main anchor, several hundred feet of anchor line, some of the safety harnesses used for racing the vessel, an aircraft locater beacon, but no sails. Someone had erected a clothesline in the storage locker, from which hung four complete sets of foul weather gear, safety harnesses, and some heavy-duty sailing gear. Also found in the locker were a chain saw and two peaveys (long levers with a hook and sharp spike at the end usually used for moving logs). The chain saw and peaveys were likely used to set the log skids on the 100-foot-high bank extending from Lund's house down to the waterfront. At the top of the high bank was the electric winch. Some people said that, when Lund returned from sailing the Joli, he would load her sails into a 25-foot skiff, take them to shore, and use the winch to hoist the skiff loaded with sails up the bank.

On June 20, three more individuals were charged in connection with the conspiracy—Homero Ospina of Los Angeles, who had provided a pump for the Helena Star; James Turner, the alleged "offloading expert;" and Eric Hale, Victorson's best pal. All three were at-large but expected to be in custody by the end of the week. That made a total of eight charged so far. Assistant U.S. Attorney Sim said there was a possibility that another individual would be indicted but indicated that the investigation was "substantially complete."

8

MY JOURNEY

I N APRIL OF 1978 I WAS THIRTY-THREE YEARS OLD. I HAD graduated from the University of Washington Law School in 1969 with a Doctor of Jurisprudence. I was second in my graduating class of a little over 100 students—second from the bottom. I distained my three years of law school. Maybe I thought I was too cool for school. It seemed to me that there was too much emphasis on theory. It seemed that little of what I learned applied to the real world. There were no clinics or internships in those days, where law students could get some practical experience. My interests during law school when I thought about it were criminal law and international law. Now that I think about it, I guess I have always been a bit fascinated with those that engage in aberrant behavior.

Speaking of aberrant behavior, John Mortimer, the extraordinary English author, playwright and barrister, wrote at the beginning of one of his books, *Rumpole and the Genuine Article*:

> I would like to dedicate this small volume of reminiscences to a much abused and under-appreciated body of men. They practice many of the virtues most in fashion today. They rely strictly on free enterprise and individual effort. They adhere to strong monetary principles. They do not join trade unions.

They never go on strike. Far from being in favour of closed shops, they do their best to see that most shops remain open, particularly during the hours of darkness. They are against state interference of any kind, being rugged individualists to a man. No. I am not referring to lawyers. Will you please raise your glasses, ladies and gentlemen, and drink to absent friends, to the criminals of England. Without these invaluable citizens there would be no lawyers, no judges, no policemen, no writers of detective stories, and absolutely nothing to put in *the News of the World.*

During my third and last year of law school in 1969 I was forced to start thinking about obtaining a job after graduation. Because I was interested in criminal law, I phoned the King County Prosecutor's Office in Seattle and arranged a job interview with the Assistant Chief Criminal Deputy. When I showed up for the interview, he was not there—not a good sign. To take care of this dilemma the Chief Criminal Deputy, Bill Kinzel, decided to interview me himself. One of his first questions to me, as you might imagine, was what my grades were in law school. I responded by saying that, if he was going to make a hiring decision based on my grade point, I might as well walk out the door and not waste his time. I can only guess that he was impressed with my candor, if not my grades in law school.

In less than half an hour Mr. Kinzel indicated he wanted me to meet the elected King County Prosecuting Attorney, Charles O. Carroll. Chuck, as he was known, had been in office for over twenty years and was a former All-American running back for my alma mater, the University of Washington Huskies. Mr. Kinzel ushered me into a plush, gigantic conference room. Mr. Carroll walked in from his adjoining office to join us. He filled the room with his stature and personality. He was big, extraordinarily handsome, imposing, and extremely charismatic. Mr. Kinzel said some flattering things about me—thankfully leaving out the unflattering things—and told Mr. Carroll he wanted to hire me. In a total time of less than one hour, I walked out of the office with a job as a King County Deputy Prosecuting Attorney, contingent on passing the bar exam, which I would take in the summer. I was ecstatic and forever grateful to both men for taking a chance on a bum like me.

Though studying was not a forte of mine in law school, I studied long and hard for the all-important bar exam. I was not about to fail and take it a second time. There was about a three-month lag time between finishing the three-day bar exam in July and the date that the bar exam results were posted in October. I did not have many friends in law school, primarily because I did not spend a whole lot of time there fraternizing. I frequently had a part time job to pay for my education, one of which was as a bartender at Dante's Tavern during my second year of law school. The erudite friends of mine, who had just finished taking the exam with me, were all spending this three-month hiatus clerking for prestigious law firms where they had jobs waiting. To me, it sounded like three months of stress—like a three-month death march.

Instead of waiting around Seattle stressing out about the bar exam, I hopped into my 1960 dark blue Porsche 1600. With $300 in my pocket I headed out of Dodge with the sunroof open—from Seattle bound for Mexico. I crossed the border in Nogales armed with a 38-caliber pistol that I bought on the street for $20 from a derelict while working at a Standard Oil gas station one summer in Spokane, Washington, where I had grown up. I left Seattle recognizing that, because of the age and number of miles on my Porsche, it might well break down in the middle of nowhere in the mountains of southern Mexico, forcing me to abandon it and find another way back to Seattle. Bear in mind that I only had $300 to my name and no credit card to bail myself out. I had been comfortable hitchhiking back and forth between Seattle and Spokane during college. That was a habit I inherited from my much older brother, who would routinely hitchhike between Spokane and Philadelphia while he was a student at the University of Pennsylvania. I did have faith that my Porsche would get me back to Seattle alive and in time to hear my fate relating to the bar exam.

Before departing Seattle, I called my girlfriend, who graduated from the University of Washington in textile design and was working for a company in Dallas. Somehow, I talked her into taking some vacation time and spending a few days with me on the road. She flew to Tucson, Arizona, and I picked her up at the airport. She had no idea what a meager amount of money I had to my name after paying 90 % of my undergraduate and law school education. We drove south to Nogales for the night, where I exceeded her worst expectations. We slept on the grass in a park with my 38-calibre under my belt. From Nogales we spent a couple of days driving south along the west coast of Mexico through Topolobampo and Culiacán to Mazatlán, where we luckily came across some friends on vacation. They let us sleep on the floor of their room in the La Siesta Hotel for two nights. The La Siesta was home to the famous El Shrimp Bucket restaurant opened in 1963 and was the beginning of the chain of Mexican restaurants, which included Señor Frog's and Carlos and Charlies. After quickly wearing out our welcome, we drove toward Puerto Vallarta, hoping to arrive by nightfall. PV had been put on the map five years earlier in 1964 with the release of the movie, *The Night of the Iguana*, starring Richard Burton. He had brought his soon-to-be wife, Elizabeth Taylor, to the location set in Mexico, setting off much drama.

Unfortunately, nightfall came more quickly than I anticipated, and there were no streetlights to light up the roads. Driving in Mexico at night can be very dangerous, because cows frequently sleep on the warm asphalt, which holds warmth from the sun, even at night. The cows are hard to spot in the darkness as you round a corner in the middle of nowhere. I had already run over a small pig and was not at all interested in having the same misfortune with a much larger animal. I pulled off the road into a deserted field in a remote part of old Mexico, and we spent the night sleeping in the Porsche. Of course, the seats folded down. I really knew how to impress my girlfriend.

The next day we drove into Puerto Vallarta, and I splurged on a cheap room in the Rio Hotel in El Centro. My girlfriend stayed with me in Vallarta long enough for me to get down on my knees and propose marriage. By this time, I knew she could handle any adversity that life might bring. We were alone on the beach when I got the surprise of my life—Laurie said, "Yes," and the next day retreated back to Dallas. Her "vacation" was finally over. Only one question remained: Would she do a background check on me?

After taking Laurie to the Puerto Vallarta airport, I continued my travels down the west coast of Mexico, then on to Guadalajara, Acapulco, and Mexico City. Since I had little dinero, I had purchased a hammock in Mazatlán and spent many a night sleeping in my hammock pitched between two palm trees on a remote beach. I did have my "piece" for protection, but with one exception, never had a serious problem with any of the Mexicans that I engaged with. There were times in small mountain villages that I would be the only gringo in the whole village. I would walk into a cantina and never have to pay for a cerveza or shot of tequila. The one exception occurred when I was sleeping one night in my car in Mexico City. I could not find an appropriate place to hang my hammock. A man, not seeing me sleeping in the folded down seat, tried to break into my car. I jerked awake and raised my head up. Our eyeballs came within inches of each other, separated only by the car window. His eyeballs practically ejected from their sockets when they encountered mine. He fled like a rabbit—maybe some whacked out American kid, who had come down from the mountains after feasting on magic, psilocybin mushrooms hoping to meet up with "Lucy in the sky"—a not uncommon occurrence back in the day.

From Mexico City I drove across southern Mexico to Veracruz on the Gulf of Mexico and from there up the eastern coast and inland through the interior of the country before crossing back into the United States at Laredo, Texas. I then headed back to the Pacific Northwest via Dallas to see if I was still engaged. Arriving in Coeur d'Alene, Idaho, with no folding money left from the original $300, I used the last of the metal in my pocket to make a phone call to my parents in Spokane to let them know that I would be passing through within the hour before leaving the next day to return to Seattle. My beloved Porsche had performed admirably, logging almost 10,000 miles before returning me to my starting point after over two months on the road.

After arriving back in Seattle, I moved into an apartment with two buddies. A couple nights later, I was in a bar when a classmate of mine walked up to me and said that the bar exam results had just been posted a little earlier in the day. A quick phone call between beers at the old Red Onion dive bar in Madison Park determined that a mistake had obviously been made and I had passed the bar.

I was sworn in and admitted to practice law in the state of Washington on October 13, 1969, and immediately began work in the King County Prosecutor's Office. As a new deputy, I was assigned to handle misdemeanor and gross misdemeanor cases in a couple of King County District Courts three days a week and the same type of cases in Seattle District Court along with preliminary hearings in felony cases the other two days of the week. My first day on the job I shadowed a more experienced deputy prosecutor in Shoreline District Court, Darrel Lee, whom I expected to replace so that he could move up into a position requiring more experience. Darrel was a no-nonsense type of guy. At the end of my first day, he dropped a bomb shell on me. My first day would be his last day at Shoreline District Court. The following day I would be the man, totally on my own trying cases like DUIs, minor assaults, minor thefts—that type of crimes. It was like being thrown into the fire. I was not prepared for this. Law School in those days consisted mostly of theoretical exercises with no practical experience. Suddenly I was thrust into a courtroom to handle several cases each day with no one to watch my back.

It turned out to be the best possible way of beginning my career if I wanted to be a trial lawyer. I was literally in court all day, most every day. It was trial by fire. I learned more about being a trial lawyer in a few days than I had ever learned in law school—probably my fault. After about three months or so on the circuit, I was moved permanently downtown to the King County Courthouse in Seattle. One year later, All-American football star Chuck Carroll was defeated in his bid for another four-year term. I had worked for him for about fifteen months before Christopher Bayley ascended to the elected office of King County Prosecuting Attorney in January of 1971. Fairly soon thereafter, Bayley promoted me to the position of Senior Deputy Prosecutor leading me to handle some of the most serious felony cases that were prosecuted in our office. I worked for him for eighteen months before resigning in July of 1972. I had worked in the office for a total of almost three years, trying felony cases day in and day out. I needed a break.

Shortly after I resigned, Bayley indicted Chuck Carroll along with a lot of policemen and at least one Seattle city council member, "Streetcar Charlie," in connection with a longstanding police payoff system—payoffs to the police from gay bars and gambling establishments. The criminal case against Carroll ended up being dismissed. I owe a great debt of gratitude to both Chuck Carroll and Chris Bayley for allowing me to progress at my own pace and for allowing me to exercise far more discretion than I was probably qualified to exercise.

After my resignation from the Prosecutor's Office, my wife, Laurie, and I bought one-way tickets to Europe. Our friends were buying houses and making babies. We had no children yet and no house. I had hoped to obtain a legal job in Paris, working in a branch of an American law firm there. Why would I flee a good job in Seattle for a questionable future somewhere else? I had no desire to be a common man. I was seeking opportunity, not security. I wanted to fail or succeed on my own terms—to make my own mark.

Once we got to Paris, I worked out a good nightly rate with a Vietnamese hotelier for a room in the Hotel St. Louis, conditioned on our staying in his small hotel at least one full month. It was a five-floor walkup located on the Ile de la St. Louis, one of the two islands in the Seine River, the other island being the Ile de la Cite, where Notre Dame Cathedral stands tall—or use to stand tall before the catastrophic fire of 2019. Bridges connect both islands to the Left Bank and the Right Bank as well as to each other. We had a sliver of a view of the Seine from a small window. It sounds romantic, but the hotel was pretty run down and decrepit. Navigating the irregular stairway up five floors was like trying to keep one's balance on a small boat in rough seas. The hotel has been substantially upgraded to a very well located three-star hotel at this time.

In order to improve my marketability to a potential employer, we enrolled in the Alliance Française to better our ability to speak French. One could show up at this school any day of the week and be immediately enrolled in classes. No English was spoken in class, in part because there would normally be people from many different countries in attendance, who did not necessarily speak English.

Unfortunately, my goal of working as a lawyer in Paris for an American law firm was totally unrealistic. I found out rather quickly that jobs of this kind were reserved for either senior lawyers from stateside, who used a stint in Paris as sort of a sabbatical, or younger lawyers, whose qualifications were comparable to being former clerks for Justices of the United States Supreme Court. Besides the obvious deficiency of not speaking French fluently, my qualifications fell far below what were required. I had to resign myself to the fact that our time in Paris would not last. One of my greatest regrets in life is that I never became fluent in a foreign language.

After spending five weeks in Paris, we continued our travels around the periphery of Europe, including two weeks in Morocco and stops in three Communist countries in Eastern Europe. After almost seven months travelling through the capitals of Europe, I ran out of money—again. We returned to Seattle in early 1973 for me to make an honest living. I decided to embark on a life of crime—becoming a criminal defense attorney. We rented a houseboat on Portage Bay, which connects Lake Union to Lake Washington, and I opened a law office on the second floor of the newly restored Grand Central on the Park building in Pioneer Square.

Most lawyers starting up a new practice can take business with them from work at a previous law firm or some other source. I, however, had been missing in action for seven months abroad and had no business to bring to the table of my sole proprietorship. In the beginning I would sit in my cool office for substantial periods of time, with my hand within easy reach to pounce on my phone if it ever rang. No one advertised in those days. Law was a profession. I never learned the art of networking, but business started to trickle in. John Mortimer in one of his many books, *Rumpole of the Bailey*, reflecting on the life of a criminal defense barrister, ruminated: "Life at the Bar has its ups and downs, and there are times when there is an appalling decrease in crime, when all the decent villains seem to have gone on holiday to the Costa Brava, and lawfulness breaks out. At such times, Rumpole is unemployed." I guess some of the villains in Seattle started returning from holiday in Las Vegas or Palm Springs as my business began to improve.

I knew I did not have much business sense when I did some very minimal legal work for my next-door neighbor, Henry Broderick—a very well-known and iconic Seattle businessman and civic leader. He never drove a car. He gave me complete discretion to handle the matter for him in any way I chose, except by filing a lawsuit. He had never sued anyone in his life and was not about to go down that route. I respected that. After completing the task—without suing anyone—I sent him a bill for my services. Two days later, I received a note back from him saying, "I have corrected your fee to bring it more in line with the value of services rendered. Thanks—'HB'." Enclosed was a check for over 50% more than the amount I had billed him. I thought to myself that this may never happen again in my lifetime. I decided I needed to raise my rates. Three years later, after buying a house and having two children, I snagged Captain Rubies as a client. They say that crime does not pay, but it is a living.

My criminal law practice at this time was evenly divided between the state and federal courts. The federal courts are known throughout our country as no-nonsense forums. You better be prepared. The federal judges had lifetime appointments, as opposed to state judges, who had to run for reelection every four years. The only way to get rid of a federal judge is impeachment. Fortunately, I had only been threatened with being sent to jail myself by a judge two times, once by a King County Superior Court Judge and once by a Federal District Court Judge in Tacoma, Washington—not for being ill prepared, but for being too aggressive.

A lot of criminal defense attorneys do not like to practice in federal court. The sentences imposed in criminal cases in the federal courts are usually much harsher, and the environment in the courtroom is much more formal. Though I had come from being a prosecutor in the state court system, as my career progressed, I did an increasingly greater share of my work as a hired gun in federal court. The cases were usually more complex and more challenging. Assistant U.S. Attorneys had a lot of cards in their hand—a seemingly unlimited number of investigators and seemingly inexhaustible amount of funds and resources to pursue those who tended to walk on the wrong side of the law. They had the ability at a moment's notice to put an FBI or DEA agent or the like on a plane to Europe, the Far East, or South America to obtain hotel records, travel records, or to tail those suspected of nefarious activities targeting the United States. I personally liked the challenge in federal court and was not dissuaded by the odds.

Criminal law is all about life, death, liberty, and the pursuit of happiness. A criminal lawyer's client's future, if not life, is in the palm of his lawyer's hand. It is a mighty burden to carry. Civil law is entirely concerned with that most odious of subjects, money. Criminal lawyers frequent the many different courtrooms of our society. Civil lawyers rarely get into court because most of their cases settle. A criminal lawyer can defend murderers without approving of murder. If the world had been created entirely without evil, it might have been a dull world leaving me without an occupation.

To be a successful criminal defense lawyer, you have to be a bit of a maverick. You also need to be thick skinned. Criminal defense lawyers are generally much maligned and under-appreciated. Most people think that they are a blight on our society—that all they do is keep violent criminals on the street—at least until they need a criminal defense attorney to represent themselves, one of their parents, or one of their children. Then they become your best friend and they do not need you tomorrow—they need you now. John Mortimer, the former barrister at the Old Bailey, London's central criminal court, whose novels formed the basis for the PBS-TV series *Rumpole of the Bailey*, once famously said:

> It's rare for a criminal lawyer to be invited into his client's home. We represent a part of their lives they would prefer to forget. Not only do they not ask us to dinner, but when catching sight of us at parties years after we have sprung them from detention, they look studiously in the opposite direction and pretend we never met. No one, I suppose, wants the neighbors to spot the sturdy figure of Rumpole climbing up their front steps. It may give rise to speculation as to whether it's murder, rape, or merely a nice clean fraud that's going on in their family.

I always thought that, whether I was a prosecutor or a criminal defense attorney, my contributions to the well-being of society were equally beneficial. A dramatic example of my contributions to the well-being of society while a defense attorney is a case that I began working on in November 1985.

I was approached by a brother of a Canadian defendant who had pleaded guilty in the United States District Court for the Northern District of California to possession of U.S. counterfeit currency. This occurred in San Francisco and on October 4, 1985, he was sentenced to three years in federal custody. He was doing his time at the Federal Correctional Institution in Milan, Michigan. I had not represented him on that charge. His brother had gotten my name from a charming, young Canadian woman, whom I had previously represented in the United States for couriering 1.5 kilos of narcotics from India to the United States. They were both from Edmonton. The brother wanted to hire me to file a Motion for Reduction of the defendant's sentence. I informed the defendant's brother that the likelihood of prevailing on such a motion was not good, unless we could offer some sort of a carrot to get the government to go along with such a request—like turning over a substantial amount of U.S. counterfeit currency that might still be on the street. The brother left my office indicating that he would get back to me after returning to Canada.

A few days later, I received a package from Fed Ex. It contained several Polaroid photographs of multiple cardboard boxes of what appeared to be uncut sheets of old U.S. counterfeit currency. Also, in the package was something remarkable— an original uncut sheet of what I assumed was also U.S. counterfeit currency—five $100 bills, one $50 bill and two $20 bills for a total of $590 on the uncut sheet. Voila! I had something to work with. I reached out to a very experienced Special Assistant U.S. Attorney in San Francisco, Sandra Teters, and sent her one of the photographs contained in the Fed Ex package I had received. She and I worked out a written agreement to the effect that, if the United States recovers more than $1,000,000 of old counterfeit U.S. currency as a result of information provided by my client or me, or as a result of my actions, the government would file with Judge Eugene Lynch a motion to modify the defendant's sentence from three years to one year. The counterfeit currency had to be obviously old so that someone could not go out and print some new currency to satisfy the agreement.

On January 9, 1986, I drove my Volvo station wagon by myself north to Vancouver, Canada, hoping to get some U.S. counterfeit currency out of circulation. I was cognizant that the source of the counterfeit currency in the photographs was a group of fairly dangerous and deranged thugs from Eastern Europe, blessed with a touch of evil. I did not need a body adjustment. I kept looking in my rear-view mirror to see if I was being followed. I could swear I was being followed but am quite sure I wasn't. I am not ashamed to admit that I was a bit on edge. Nothing ventured, nothing gained! I had two requirements for my involvement in this caper—the counterfeit currency had to be well packaged in cardboard boxes and secured with duct tape, and I would have no personal contact with anyone associated with the currency to be picked up by me. I crossed the border into Canada, Vancouver, and parked my car in an underground parking lot b shopping mall. Pursuant to a prearranged plan, I left the car unl went up into the mall for a cup of coffee, and returned to my Vol half an hour later. Inside my car were five heavy cardboard boxes we secured with duct tape. I assumed they contained a monstrous amount of U.S. counterfeit currency but had no idea how much. I now had to figure out how to get the bounty into the United States.

I was reluctant to drive my find across the border. If I was stopped at the crossing, it would take a lot of explaining to U.S. Customs. I was also concerned that I might well be detained, as the Special Assistant U.S. Attorney in San Francisco was not privy to the timing or details of my caper. I had purposely wanted to keep the details under wrap for fear of spooking anyone. As I was heading south toward the border, I decided to go to Vancouver International Airport, where I stopped at the office of international courier, DHL.

I advised the DHL office manager that I had five boxes that I wanted shipped by air to the San Francisco airport for pickup by the U.S. Secret Service. Besides guarding the President of the United States, Vice Presidents, and their families and former presidents, the Secret Service is the federal agency responsible for investigating counterfeit currency crimes. It was created after the Civil War to control the influx of counterfeit currency following the war. It was only after the assassination of President William McKinley in 1901 that the Secret Service was assigned to protection duties.

The DHL manager at the airport asked me what the five boxes contained. I responded, "Legal documents." I did not tell him they were counterfeit legal documents. The boxes were weighed; I paid the freight with my credit card and left for the border. I called the Special Assistant U.S. Attorney and Secret Service to let them know that there would soon be five presents wrapped with gray ribbon arriving at DHL SFO by Learjet. That afternoon the Secret Service picked up the five boxes at the San Francisco airport. My contribution to the well-being of society was concluded.

he Secret Service to arrive at an accurate
weeks. The stash was estimated by the
3 million dollars' worth of U.S. coun-
ne the largest recovery of counterfeit
.. Judge Lynch reduced my client's sentence
..o one year and he was released from FCI Milan the
month. I kept the $590 uncut sheet of counterfeit currency
...at had been sent to me by Fed Ex as a reminder of this extraordinary
seizure. I was beginning to become fond of enormous, record breaking seizures of contraband.

Unlike the seizure of the Helena Star and its 37 tons of marijuana by the Coast Guard, my seizure of 2.3 to 3 million dollars'
worth of counterfeit currency received absolutely no publicity before
my client's sentence was reduced. I was concerned that any publicity prior to the Judge's ruling might incur a public outcry that I had
bought my client's freedom, albeit with U.S. counterfeit currency. I
was concerned that such an outcry might affect the Judge's decision
as to whether he should go along with the joint recommendation by
me and the assistant U.S. Attorney in San Francisco. I had, therefore,
required the government to agree not to disclose our involvement in
the seizure before Judge Lynch had time to rule on our joint request
for a reduction of my client's sentence.

I have always tried to keep my clients out of the newspapers and,
now, the internet. Publicity may be good for the lawyer, but it almost
always works against the defendant.

The federal judges in both the Western District and Eastern
District of Washington were, with few exceptions, highly intelligent,
diligent, and respected by those of us who had the privilege of appear-
ing before them. As I say, the setting in federal court was usually very
formal—almost always. During one of my early forays in federal
court as a young defense attorney, however, I experienced my first
appearance in the court of the Honorable Walter T. McGovern, Chief
Federal District Court Judge of the Western District of Washington
from 1975 to 1987. He was appointed to this lifetime position by

President Nixon in 1971, taking over the vacated position of Judge William Lindberg.

I happened to be representing a man, who had earlier pleaded guilty to a serious illegal drug charge. He was waiting to be sentenced. Sentence impositions were usually held on Friday mornings, and generally a judge would sentence half a dozen or so unlucky defendants at that time. My client, Freddy, was a black man from San Francisco in his 40s and one of my favorite clients. He had a great personality, attitude, sense of humor, and was appropriately remorseful for his drug-dealing activities. He was not in custody. I was wearing a typical dark, conservative, pin-striped suit.

As Freddy walked into the courtroom to meet me, he was wearing a loud, multi-colored, flashy suit, and an equally flashy pair of shoes. He looked like he had come straight from the circus or the racetrack. Some in the courtroom thought he was probably a pimp as well as a drug dealer. He had a toothbrush prominently sticking out of the breast pocket of his coat. I liked that. A little humor can play well in the courtroom if it is not overdone. He knew he was headed for the slammer, the only question being for how long. This day the courtroom was quite full of other attorneys, their clients, loved ones, assistant U.S. Attorneys, and spectators. The bailiff called the court to order and Judge McGovern came out from his chambers to preside over the various sentencings. Our case was called. Freddy and I strode to the lectern, me wearing my traditional, dark, pin-striped suit and flashy Freddy standing out—as conspicuously out of place as a porcupine riding a Ferris wheel.

Judge McGovern looked down at us from his high perch and asked: "Which one of you is the lawyer?" The courtroom exploded in laughter. I sheepishly raised my hand—guilty.

Over the years, I got to know Judge McGovern quite well and considered him a true friend. I always enjoyed being in the courtroom of such a well-respected jurist, who had a sense of humor but ruled with a steady iron hand. Most judges never refer to lawyers in their courtroom by their first name only. With those he knew well and liked, Judge McGovern would frequently refer to them using their first names. After a time, I was lucky enough to have achieved that status in his courtroom. It gave me a real leg up with my clients, who could not help but think I had a real in with the Judge that would bode well for them in future court appearances. Judge McGovern was also an incredible athlete. His phenomenal collegiate basketball career at Santa Clara and Gonzaga was cut short by his call to active duty. Before the end of World War II, he would be named an honorable mention All American. In 2013, at age 90, he won a National Over-90's Indoor Doubles Tennis Tournament, qualifying him to receive what tennis junkies refer to as a "gold ball," an extremely prestigious accomplishment.

9

THE DEFENSE

W HILE LEGAL PROCEEDINGS WERE PENDING AGAINST Captain Rubies and First Mate Pedro Vera, they were incarcerated in the King County Jail. They would have to be transferred from the jail a few blocks to the United States Courthouse for every court appearance they had. On May 3, 1978, they were arraigned on the charges against them and, as is customary at a defendant's first court appearance and pursuant to advice of counsel, they pleaded not guilty.

Assistant United States Attorney Ron Sim sought to increase their bail which had been originally set at $25,000 for the captain and $10,000 for the first mate. Mr. Sim advised U.S. Magistrate John Weinberg that the government had recently discovered that marijuana had been transferred from the Helena Star to an unidentified sailboat before the freighter's seizure on the high seas of the North Pacific. He said, "Our investigation has expanded and we are now beyond the point of the Helena Star and the Colombians, and we expect to be indicting some Americans next Tuesday." Sim said arrangements had been made in San Francisco to post bail for Rubies and Vera, but that the government had not been told what the relationship was between the two defendants and the person or persons who were arranging for their release on bail. Sim went on to say, "the people arranging bail might be the people who might be discovered as a result of our investigation and might want to get these people (Rubies and Vera) out of the country." I was not aware of any plan to bail out the captain and first mate and spirit them out of the United States. However, years later, David Victorson and Eric Hale apparently advised the government that, indeed, there had been a scheme to bail them out and spirit them out of the country.

I argued against increasing the bail for a number of reasons including the unfairness of raising bail when it appears that the seamen were on the cusp of bailing out and raising bail after it had already been set at the request of the government. Magistrate Weinberg refused to raise their bail stating, "When it became apparent to the Government that defendants were in a position to post those amounts, the Government sought to increase bond to $250,000 each. The Court should not participate in, or give the appearance of participating in, any effort to manipulate previously set bail figures for the purpose of keeping them beyond the reach of a defendant. This would deny him his right to bail. In the absence of any showing of material new information, the integrity of the Court's initial order requires that the motion to increase bail be denied."

Assistant U.S. Attorney Sim, however, persuaded U.S. District Court Judge Donald Voorhees (a federal judge instead of a magistrate and who had been assigned to handle the case) to hold off on the release of the two defendants until he reheard Sim's motion set for the following day. Sim filed a memorandum in support of his motion to increase bail expressing his concern that the two seamen would flee the United States. He said that widespread publicity about the case had appeared to jeopardize chances for continuing a successful investigation, but added, "A combination of good fortune and good investigation has resulted in many unexpected developments." Not surprisingly, on May 4 Judge Voorhees did raise the bail of both men to $250,000.

During the end of April and much of May I spent doing a wide variety of things. On April 21, I went aboard the old, rusty bucket freighter to get a feel for it and took some photographs. On May 4, I repeated the same type of excursion to see the Joli. I spent a lot of time meeting with my client and other lawyers and reviewing documents, nautical charts, and evidence seized from the Helena Star, the Joli, Michael Lund's house, and the pickup that Patricia Karnik had been driving when she was stopped by the DEA. I corresponded with Roman's wife, Lola, who was in Cartagena. My letters were in English. Hers were in Spanish. I would hire an interpreter to translate them for me. Also time consuming was research regarding other similar, multi-ton marijuana mothership seizures that had emanated in the Caribbean or waters off the coast of Florida. Some of these cases had not only gone to trial in federal court, but also had been appealed to the United States Court of Appeals for the Fifth Circuit, which decides appeals out of Florida and other southeastern states. Of course, I had to make sure that the captain's assurances that I would be timely paid and paid in full for my services would be met.

It is one thing for a criminal defense attorney to represent a corporation in a criminal case or an officer or director of a corporation. A corporation usually has deep pockets and frequently must pay the legal expenses of its officers and directors in a criminal case if their alleged criminal activity was carried out in the course of their employment. Representing an individual, whose legal expenses will not be paid by a corporation, however, can be a totally different matter. In such a situation one of the first subjects that a criminal defense lawyer has to address is to find out where the potential client's money is. Once a lawyer appears in court on behalf of the client, withdrawing from representing the client that cannot pay the freight can be difficult. Once the lawyer finds out where the client's money is, he must then find a way to separate the client from his money—lighten the client's wallet. This might sound crass, but no one likes to work for free. In addition, the lawyer must make sure that he or she does not knowingly accept dirty money—money derived from an illegal source, like the sale of narcotics. If that occurs, the lawyer could have his fees forfeited or find out that he is now the subject of a criminal investigation.

Collecting legal fees in criminal cases is an art. If a lawyer isn't good at it, he goes broke. Thus, many criminal defense lawyers charge a flat fee and require a sizeable retainer to be paid up front, if not the entire fee. After all, if the client pleads guilty or is convicted after trial and is sentenced to prison, the lawyer may have no way of collecting outstanding fees owed for his services.

Because contingent fees (where a fee is only due if the lawyer wins the case) are deemed unethical in criminal cases, the only other means of charging fees in a criminal case is charging by the hour. I was charging the captain by the hour, so I had to be quite confident that there were resources available to be paid in a case that was sure to generate a lot of work and attention—in the end over three-year's worth. Fortunately, the captain, who was in custody for the duration, had people on the outside who seemed reasonably eager to help pay my fees or be a conduit for payment to me by other sources. Of much fascination to me were three checks that I received from "Jose Smith" drawn on the Pan American Bank of Miami Beach, the amounts of which were written on the face of the checks in Spanish. It was the first and last time that I ever received a check drawn on an American bank that was written in a foreign language. I never met Jose. No fear—the checks were cashed without question.

I have frequently been asked how I could transition from being a prosecutor to being a criminal defense attorney. For me, it was easy. The only real difference for me was that I had a different client. As a prosecutor your client is an individual state or the United States and its people. As a criminal defense attorney, you represent one person or one corporation. My approach to representing each client remained the same. Do the best job you can for whichever client you represent, whether it be a government or a human being. In addition, I have found it challenging to go up against the vast resources of the United States government. I looked upon myself as a hired gunslinger.

So how does one defend someone in charge of a drug store—someone sitting on many tons of marijuana for over a month on the high seas from equatorial Pacific Ocean to the North Pacific? I am often asked how I can defend someone I know to be guilty. It is another easy question for me to answer. Aside from carrying out the constitutional right that all defendants must be represented by counsel, representing someone you know to be guilty is much easier than representing someone you think is innocent. There is not nearly as much pressure or stress representing someone you know to be guilty. In those cases, the job of counsel is normally to work out a fair plea bargain with the prosecutor. If the client wants to have a trial, the defense lawyer does the best he can under the circumstances with the understanding that he can't put the client on the witness stand to testify if he knows he or she is going to commit perjury. If the client is convicted, no one can say that justice wasn't served. If found not guilty, it is the jury that makes that decision and their decision would be based on guilt not being proven by the prosecution beyond a reasonable doubt. That is the standard of proof in our great country, a standard that has stood the test of time and that separates the United States from many other uncivilized or autocratic countries.

The great pressure and stress for a criminal defense attorney occurs when one represents someone you think is innocent of the charges. On rare occasions, I have represented clients, who were totally innocent of any wrongdoing. The defendant's liberty, if not life, is literally in your hands. Nothing can be more difficult. An error in arresting or charging an innocent person is usually a result of a problem with the law enforcement investigation, which in some cases can be disastrous. A dramatic result of such a mistake occurred when a client of mine was arrested in 1983 for the rape of four women on Queen Anne Hill in Seattle. Lucky for him, his U.S. passport indicated that he was out of the country on the date of one of the alleged rapes, but, unlucky for him, the investigating detective chose to disregard my client's suggestion that the detective check his passport. Fortunately, I was able to prove to the Chief Deputy King County Prosecutor that my client was having dinner in Paris with his father at the home of the United States Ambassador to the Organization for Economic Cooperation and Development at the time one of the rapes had been committed.

My client had even signed the guest book at the Ambassador's home. The real culprit of these rapes, Dean Carter, had moved from Seattle and was eventually arrested, but not before murdering three women in southern California. He was sentenced to death. My client was fully exonerated two months after the rapes as a result of blood tests and other evidence.

Getting back to my defense of Captain Rubies, there is an old saying among lawyers that when the law is against you, you should pound the facts; when the facts are against you, you should pound the law; and when both law and facts are against you, you should pound the table. Because my client was arrested while Captain of a ship loaded with 37 tons of Colombian Gold, I decided to pound the law. United States District Court Judge Edward B. Davis in Miami in another marijuana mothership case succinctly stated the main legal issue: "The question here is whether the United States overreaches the international law of jurisdiction when it tries to prosecute foreign crewmen of a stateless ship stopped on the high seas." My decision was made—I would endeavor to make the high seas my "loophole."

I was very fortunate to have a bit of a head start on the law of the sea, because I had authored a treatise entitled, *The Legal Implications of the Sea Use Program*, which was published in a 1970 issue of the *Marine Technology Society Journal*. The Sea Use Program was sponsored by the Oceanographic Commission of Washington and had as its goal the possible placement of an undersea habitat on the top of Cobb Seamount. This unique underwater mountain is located approximately 270 nautical miles from Grays Harbor, Washington, and a slightly lesser distance southwest of Vancouver Island, Canada. Strangely enough, this is the same Grays Harbor, west of which the 19-year-old seaman on the Coast Guard Cutter Yocona spotted the flashing lights of a small, low flying aircraft to the west—the same low flying aircraft that Captain Morgan thought might be looking for a vessel, because small aircraft don't normally fly fifteen miles off the coast. It is also the same Grays Harbor that is located three miles south of the uniquely remote and unpublicized Copalis Beach Airport from which this low flying, small aircraft might have taken off—the same beach airport that is underwater every day at high tide.

Cobb Seamount is a 10,000-foot undersea mountain that comes within about 150 feet of the surface of the North Pacific. Because the Sea Use Program had plans for an eventual investment of over $2,000,000, its proponents were concerned about their legal rights in undertaking scientific research on the high seas and possibly placing an undersea habitat on the top of this undersea mountain. Hence, I became familiar with the law of the sea, and eight years after the publication of my treatise the Helena Star had sailed very near the submerged seamount, if not right over it.

On May 28, Larry Finegold, a very accomplished former Assistant U.S. Attorney who represented David Victorson, and I flew to San Francisco for a strategy session with at least four other lawyers involved in the case. The meeting was held in the conference room of the offices of Robert Moran, the lawyer who was responsible for getting Bob Morton paid for the sale of the Knik Wind tug boat and the Chignik 105 barge, when Morton was threatening to contact the authorities if he didn't get paid immediately. The other lawyers present for this meeting were Moran, Bill O'Brien, another prominent San Francisco lawyer, William Urich, from Moran's office who was a graduate of Yale and the University of Pennsylvania Law School, and another lawyer who had flown in from Miami to consult because of his expertise in defending big-time narcotics cases in Florida. I believe David Victorson was also present. Victorson had been using Bob Moran as his legal counsel, business consultant, and consigliere for quite some time. Moran was basically trying to control the case behind the scenes. To represent Eric Hale, he brought in Ivan Fisher, a well-known and high-priced mouthpiece from New York City. I had a feeling that Moran might try to replace me as the captain's attorney for fear that I would not be a team player.

Replacing me was not going to happen, particularly after I began discussing the potential jurisdictional and search-and-seizure issues affecting the legality of the seizure of the Helena Star on the high seas. When I stated that the main legal issue in the case would most likely be substantially affected by the 1958 Geneva Convention on the High Seas, I detected a certain amount of disbelief in the room. Criminal defense lawyers, as a rule, don't deal with criminal cases that have international implications or ramifications. At any rate, I knew that I would not be replaced as Roman's attorney by Moran or anyone else. I continued to be wary of Mr. Moran and had no further dealings with him. My view of him was confirmed sometime later when Larry Finegold found out that most of our conversations in Moran's office were being surreptitiously and illegally tape recorded by him. On a later trip to San Francisco to strategize in Moran's office, Larry asked to use one of Moran's tapes. The one provided to him had not been fully erased and had Larry's voice on it from our previous meeting in Moran's office.

Three days after our initial meeting in San Francisco, I filed a fifteen-page motion and supporting brief with the Court challenging the Coast Guard's jurisdiction to detain, board, search, and seize the Helena Star under American or international law and alleging an unreasonable search and seizure under the Fourth Amendment to the United States Constitution. The United States had duly ratified the treaty involved in this case, the Geneva Convention on the High Seas, and thus it had become part of the supreme law of the land in 1962. It superseded any American legislation passed either before or after its ratification.

The major intent of the Convention on the High Seas was to guarantee the freedom of the seas. The Coast Guard Cutter Yocona's Captain Morgan had been given the green light to board the Helena Star because our government had determined it to be a "stateless" vessel, whose British registration had expired. The only reference to a stateless vessel in the Convention, however, is in Article 6, which indicates that a vessel sailing "under the flags of two or more States may be assimilated to a ship without nationality." The freighter did not fall within that category. Article 22 of the Convention provides the only other basis for a country's warship, like the Yocona, to board a foreign merchant ship. Boarding would only be legal if the ship was engaged in piracy, the slave trade or, if in our case, the vessel was of the "same nationality as the warship." Clearly the Helena Star did not fall within any of these three categories.

This case was one of first impression in the courts of the United States. That is to say no court had ever ruled on this exact issue. A court in Florida, discussing a similar seizure of a freighter loaded with marijuana, stated: "Like the seas where the vessel was boarded, the problem is deep and shark infested. Unlike the seas, the answer is not clearly charted." We had a strong argument. Our biggest problem, however, was getting a federal judge to buy into it. What judge is going to dump a case involving the alleged attempted importation of 50 tons of Colombian Gold into the United States—the largest quantity of marijuana ever seized on the west coast of North America?

If we were successful with our illegal boarding argument, the evidence would be suppressed and the case dismissed. If we were unsuccessful, we would then have to rely on the factual defense that the captain had no knowledge of the ultimate destination of the marijuana. If, for example, the load was destined for Canada, he could not be found guilty of conspiracy to import marijuana into the United States.

10

THE TRIAL

ONE OF THE ALTERNATIVES TO GOING TO TRIAL IS TO ENGAGE in negotiations that potentially lead to a plea of guilty by a defendant—called a plea bargain. By letter dated July 3, 1978, Assistant U.S. Attorney Ron Sim set forth a possible plea agreement that would dispose of Captain Rubies' case. I had advised Mr. Sim earlier that the captain was anxious to challenge the right of the Coast Guard to seize the Helena Star and to pursue our motion to dismiss for lack of jurisdiction. Mr. Sim was also anxious—anxious to obtain Rubies' cooperation against other persons involved in the conspiracy and to have DEA agents interview him at once regarding his identification of other participants. Assuming the pretrial motions were decided in favor of the government and in return for the captain's cooperation, Mr. Sim would agree to allow him to plead guilty to Count 1 (Conspiracy to import marijuana), would dismiss Count 2 at the time of sentencing, and recommend that the appropriate sentence for Captain Rubies would be imprisonment for a term of eight months. The agreement, if consummated, would require the Captain to cooperate fully and to testify truthfully at all trials or grand jury proceedings relating to this case.

The captain and first mate were scheduled to be tried first. However, before any trial could commence, pretrial motions had to be decided by Judge Voorhees after hearing evidence. The most important motion to be determined obviously was the legality of the boarding by the Coast Guard of the Helena Star.

Courtrooms, especially federal courtrooms, can be very intimidating places. Defendants' lives are literally at stake, and the pressure on defense lawyers can be immense. United States Attorneys have the awesome responsibility of representing the people of the United States. I would get extremely nervous, if not fearful, before court appearances. It finally dawned on me that all the participants in a courtroom are fearful. Defendants fear that their lawyer may not be up to the task. They fear for their future and the unknown. Judges have enormous power. Will they exercise it fairly and correctly? They fear making a wrong decision on legal issues during trial and being reversed on appeal by a higher court. Prosecutors fear a not-guilty verdict and having to go home and tell his or her spouse that Stew Riley or some other lightweight mouthpiece has beaten them once again.

Evidentiary hearings on the pretrial motions began on July 12, 1978. The government was represented by Assistant U.S. Attorneys Ron Sim and Richard Jones, as well as Lieutenant Andrew Anderson from the Coast Guard, who was only admitted to practice law before the U.S. District Courts in Florida. As a result, Anderson had to be specially admitted for this case only, to practice before the U.S. District Court in Seattle. Seven of the eight defendants were present in court with their respective attorneys. Three of us were from Seattle—Larry Finegold, Dan Smith, and me. The other four were from New York City, San Diego, Miami, and Los Angeles. Each of them had to be specially admitted as well and have local counsel back them up, because they had not been admitted to practice law in the Western District of Washington. The eighth defendant, Michael Lund, was still a fugitive. There was rampant speculation in the Seattle sailing community that the drug cartel that fronted the money for the botched offloading operation had killed him for screwing up and that he was probably swimming with the fish.

Eric Hale was represented by Manhattan attorney, Ivan Fisher, who reportedly had a car and driver outside his office waiting to transport him wherever he needed to go at a moment's notice. As a young lawyer he had been counsel for Joseph Bonanno, also known as "Joey Bananas," the boss of the Bonanno mafia crime family, and later in the 1980s represented another New York mafia crime boss in the well-known Pizza Connection case, the longest federal criminal trial in U.S. history at the time. In 1980 the *New York Times* listed Fisher as one of the top five criminal defense attorneys in New York City and in a separate article described him as "one of the nation's most sought-after and highly paid criminal lawyers." Fisher reportedly once counseled law students to look in the mirror and practice telling potential clients that their retainer would be $100,000.

The pretrial hearings lasted five days, concluding on July 19. Testifying for the government were Commander Charles Morgan, Captain of the Coast Guard Cutter Yocona; Lieutenant Commander Walter John, who led the armed boarding party; several DEA agents who interviewed the first mate, Pedro Vera, and stopped Patricia Karnik at Ray's Boathouse in Seattle. Steve Winston, the Fines and Penalties Officer for U.S. Customs in Seattle, testified that no one had filed a claim of ownership of the Helena Star. Who is likely to file a claim to a vessel loaded with 37 tons of Colombian Gold? Henry Clay Black, a Foreign Service officer assigned to the U.S. Embassy in London, testified that, upon the Coast Guard's request, he attempted to find the Helena Star's registry through the British foreign office in London, but was unsuccessful.

Also testifying was Rear Admiral Alfred Manning, Chief of the Operations Division in Coast Guard District 17 in Seattle. His duty officer in the Operations Center had been in contact with the Royal Canadian Mounted Police to determine whether they had anything on the vessel. Manning received a copy of a message from the U.S. Embassy in London to the U.S. State Department that stated: "U.K. Foreign and Commonwealth office advises that the M/V Helena Star is not U.K. registered." A copy also went to the White House. He then received a message from Deputy Secretary of State Warren Christopher that the State Department concurred with the Coast Guard proposal to board the MV Helena Star as a stateless vessel. Christopher was serving at the time under President Jimmy Carter and later took office in 1993 as Secretary of State in the Clinton administration. Under my cross-examination, Manning testified that, at the time he communicated information to the Cutter Yocona that there was no objection to boarding the freighter, he had no reason to believe that the Helena Star had actually off loaded any marijuana, that it had been in United States waters, or that it had violated any United States laws.

Patricia Karnik, Mike Lund's girlfriend from La Jolla, California, also testified during the pretrial hearings in her lawyer's effort to suppress statements made by her before being advised of her constitutional rights and his effort to suppress the seizure of evidence taken from Lund's pickup when she was stopped by the DEA at Ray's Boathouse. Judge Voorhees thought she was lying during her testimony. "I just cannot believe the testimony that you've given the last couple of minutes. I don't think I've ever said this to a witness before, but I just cannot believe the testimony you've given here, and I think you would be well advised to be sure you tell the truth under oath."

After hearing eleven witnesses testify over a period of five days, the Court heard oral argument from six lawyers, two representing the United States and four representing their clients. Much of the testimony had centered on the confusing registration history of the Helena Star. Assistant U.S. Attorney Ron Sim said to the Judge, "The Court has listened to at least ten lawyers for four days and I think still doesn't know where that ship is registered."

Judge Voorhees graduated from Harvard Law School in 1946. He had been a United States Naval Reserve Lieutenant from 1942 to 1946. During the hearings, it was obvious he had great knowledge of ships and the sea. He was nominated by President Nixon to a seat on the United States District Court for the Western District of Washington and confirmed by the United States Senate in 1974. Probably his most noteworthy decision during his twelve years on the Federal bench was a decision in 1986 in which he found that the Government improperly concealed evidence from the courts at a 1944 hearing on whether there was a military necessity to remove Japanese Americans (U.S. citizens) from their homes in the Western states to internment camps. The ruling overturned the conviction of Gordon K. Hirabayashi, who had fought exclusion, and was viewed by Japanese Americans as a landmark vindication of their long-held belief that their civil rights were violated during World War II.

At the conclusion of oral arguments on July 19, Judge Voorhees ruled:

> The Helena Star was apparently stateless and the Coast Guard was entitled to act upon that appearance. Even though controlling law is not only sparse but is seemingly nonexistent, I find that the Helena Star, by reason of being stateless, was subject to being stopped and boarded by authorized representatives of any nation as if the Helena Star was flying the flag of that nation. Hence, the Helena Star could be boarded on the high seas by the Coast Guard of this country. Upon boarding, the Coast Guard found no current certificate of registration from any country. They found a welter of confusing names and papers. There was no cargo manifest. The Master said that there were no logs. The Master refused to open the hold and very significantly, cartons of Olympia beer were observed aboard that vessel.

Captain Rubies, First Mate Vera, and Patricia Karnik were scheduled to start trial the following day. In spite of her perceived perjury, Judge Voorhees granted Karnik's motion to keep out statements made by her prior to being advised of her constitutional rights and her motion to keep out evidence seized from the pickup that she had been driving because DEA had searched the vehicle without obtaining a search warrant. The Judge also severed her case from ours and continued her trial date. Trial for the other four defendants had already been scheduled for September.

Mr. Sim's offer in his letter to me of July 3 would have allowed Captain Rubies to get out of jail after serving only eight months behind bars with credit for time served, if he cooperated with the government and testified against the other conspirators. The seizure of the Helena Star and 37 tons of marijuana was the result of the lack of preparation by the Americans to offload all the marijuana at one time. In a sense, Roman had been victimized by the Americans, his fellow unknown coconspirators. I was anticipating the next morning before trial started that the captain might accept the proposed plea bargain and enter a plea of guilty to one count of the Indictment.

That afternoon, after hearing Judge Voorhees deny our motions, I returned to my office. On my desk was a Western Union Telegram in Spanish dated the same day from Rubies' wife in Cartagena, Colombia. It said: "Inform Roman immediately. Relatives say not to proceed. Extremely worried. Tell Roman to call me. Greetings— Lola." Roman's relatives obviously did not want him to proceed with the plea bargain and were concerned. His wife wanted him to call her immediately. I took this as an indication that his life and the lives of his family might be in danger if he agreed to cooperate and testify against other charged or uncharged coconspirators. Michael Lund was still wanted, dead or alive. The next morning, prior to the start of trial, I arranged for my client to make a long-distance call to his wife in Cartagena. After speaking with his wife, the captain decided to turn down the government's proposed plea bargain and go to trial.

The trial of Captain Rubies and First Mate Vera began on July 20. Jury selection began with Judge Voorhees cautioning the jury not to be influenced by all of the publicity in newspapers and on television that resulted from the seizure of the Helena Star. There was no one in the courtroom of prospective jurors that had not heard of this case. Jury selection went quickly and smoothly. I challenged one juror's suitability for service in this case, who had retired from the Bureau of Narcotics, which had morphed into the Drug Enforcement

Administration. When I questioned her, she admitted that there was a possibility that her past employment might affect her deliberations in this case. The judge granted my request that she be excused from the jury. A jury of twelve was eventually sworn in to try the case. Two alternates were also sworn in, in case any of the twelve selected could not complete their jury service.

Many criminal defense lawyers like to use a scattershot approach to convincing a jury—throw everything but the kitchen sink at the jury and see if anything sticks. It is commonly referred to as the octopus defense. When attacked by a predator, the octopus sprays a cloud of black ink to befuddle its attacker and slips away in the confusion. Sometimes that works. I preferred to rely on one or two strong arguments, rather than a lot of weak ones. I looked to our northern neighbor, Canada, for our defense in this case.

Opening statements were given by Assistant U.S. Attorney Sim, Dan Smith representing First Mate Pedro Vera and me. I acknowledged that my client was the captain of the Helena Star carrying a massive load of marijuana in its hold. I provided the jury with some background information on my client and then got straight to the crux of the case. Captain Rubies was charged in Count I with conspiracy to import marijuana into the United States and in Count II with actual importation of marijuana into the United States—the crucial words being "into the United States."

I told the jury that the Helena Star, when first sighted by the Coast Guard, "was headed toward the Strait of Juan de Fuca on a course which was consistent with the vessel proceeding either to Canada or the United States. The closest that the vessel was ever seen to the United States was approximately eighteen to twenty miles" and "that at all times the vessel was within the observation of the Coast Guard, it was actually closer to Canada than it was to the United States. The vessel was at no time within the territorial waters of the United States, the customs waters, or even within the 200-mile fishery conservation zone of the United States—that at all times the vessel was observed only within the 200-mile fishing zone of Canada."

I informed the jury that the captain had been given a set of coordinates, latitude and longitude of a particular point on the high seas that was in fact closer to Canada than the United States and was the expected point for transferring the marijuana from the mothership. Finally, I pointed out that, three days after the seizure of the Helena Star on April 17, the Knik Wind tug was located at Port Alberni, Canada, with the Chignik 105 barge located nearby. They were expected to be used to offload the marijuana. There was little if any evidence that Captain Rubies knew the ultimate destination of his cargo. Possession of marijuana on the high seas is not a crime without the requisite intent to import it into the United States.

The trial lasted four days, one day less than the length of the pretrial hearings. Most of the witnesses that testified in the pretrial hearings testified at trial regarding the same facts that they testified to in the pretrial hearings. Aside from testimony regarding the seizure of the Helena Star on the high seas of the North Pacific, most of the rest of the testimony related to the investigation conducted by the DEA from the date of the seizure until the time of the pretrial hearings, a period of about three months. The government called twenty witnesses before resting its case. Dan Smith, attorney for First Mate Pedro Vera, called his client to testify. Unlike Captain Rubies, Vera asked for an interpreter.

The first mate testified that, before he boarded the Helena Star on March 3, 1978, he had asked the captain for work. Vera testified: "He (Captain Rubies) said that his economic situation was not as before. He said that he could not give me a job on his boat because, practically speaking, he had no boat. He found himself in the situation of having to make a trip, and that it was going to be a trip transporting marijuana. I asked him if I could go on that trip." Vera referred to the fact that Captain Rubies got off the ship in Colon, Panama, just before transiting the Canal, to meet with a man named Gomez. Vera said that Rubies came back from the meeting angry because "Gomez wanted us to take the cargo practically to his house."

Surprising me, Vera said that he had never seen the Joli and, furthermore, had no knowledge that any marijuana had been transferred to another vessel from the freighter at any time. He did admit to knowing "that supplies had been brought, water and food" to the Helena Star. He said the captain told him that they "were going to unload very far upward in Canadian waters, in high seas." He said he and the other crew members never spoke of importing marijuana into the United States. He concluded: "And I don't know that transporting marijuana on the high seas would be punishable by any country."

In response to cross-examination by Mr. Sim, First Mate Vera indicated that the Helena Star spent four or five days outside of the Strait of Juan de Fuca before contact was made with the Coast Guard. "I think we were waiting for the boat that was supposed to be coming from Canada. I saw the Canadian mountains in front of me for four or five days." Sim asked Vera if he thought "that you could sail around the world with a boat load of marijuana and stay on the high seas and dispense it to other boats and not be arrested?" I thought that was a rather good question. Vera responded: "That was not my intention and I didn't think about it." After being contacted by the Coast Guard, reversing course and heading toward China, he said "the captain and I and the first engineer spoke of throwing the cargo out into the water." He did not explain why the cargo wasn't jettisoned.

The last witness called at the trial was DEA case agent, James Prange, an excellent agent. I had him identify a record seized from the Joli as a result of a search warrant, which verified that the Joli had been out of the United States and had come through U.S. Customs in January 1978. I chose not to call Captain Rubies to testify at trial because he had already given a statement to the DEA, which had been introduced into evidence. In addition, I had come to my own conclusion that Pedro Vera had in all probability perjured himself when he testified that he had no knowledge that any marijuana had been transferred to another vessel from the freighter at any time. He had totally lost credibility by his performance on the witness stand—playing fast and loose with the facts. I did not want to take the risk that Roman

126

might fall into the same trap. It is always better for a defendant to rely on his right to remain silent and not testify than to get up on the witness stand and lie under oath.

The decision to testify was Roman's and his only. I would not countenance allowing a client of mine to take the witness stand and lie to the jury. I advised him that he had three choices when it came to testifying: (1) testify and tell the whole unvarnished truth, (2) testify and lie or (3) rely on his right to remain silent. I further advised him, as I do all clients, that option (2) was not really an option that he could choose if he wanted me to remain as his attorney. He took my advice not to testify and, by doing so, kept a modicum of credibility intact. The defense and the government then rested their cases.

There was one final issue to take up that day before adjourning till the next morning for closing arguments. There were core samples of marijuana taken by DEA agents from the 1239 bales that had been found on board the mothership. These samples had been introduced as exhibits by the government at trial. Judge Voorhees said: "The odor is permeating my chambers." He did not want the samples to go to the jury room when the jury started to deliberate after closing arguments the next day. The jurors were not asked whether they wanted to deal with the odor or not. The judge didn't say that he was concerned with the prospect of some surreptitious petty theft of weed in the jury deliberation room or that the jury might come up with some whacked out verdict, but the bottom line was that the Judge would not allow the samples to be available to the jury while it deliberated.

The following morning, all parties having rested their cases, Judge Voorhees instructed the jury as to the law relating to this case and closing arguments began. Because the prosecution has the difficult burden of proving guilt beyond a reasonable doubt, it has two bites at the apple. They give an opening argument and then have another opportunity to clean up after counsel for the captain and first mate have said their piece. As a defense attorney, it is very frustrating to give your closing argument and then have to sit down and listen to the government pick away at your argument with no way of responding to any particularly convincing argument that the prosecution may have offered the jury in its rebuttal argument.

Assistant U.S. Attorney Richard Jones led off for the government. As I expected, he made much out of the fact that Pedro Vera lied to the DEA and when he testified at trial that he had never seen the Joli and had no idea any marijuana had been transferred from the freighter to the sailboat. Jones compared the first mate's version of the facts negatively in comparison to the captain's version, but then referred to the captain neglecting to tell the DEA that the Joli had made two trips instead of one to meet the mothership and that a substantial load of marijuana had already been transferred to the Joli, unbeknownst to the DEA at the time of the captain's interview on board the Coast Guard Cutter Yocona.

In order to dispel our position that the load was destined for Canada, the Assistant U.S. Attorney referred to evidence of meat products, Olympia beer (brewed in Tumwater near the capital of the state of Washington) and other items of food that had been produced in the United States that were found on the freighter, thirty-five small sail bags that Lund purchased presumably to fill with marijuana and the rental of U-Haul trucks to store the sail bags and marijuana in a barn rented by David Victorson. Jones summed up: "If this trial were being held in Victoria (Canada) today, the same argument could be made (that the load was destined for the United States)."

I was next. In response first to Jones' argument that this same type of argument might be made in Canada, I said, "There's one place that this argument would have no use and that is in Colombia where they hopefully, eventually, will be returned and may unfortunately face prosecution." I indicated that my job in this case is "to insure that Roman Rubies is not unjustly convicted of something that he is not guilty of, and I sincerely hope that by the conclusion of this particular case, I will have met that challenge. They are foreigners in a foreign country, their families are located several thousand miles away in Colombia, and their friends and fellow crew members aboard the Helena Star have been deported to Colombia."

Credibility in addressing a jury, judge or prosecutor is of paramount importance in representing someone charged with a crime. I always tried to be candid with judges and prosecutors. I wanted to make sure that, if I made any kind of statement, a judge or prosecutor could rely on my representation and take it to the bank. As a result, I did not insult the jury's intelligence in my closing argument by suggesting that the captain thought he was transporting coffee beans or alfalfa.

There was only one real issue in this case—the destination of the freighter's load and whether the captain had any intention of importing his load into the United States. The judge had already instructed the jury that mere transportation or possession of marijuana on the high seas is not a crime unless there is an intent to import it into the United States.

I urged the jury to check the freighter's navigational charts and they would see that the vessel was always hovering closer to the coast of Canada rather than the United States. The captain's call name for contact with his Colombian handlers was "Vancouver," not "Seattle." Roman gave the names of three Colombian coconspirators to the DEA. He could not give them names of any Americans because he didn't know that there were any Americans involved. Mr. Lund's house was in Washington State, but just across the Strait of Juan de Fuca from Canada. American involvement does not necessarily equate to importation into America. Chet Miller, Lund's neighbor, was told by Lund after being gone with the Joli for several days in early March, that they "had gone up the west coast of Vancouver Island to an area around Port Alberni, Canada." Guess what? Three days after the seizure of the Helena Star, the tug Knik Wind and barge Chignik were both located in the Port Alberni area. The next day the tug was back in American waters at a marina in Anacortes, Washington.

I told the jury that I guessed "the Government would have you believe that the Knik Wind tugboat would steam up the Strait of Juan de Fuca pulling a barge containing 37 tons of marijuana. I assume that's the theory of their case and that this 37 tons would be essentially deposited in Mr. Lund's front yard by means of this tugboat." I told the jury I could not imagine a barge 82 ½ feet long and 34 feet wide being offloaded in front of Mr. Lund's Sequim Bay house without grabbing a lot of attention and speculation. Finally, the captain's involvement was simple—transporting a ton or rather many tons of marijuana from Colombia to a point on the high seas of the North Pacific. I did not condone what he did, it was wrong, but transportation of marijuana without any intent to import it into the United States is not a crime.

Dan Smith, attorney for the first mate and a fine lawyer who had graduated with me from the University of Washington Law School, followed me to the podium. He told the jury, "Even today we don't know beyond a reasonable doubt what the actual destination was, let alone the question of whether Pedro Vera knew what the destination was. Until Pedro Vera saw the commercials, he had never heard of Olympia beer. What he had in front of him, as he testified, was the mountains of Vancouver Island. He did not close his eyes to that. The agreement was not to bring marijuana to Sequim Bay. The agreement was not even to bring marijuana to Port Alberni. The agreement was to bring marijuana to this point on the high seas."

Dan mentioned the fact that none of the American coconspirators knew Pedro and none had testified as to the ultimate destination of the marijuana. None of them testified at all. "You don't have to consider whether bringing marijuana to the United States is wrong or not, or whether people in the White House are smoking it or not; all those things are irrelevant to the case. Now in a couple minutes I will sit and I have no way of knowing what Mr. Sim is going to say. The law says that you cannot bring up new points, and I want you to realize that my silence is not because I do not have answers to them. I know there are answers to each point that he'll bring up, and at this point I rely on you from what you've heard and from your experience in this trial to answer those questions, because I know there are answers and if there aren't answers there are doubts."

Assistant U.S. Attorney Ron Sim then stepped to the podium to attempt to rebut any particularly logical, persuasive, or prudent points that either Dan Smith or I had made in our closing arguments. Mr. Sim was a very gifted, shrewd, and skilled advocate for the government. As a prosecutor, you want to leave a few zingers in your back pocket for your second crack at the jury, when the defense has no opportunity to respond.

Mr. Sim wasted no time hitting home on the indications that marijuana from the Helena Star had reached the shore of the United States. He referred to the 26-foot landing craft at Lund's house, David Victorson renting Mr. Hall's barn not far away, keeping a U-Haul truck in the barn to keep it dry, a U-Haul truck seen at Lund's house, and traces of marijuana all over the place. "Everything that was done at Lund's property over on Sequim Bay, the installation of the winch, the purchase of the property in the first place, the purchase of the Joli, all suggest that that was the original intended destination of the marijuana, and in fact one load went through there. As the tug and barge were headed out to sea, who was coming in but the Coast Guard and the Helena Star in tow under arrest. So as the tug and barge get to the outside of the Strait of Juan de Fuca, they make a right turn and go up and hide. Port Alberni isn't an intended destination."

Once Mr. Sim finished his argument, the Judge dismissed the two alternate jurors. He then sent the jury along with the exhibits that had been admitted at trial (except the core samples of marijuana, whose odor was permeating the Judge's chambers) to the jury room to elect a foreperson. The jurors would then deliberate the fate of the captain and first mate of the Helena Star. It was 1:30 p.m. on Wednesday, July 26. A glimmer of hope aroused me as I left the courtroom, when one of the dismissed alternate jurors approached me and said that she would have voted "not guilty" if she had been allowed to deliberate. I started to think that the seemingly impossible, a not guilty verdict, might be possible. Then the worst time for defendants and lawyers began—waiting for twelve strangers to reach its verdict—to decide the fate of our clients.

11

THE VERDICT

A T 3:30 P.M. THE FOLLOWING DAY, JULY 27, 1978, THE JURY advised the Court Clerk that it had reached a verdict. All five attorneys were summoned to the courtroom and the two defendants were brought to court from the confines of their cell in the U.S. Marshal's lockup. The jury was escorted from the jury deliberation room to announce its verdict. Plenty of media were present to spread the word to their respective newspapers and television stations. When everyone was present, Judge Voorhees returned to the bench and asked the jury if it had reached a verdict. The jury foreman announced that the jury had found both Roman Rubies and Pedro Vera guilty as charged in both counts—conspiring to import and actual importation of marijuana into the United States. Sentencing was scheduled for August 25.

Jurors, who declined to be identified, said the crucial part of the deliberations was deciding that the 37 tons of marijuana seized on the Helena Star on April 17, 1978, were bound for the United States. One juror said, "They just weren't set up in Canada." The juror told the *Seattle Times* they did not believe the first mate when he said he had never seen a blue-hulled, 61-foot sailboat, the Joli, which brought provisions to the Helena Star and carried marijuana into the United States. "We didn't believe he was asleep; he was the mate, he had to be there." Vera had testified that he was not on watch when the Joli met with the freighter.

Peyton Whitely of the *Seattle Times* went on to report that Assistant United States Attorney J. Ronald Sim in charge of the trial division and Assistant United States Attorney Dick Jones, who prosecuted the case, shared a bit of booty after the verdict was returned. "Stewart Riley, Seattle attorney who represented Rubies in the trial, stopped by Sim's office to offer him a present. He brought both Sim and Jones T-shirts with a legend across the front: 'Helena Star Crew.'"

I was not used to failure and did not and do not like to lose, but I couldn't fault the jury or say that justice wasn't done. I felt that ensuring that a defendant received a fair trial under the United States Constitution was the highest and toughest calling of my profession and felt that I had carried out my duty to my client. The concepts of winning or losing a trial are not always the best way to judge a jury's verdict.

In anticipation of the upcoming sentencing of the captain and the first mate, I prepared a fairly lengthy presentence report to the Judge with copies to Assistant U.S. Attorney Sim and U.S. Probation Officer Walt Myers, who would likely be making a recommendation to Judge Voorhees regarding sentences to be imposed. I had a lot of respect for Mr. Myers based on my past involvement with him. Because of the contents of my report, I requested that the Judge keep its contents confidential and not make it a part of the court file—in essence, seal it from the public eye.

Normally plea bargain negotiations are not an area that I would address in such a report when my client has chosen to proceed to a jury trial, but this case was exceptional. I wanted the Court to be aware of the captain's frame of mind subsequent to his arrest and the reason why he chose not to plead guilty and take advantage of a reasonable plea bargain offered by Mr. Sim, but rather proceed to trial. The proposed bargain would have required Roman to cooperate fully with the government and to testify against the other coconspirators, whether American or South American.

I explained in my report to the Court that, during Roman's stay in jail, he had been communicating with his wife, Lola, in Cartagena, Colombia, by letter and an occasional long-distance phone call. His wife had been residing alone with their twenty-month old son since Roman's departure in February. The captain began receiving an indication from his wife, which caused him concern for her and their son's safety. Since Judge Voorhees ruled adversely on our motions, I had expected that Roman might plead guilty pursuant to the proposed plea bargain. It was the afternoon of that adverse ruling that I returned to my office to find the telegram from his wife wanting him to call her immediately. I advised the Judge in my report that it "became readily apparent that whether or not Roman pleaded guilty and cooperated with the government would be determined largely by to what extent he thought his wife and son would be in danger if he pursued the plea bargain. I then arranged with Mr. Sim to have Roman taken to a private office within the U.S. Attorney's Office so he could make a long-distance call to his wife in Cartagena."

I sat in the office while Roman made the phone call. At the end of their conversation, he turned and faced the wall for about five minutes not saying a word. Finally, he turned around and, as he faced me, ran his forefinger across his throat. This was meant to be a graphic indication to me of the probable consequences if he decided to plead guilty and cooperate. He then made it clear that his only alternative was to proceed to trial. It was one of the most touching moments that I have encountered in my fifty-year career in the practice of criminal law. I had come to learn that life in Colombia was cheap at that time. Senor Osorio, one of the two Colombian businessmen who had pressured Rubies to become involved in the conspiracy, had paid Roman's wife a visit the day before the phone call. The proposed plea agreement was discarded like garbage going into a garbage truck and Michael Lund was still wanted by the authorities, and perhaps by the Colombians, dead or alive.

I attached a copy to my report to the Judge of the captain's statement to the DEA, noting that nothing in that statement had proven to be untruthful by the evidence produced at trial, with one caveat. He did not advise the DEA that thirteen tons of marijuana had already been offloaded prior to the seizure of the Helena Star, but neither was he asked about that, because the DEA had no knowledge till later that some marijuana had already been offloaded and disappeared into the night. To prove that Roman had no prior criminal record, I also attached to my report a certificate from the Spanish Minister of Justice which was obtained before Roman's arrest in anticipation of his application for Colombian citizenship.

In my report I went on to discuss my client's background and involvement in the conspiracy. I could not argue to the Court that his role was minor, in that he was an experienced Captain in command of a 161-foot freighter and eight crew members under him during a two month voyage from the Caribbean Sea, through the Panama Canal, south along the west coast of Colombia to load 50 tons of marijuana before heading north from the equator, past all of Central America and the western United States to a point on the high seas of the North Pacific Ocean. It did, however, appear that his involvement was limited to being a glorified courier of a large amount of marijuana, rather than as an entrepreneur. Once news of his arrest on the high seas of the North Pacific came out in the Colombian press, his fishing permit was revoked. The revocation of his Captain's license would probably not be far behind. During his incarceration in the United States, his wife had to sell their fishing boat to pay off the fish processing company, Vikingos de Colombia S.A., Compania Pesquera.

I emphasized in my report that, once Colombian Gold was found on board the Helena Star, the captain became very cooperative. He translated Miranda rights warnings to his crew members, advised Coast Guard Lt. Commander John how to run the freighter and remained on the vessel to provide assistance in bringing the ship to Seattle. Roman was not armed and no weapons were found on the freighter.

I went on to report that there had been an enormous amount of pressure on Roman during his stay in jail in Seattle. Being a foreigner in a foreign country, he had suffered an unusual amount of anxiety and apprehension. "This, of course, is heightened by the fact that his wife and young son are located some 5,000 miles away from him. He appears to have aged dramatically in the last four months. Several people have commented to me how pale and thin Roman has become since his arrest. By attempting to alleviate some financial problems by agreeing to captain the Helena Star, Roman ended up greatly increasing his financial problems because of his arrest. Since he boarded the Helena Star in mid-February of 1978, he has not been able to support his wife and child. His wife does not work and his child is so young that he requires constant attention. Obviously, his family faces great hardship and the future does not look very bright for Roman Rubies." My report stated that, because he was a citizen of Spain and a resident of Colombia, it was difficult to assess how he would be treated by the government of Colombia upon his arrival, if allowed to return to Colombia. If not allowed by Colombia to return to his current home, he might be forced to relocate his family to Spain with great cost and family upheaval.

In determining an appropriate sentence for the captain, I tried to think of defendants that Judge Voorhees had previously sentenced, who found themselves in a comparable situation. There had been no one sentenced in Seattle whose case was anywhere close to that of the captain. There was, however, a case that I was involved in the year before, during which I represented a courier who smuggled cocaine from South America into the United States in a suitcase with false sides.

It was a celebrated case known primarily for the American, who was the head of the American side of a multimillion-dollar cocaine smuggling scheme, an entrepreneur by the name of Herb O'Brien. It was called at the time one of the largest illegal drug importation operations on the West Coast. Mr. O'Brien founded the well-known O'Brien Water Ski Company as a teenager in 1966 in the basement of his family home on Lake Sammamish near Seattle, where he tested combinations of exotic wood. He was a legend in the water ski industry, referred after his death in 2012 as the "Godfather of water skiing." O'Brien and his coconspirators were convicted of smuggling over 200 pounds of cocaine—said to have been worth $3 million at the time—from Chile in hollowed out O'Brien water skis and false-bottomed suitcases. Word on the street was that the smuggling operation was put in place to offset the ski manufacturer's financial losses.

Ron Sim was also the Assistant U.S. Attorney in that case. He was quoted in *The Seattle Times* saying, "The amount of cocaine involved in the case was three times more than all the cocaine seized by the Seattle DEA office in the past five years." The top banana and former President of O'Brien Water Ski Co., Herb O'Brien, was given a ten-year prison sentence and lost everything, including his company, which was sold to an out-of-state investor.

At any rate, I concluded that several of the defendants in the O'Brien water ski case were in somewhat comparable situations to Captain Rubies, though the illegal drug involved in that case was cocaine rather than marijuana and the quantity of marijuana smuggled by the captain was far greater in weight than the amount the couriers in the O'Brien case carried in suitcases or pairs of water skis. The organizers in the O'Brien case were given substantial prison sentences, while the couriers including my former client and the alien defendants were treated much more leniently. Obviously, I was suggesting to the Judge that Roman be treated substantially different from any American organizers that may be convicted in the future, like David Victorson and Eric Hale, for example. Roman should be sentenced more like two of the couriers in the O'Brien case, who made one round trip to Chile and were given one-year prison sentences. In addition, I pointed out to the Judge in my report that seven of the crew members on the Helena Star were not charged at all but were deported back to their home countries.

Mr. Sim responded to my sentencing memorandum agreeing with me that it would best be kept confidential at the time because of the cases pending against the other defendants. Sim wrote as follows: "By and large, I have no dispute with the factual presentation Mr. Riley makes concerning his client's background and role in the case. I think it is noteworthy that, although Captain Rubies was more candid with DEA than was Pedro Vera, he did not acknowledge the first trip by the Joli to meet the Helena Star during which marijuana was taken off. On the other hand, I think it is to Rubies' credit that he did not take the stand and lie to the jury."

In arguing for a substantial prison sentence for the captain, Sim indicated that, had the financiers of the conspiracy been unable to find a qualified ship's captain, the venture never could have begun. He went on to say, "News that the captain of a marijuana mothership had received a substantial prison sentence for smuggling in the United States will also reach Colombia and will have a substantial deterrent effect on other persons with the know-how to bring a ship from South America to the United States. This sort of major smuggling operation is occurring with increasing frequency." In short, Mr. Sim succinctly suggested that a harsh sentence would deter others from making a similar ill-fated decision.

On August 25, 1978, Mr. Sim, Dan Smith, and I returned to court with our two clients to hear their fate. Judge Voorhees took the bench. I approached the podium first, just to add a few comments in addition to what I had already covered in writing. I responded to Mr. Sim's deterrence argument by suggesting that it did not hold much weight—that "probably the best deterrence for ship captains coming up the west coast of the United States was Your Honor's pretrial ruling and the upshot of that is that probably most of these vessels are going to go to Florida rather than up along the Washington coast due to the difference in treatment of the courts down there." I went on to urge "that we not lose sight of the fact that in this particular case we are dealing with a drug that has become essentially so popular in the United States that, in various parts of the United States, it has even become legal to possess small amounts of it, and I think even in the City of Seattle, it is treated more like a traffic conviction than anything else." The Judge interrupted me stating, "However, there is a distinction between a joint and 37 tons." I knew I had just been had.

I reminded the Judge that Roman would be deported after serving his sentence and that a notation would be placed in his passport indicating that his American visa, which he'd had for many years, would be cancelled due to his drug conviction. He would be an outcast and probably have difficulty going into any country aside from Spain, where he is a citizen. His wife, a Colombian citizen, may be forced to leave her parents and family in Colombia if she intends to live with her husband for the remainder of her life. When a defendant is sentenced to prison, it is always the prisoner's loved ones—parents, spouse and children—who suffer the most from the transgressions of the defendant. I told the Judge that I had come to know the captain very well over the last four months, in large part because I was the only one here in the United States that he could turn to. "I sincerely hope that Your Honor recognizes what he has gone through and what he will go through in the future. He is definitely paying the price for his actions no matter what sentence the Court imposes this morning."

Judge Voorhees then asked Captain Rubies if he cared to say anything before the Court imposed sentence. He ascended to the podium, looking sad and beyond his years, and stated:

> I want the Court to know that, despite the fact that I had declared not guilty to the charges—to the specific charges that were made against me, I feel a deep feeling of guilt. I know and I knew that what I did was wrong. The circumstances that put me to it—no, the circumstances pushed me to it and I did not have the sufficient moral strength—moral and physical strength to withstand the pressure. I am very sorry and I repent, I am very sorry.

Mr. Smith then rose to advocate for First Mate Pedro Vera. He very cogently argued that "the evidence is that marijuana does not cause crime and violence, does not cause addiction and generally no demonstrable harm to the individual or society, and that speaks equally to the gravity of possessing a large amount for distribution. This is truly a victimless crime." He went on to say, "Mr. Vera has never complained of his treatment. In fact, throughout the proceedings he has continuously expressed to me his appreciation and his respect for the treatment that he has gotten from the United States legal system." After Mr. Smith was finished, Mr. Vera declined to address the Court. He had privately stated that he had not felt the slightest moral failure for having transported marijuana.

Assistant U.S. Attorney Sim then addressed the Court saying that he had already expressed his views regarding the captain in his sentencing memorandum responding to my earlier memorandum. He finished by stating: "I would only like to invite the Court's attention to the fact that these offenses in the case of both defendants were profit-motivated. Both defendants saw an opportunity to make money, they made a risk, weighing a risk analysis and entered into this knowingly and, I think, saw the consequences in committing a serious crime against American law."

Finally, the time had come for Judge Voorhees to pronounce sentences:

> This sentence is a delicate one for this Court because the two defendants are not citizens of this country, and I want to be sure that this Court treats them at least as well as I treat a citizen of the United States. The presentence reports (done by U.S. Probation Officer Walt Myers) indicate that they are both honorable, hard-working people and that this is the first time they have ever been prosecuted for any crime any place. I know the Court would be tempted to be lenient with them, but this is a serious matter and I think that I must consider the deterrent effect upon others in South America, licensed mariners, who are tempted to operate ships bringing contraband into this country, and I think the only way that I can do that is to indicate that even to those who are tempted to do it, that even though the financial rewards are high, as in this case, the potential risk is very high, and if they do it, they subject themselves to the possibility of imprisonment."

The maximum sentence for each of the two counts the defendants were convicted of was five years on each count for a total maximum exposure of ten years. With respect to the captain, Judge Voorhees imposed a four-year sentence on each count to be served concurrently with each other (at the same time). Had the Judge given my client consecutive sentences, he would have had to serve eight years. The Judge rightly said that Mr. Vera's involvement was much less serious than Captain Rubies and imposed a two-year sentence on him on each count to also be served concurrently with each other. I couldn't question the fairness of the sentences. With credit for good time, Roman could be released from prison after serving two years and eight months.

The penalties for possession, sale, or importation of marijuana were low in the 1970's, because the concept of multi-ton seizures of marijuana was inconceivable to Congress. Once these multi-ton seizures began to proliferate, Congress decided that something needed to be done. Not only were the maximum sentences raised, but mandatory minimum sentences were mandated. In 1984, the penalties for possession or distribution of over 1,000 kilograms of marijuana jumped to a *mandatory minimum* of ten years in prison and a maximum of life in prison. If a defendant had a prior felony drug offense, he or she would be looking at a *mandatory minimum* of twenty years in prison and a maximum of life. By the time Congress decided enough was enough, I had already been involved in handling at least five more marijuana seizures of at least one ton, the biggest of which was 72 tons coming by ship from Thailand.

After our clients were sentenced, Dan Smith and I filed notices of appeal of the case on behalf of our clients to the United States Court of Appeals for the Ninth Circuit in San Francisco. The Ninth Circuit handles appeals from the western region of the United States. I had already been admitted to practice before the Ninth Circuit. On November 13, 1978, a couple months later, I was admitted to practice before the United States Supreme Court. Chief Judge, John Roberts, recently said that only about five percent of lawyers are admitted to the Supreme Court of the United States. They obviously did not do a background check on me. I wasn't finished with this case yet. If we lost in the Ninth Circuit, I would attempt to get the Supreme Court to hear the case.

I did not question Judge Voorhees judgment in this case. I appeared in front of him many times, mostly after the Helena Star case was finished. He was highly respected as a judge and I held him in high esteem. He was a true gentleman. As time went on, I felt that I had developed a good relationship with him. That conclusion was borne out when he hired me to represent one of his adult children, who was charged in King County Superior Court with a crime. I will always treasure the confidence that he had in me to place the life of his son in my hands.

12

AUCTIONS

C IVIL COMPLAINTS FOR FORFEITURE OF THE JOLI AND HELENA Star had already been filed by Assistant U.S. Attorney Charlie Pinnell, including the vessels' tackle and equipment. There was an expensive Navistar sextant on the freighter that was the personal property of Captain Rubies that he had brought onto the Helena Star when he boarded her in February 1978. I made a special request of Mr. Pinnell that he return it to me, because it was not a fixture of the Helena Star and was grateful when he decided that my request was reasonable. I took receipt and sent the sextant to Roman's wife.

By this time, the captain had been transferred to serve his time at the Federal Correctional Institution on Terminal Island, located in Los Angeles Harbor between San Pedro and Long Beach. For him, compared to the King County Jail in Seattle, Terminal Island was a paradise. He wrote: "There is sun, fresh air and a lot of space to walk around. The trip from Seattle was hell. It was by bus and it took two days, manacled all the time. I am afraid that if the dollar continues to fall in the international market, they will send the next ones walking."

The first mate had been transferred to serve his time at the Federal Penitentiary on McNeil Island in south Puget Sound not far from Seattle. In order to visit a client there, a lawyer had to take a

Penitentiary boat with regularly scheduled sailings between Fort Steilacoom and the Island. It was a pleasant crossing if the weather was nice. Once when I made the crossing to visit a client, one of my former clients had good work duty—manning the mooring lines on the boat. I did not visit the first mate there, but I did send him a check for $300 that I had received from Roman's wife for Pedro to have some spending money at the commissary while imprisoned—a nice gesture on Roman's part. On October 26, 1978, Roman's wife advised me that the captain had been transferred to serve the remainder of his sentence at the Federal Correctional Institution in Texarkana, Texas, right next to the Arkansas border.

On September 22, 1978, an auction was conducted by a U.S. Marshal to sell the Joli, which had been seized by the DEA on May 1. About 100 people crowded the docks to observe the proceedings. A sealed bid for $175,000 on the yacht had already been made by Old National Bank, the bank that held the preferred ship's mortgage on the sailboat, which was guaranteed by its previous owner, Bill Niemi. According to the *Seattle Times*, Niemi showed up at the auction wanting "to look inconspicuous" wearing a wide-brimmed leather hat, an old sea jacket and blue jeans. He had originally bought the Joli for $390,000 in 1974 and sold it to Mike Lund for $255,000.

Only two people bid at the auction held at Cadranell's Yacht Landing on Lake Union. After hearing the Bank's bid, Larry Spira, a Doctor from Los Angeles, immediately bid $176,000. His bid was followed by $180,000 from Niemi, $181,000 from Spira and the winning bid of $190,000 from Niemi. Niemi essentially was bidding to protect his interest in the Joli. When the boat was sold to Lund, Niemi co-signed Lund's loan at the Old National Bank, which also explains the bank's bid. If the boat had been sold to another bidder for $50, for example, Niemi still would have been obligated to the bank for $211,000. That is the amount, with interest, that Lund still owed, which amount Niemi had guaranteed would be paid to the bank. Niemi, however, would have had no collateral to secure the loan, which necessitated his bidding on the yacht. Niemi provided a cashier's check for $22,500 to the Marshal toward the purchase back of the vessel with ten days to pay the balance.

Niemi said he planned to sell the Joli after making some minor repairs. He still had not recovered more than $25,000 worth of sails, anchors and other gear that had been stripped from the sailboat by Mike Lund. Larry Spira, the other bidder, stopped by for a drink in the Joli's cabin after the auction, introducing himself as a slot-machine dealer from Las Vegas when reporters tried to find out who he was and what his interest was in buying the Joli. Niemi said the $190,000 that he paid to get the boat back was a steal. He had an advantage over other prospective bidders because he knew the Joli and the terms of the Marshal's auction prevented a survey by anyone else before the auction. Niemi turned around and sold the yacht the following day for $225,000 to an unidentified buyer from San Francisco—subject to a marine survey. It was later seen in the 1980s on the Great Lakes, renamed "Triumph."

Two days after Niemi resold the Joli, four of the remaining untried defendants, David Victorson, Eric Hale, James Turner and Homero Ospina, were supposed to begin an expected month-long trial. The government planned to call 65 witnesses at the trial scheduled for September 25, 1978. Assistant U.S. Attorney Ron Sim had advised me that he planned to call my client, Captain Rubies, to testify against the defendants at their trial. Sim already knew that the captain had no interest in testifying against his remaining codefendants, because he felt that his family in Colombia would be in danger if he did so. That was the reason that he turned down the very favorable plea bargain that Sim had earlier offered. Now Sim was trying to force the captain to testify, because he was not going to testify voluntarily. Three days before trial, I advised the Court that, if the government called the captain to testify, he would invoke his Fifth Amendment right to remain silent based on the fact that his answers might tend to incriminate him and lead to a second prosecution in Colombia. If granted immunity from further prosecution in the United States, such immunity would not benefit him if he is charged in Colombia. I needed to protect the captain from the risk of foreign prosecution there. It was clear that he would not remain in the United States after serving his prison sentence, because an immigration detainer had been obtained to deport him. Assuming that he would be deported, his probable forced destination was likely to be Spain, where he was a citizen, or Colombia, his country of residence and where his family lived.

The captain faced a Hobson's choice. If he testified, his family might be eliminated and he might end up being prosecuted in Colombia. If he did not testify, he could be found in contempt of court and receive an additional sentence to serve in the United States. The possibility of foreign prosecution was real, not imagined. News of the seizure of the Helena Star had reached the press in Colombia. The DEA Administrative District Offices in Madrid, Spain, Bogota, Colombia, and Panama had all received information regarding the case. The penalty in Colombia for the captain's role in the conspiracy was three to twelve years imprisonment and a fine of Five to Fifty Thousand pesos. Conspiracy charges carried a penalty of five to fourteen years in Colombia. Captain Rubies didn't set foot in the United States till after he was arrested on the high seas of the North Pacific, so that any questions of him at a trial would of necessity be limited to his activities outside the United States—that is, activities in Colombia and Panama and on the high seas. The United States government was clearly interested in finding out more about the Colombian aspect of the conspiracy.

There was little if any precedent (case authority) on the question of whether a judge could require someone to testify if the witness relied on his Fifth Amendment right to remain silent and there was a real possible risk of the witness being prosecuted in a foreign country. The United States Supreme Court had never ruled on the question.

The potential problem facing the captain, however, was quickly alleviated when three of the defendants set to go to trial, David Victorson, Eric Hale and James Turner, agreed to an abbreviated non-jury trial on stipulated (agreed) facts, with the understanding that Judge Voorhees would probably find them guilty. Such a resolution would preserve their right to appeal to the Ninth Circuit the Judge's earlier decision validating the legality of the seizure of the Helena Star. The result for the captain was that the prospect of having to testify was eliminated and Judge Voorhees did not have to address the risk of foreign prosecution issue. The fourth defendant, Homero Ospina, pleaded guilty to providing a water pump for the freighter. He had purchased the pump in Los Angeles under a phony business name and had it flown to Seattle and delivered by chartered float plane on April 2, 1978, to Mike Lund's house on Sequim Bay. Judge Voorhees gave him a fine of $15,000, but no prison time, considering his rather minor involvement in the conspiracy. Ospina had agreed to transfer his $10,000 bond toward payment of the fine. His very capable Miami attorney, Irwin Lichter, considered it a victory because his client would not be serving any time behind bars.

On October 5, 1978, David Victorson and Eric Hale appeared with their respective attorneys before Judge Voorhees for what amounted to little more than a formality because both had waived their right to a jury trial and agreed to a stipulated trial in which the evidence was not disputed. This method of resolving their cases preserved their right to appeal their convictions based on an illegal seizure of the Helena Star to the Ninth Circuit Court of Appeals in San Francisco along with Captain Rubies and First Mate Vera.

The stipulation alluded to, among other things, the fact that Eric Hale had rented a U-Haul truck in Port Angeles on April 7, which was turned in to a U-Haul rental agency in Elk Grove, Illinois, on April 26 after the seizure of the Helena Star. It also referred to the fact that Mike Lund had no apparent wealth before the summer of 1977, frequently having to borrow from friends to meet living expenses. However, from that point on until his disappearance, Lund displayed a seemingly inexhaustible supply of money. Based on the agreed facts, Judge Voorhees found Victorson and Hale guilty.

At their sentencings on December 8, 1978, Assistant U.S. Attorney Ron Sim recommended the Judge impose two five-year sentences for Victorson and Hale to run consecutively for a total of

10 years. Their lawyers, Larry Finegold and Ivan Fisher, each recommended no more than five-year sentences for their clients. Mr. Sim reminded Judge Voorhees that, about three years earlier, Judge Voorhees' fellow judge on the bench, Morrell Sharp, had handed out a sentence in a nine-ton marijuana case of two five-year consecutive sentences for a total of ten years. Unlike the captain of the Helena Star, neither Victorson nor Hale spoke at their sentencing hearing. Both were given five-year prison sentences by Judge Voorhees on one count and three-year sentences on the other count, the sentences on each count to run concurrently with the other. Both were also fined $30,000. They were allowed to remain free until their appeals to the Ninth Circuit were decided.

On February 3, 1979, Patricia Karnik, Mike Lund's girlfriend, was convicted of conspiracy and ordered to perform 300 hours of community service and serve five days in custody. James Turner, the offloading expert, added his name to the list of fugitives when he failed to appear for his scheduled plea of guilty on June 15, 1979. His $5,000 cash bail previously posted was forfeited to the government. Turner would surface later in a jail in California, having been arrested on another drug charge.

The Helena Star was scheduled to be auctioned off on February 21, 1979, at her berth at the Lake Union Naval Reserve Center. No minimum bid was required. In anticipation of the auction, the U.S. Marshal's office had been receiving an average of ten phone calls a day about her, many from Alaska. A comparable ship would cost several million dollars if constructed in 1979. The *Seattle Times* put it this way: "Her value is enhanced because she is a prize of Uncle Sam and will carry no restrictions as an American-flag vessel. She can be used for coastal trade after documentation. The federal maritime Jones Act prohibits foreign-built ships from calling directly between two American ports. In this case, as property of Uncle Sam, she's an exception to the law." Prospective buyers, however, "will have to assume the risk when she's auctioned where is, as is."

The bidding for the freighter started with a very experienced U.S. Marshal, Jack Tait, handling the auction. The first bid was for $50,000. The bidding escalated through levels of $100,000, $150,000, $200,000, $225,000 and $250,000 before Jim Capron, a Friday Harbor, San Juan Island, commercial fisherman submitted the winning bid of $260,000. He said that he and his two partners bought the vessel for their own use, but that the ship could be used for ocean research or leased to an oil company. According to reporter, Peyton Whitely, Capron said that "it would be a few days before he knew exactly what he bought this morning. It wasn't possible to have the vessel surveyed before the sale, although Capron said he did send a diver down to inspect the Helena Star's hull. Capron estimated that it could cost $1 million to prepare the ship for its new role. He estimated it would cost $2 million to build a similar vessel. Capron just laughed when someone asked if he was planning any trips to South America."

After purchasing the Helena Star, Mr. Capron was able to contact Captain Rubies, while he was serving his time in Texarkana. Roman provided some help in advising him concerning the operation of the vessel. Shortly after, Capron contacted me to see about the possibility of getting Roman out of prison temporarily to further assist him with the operation of the vessel. I explained that that was not going to happen, given that the U.S. Immigration and Naturalization Service had placed an immigration hold on Roman for deportation after Roman finished the term of his sentence. I had a feeling that Capron's tenure with the decrepit vessel was going to have a bumpy future.

13

THE APPEAL

I HAD BEGUN TO WORK ON CAPTAIN RUBIES' APPEAL. IVAN FISHER, Eric Hale's lawyer, called me from Switzerland to ask me if he could be co-counsel with me on the appeal. He told me that the Cartel's "court" in Colombia had found Rubies not guilty but found the first mate guilty. He told me that Roman's family in Cartagena would be taken care of. I took that all with a grain of salt. We later agreed that he would not be my co-counsel on the appeal. In late December of 1978 I filed a 36-page memorandum on behalf of the captain in the United States Court of Appeals for the Ninth Circuit appealing his conviction. The legal brief raised three issues on appeal, the primary one relating to the legality of the seizure of the Helena Star and search of the vessel. Dan Smith, attorney for the first mate, also filed a memorandum. By this time Rubies had been transferred from Terminal Island in California to the Federal Correctional Institution in Texarkana, Texas. His new identity as a convicted felon, which followed him from Terminal Island, was prisoner #20521-148.

On May 17, 1979, Dan Smith and I presented our oral arguments to a three-judge panel at the United States Courthouse for the Ninth Circuit Court of Appeals in San Francisco. We had to share our allotted time of only 30 minutes. Assistant U.S. Attorney Sim also appeared and was allotted 30 minutes of time for his response.

Though he was confident of victory, because the issue in our case was novel, he knew there was still a possibility that the convictions could be reversed. When a lawyer walks into a trial court room or an appellate court room, there is no such thing as a slam dunk. Over the years, I had won cases I had no business winning and lost a few cases I thought I should have won. It is always somewhat of a crap shoot. Nothing ever seems to be black and white, just a shade of gray. In an affidavit filed after oral argument, Ron Sim stated, "I felt that there was a real possibility of reversal on appeal."

Time spent at my office was not always all work and no play. While waiting for the Ninth Circuit to rule on our appeal, I decided to attempt to engage in some *pro bono* work. *Pro bono* is a Latin term, which means doing unpaid legal work for the good of the public. On July 17, 1979, the Major League Baseball All-Star game was played in Seattle. The crowd included former President Gerald Ford. Also in the crowd was a famous exotic dancer, who happened to be a big baseball fan, or was it the other way around—a big baseball fan who happened to be a famous stripper. She was known as Morganna, baseball's Kissing Bandit. She was extremely well-proportioned—some would say she was extremely top heavy.

As Morganna had done in other All-Star games since 1971, she quickly tumbled over the Kingdome fence and ran onto the field with the Kansas City Royals star player, George Brett, as her target. She eluded transfixed security officers, streaked across the infield in red jogging shorts and a T-shirt taxed beyond capacity, and landed a lip-locker on the batter in the on-deck circle. George Brett surrendered with no discernable struggle. Morganna was arrested by the local cops, taken to the station and charged with criminal trespass.

A couple of days later, my associates, including my esteemed partner, Roger Johnson, and I were sitting around our second office in the secluded, almost secret bar in the back of the City Loan Pavilion Restaurant, one floor down from our offices. It was late in the afternoon. We were kicking back and thinking how much fun it would be to represent Morganna on a *pro bono* basis—representing her for free for the good of the public. I decided I would stop talking and actually do something about it. I would compose a letter to this splendid young lady offering my services. The only problem was that I had no address for her. The internet had yet to be invented. I did have her last name from the newspaper. I thought the court file might contain her address.

Not to be deterred, the next day I sprinted up to the Seattle Municipal Court Clerk's Office and sheepishly approached one of the clerks and asked her to see the court file of a defendant with the last name of Cottrell. The clerk left to search for the file. She returned empty handed, saying that she was unable to find such a file. She asked me for the first name of the defendant and I responded in a rather hushed voice, "Morganna." The clerk quickly responded, "Why didn't you say that to begin with?" She left for a moment, returning in a flash with Morganna's court file, which had obviously been put in a special place, probably because of so many press inquiries. I am sure I was blushing—I know I was embarrassed. I thanked the clerk, grabbed the file and snuck away to a far corner of the office to inspect the file. Voila! I jotted down Morganna's address in Columbus, Ohio, returned the file, slunk out the door and fled back to my office.

Following is part of my letter to baseball's Kissing Bandit:

Dear Morganna:

Allow me to introduce myself as one of the smoothest and slickest criminal lawyers in the city of Seattle as well as one of your greatest fans. In my capacity as a criminal defense lawyer, I frequently represent dainty young damsels in distress like yourself. I greatly admired the way you welcomed George Brett to the Kingdome during the recent All-Star game in Seattle, but I understand via the papers that you were pinched by the local gendarmes here for "criminal trespass." No doubt all the cops wanted to do was frisk you. Since you are from out of town and probably don't know any criminal lawyers in Seattle, I though it appropriate to offer you my legal services for free. Please let me know if I can assist you in your time of crisis.

Fondly, Stewart "Loophole" Riley

A couple days later, I was in my office when our receptionist let me know that someone named "Morganna" was on line 2. I immediately thought that one of my friends was pulling my leg. I answered the phone to hear the sultry voice of the one and only Kissing Bandit telling me how delighted she was to get my letter, but that she had just been allowed by the Seattle City Attorney and the Judge to forfeit the $115 she had posted as bail to gain her freedom. Unfortunately, her case was finished and I was out of luck.

Several days later the U.S. Mail brought me an autographed glossy photograph of Morganna with a note to "Loophole" saying, "If I'm ever in trouble, I'll make my one phone call to you—your breast friend, Morganna." She is the only person I've ever known who dots her "M"s. Sure enough, the next couple of years she got arrested at All-Star games in Los Angeles and on the East Coast. I was the first one she called. I assisted her in getting legal counsel in both cities— *pro bono*, of course.

Lawyers for David Victorson and Eric Hale had also appealed their convictions to the Ninth Circuit, but a motion by Ron Sim to consolidate their appeal with ours was denied by the Court. The three-judge panel before which Dan Smith and I argued the appeal in San Francisco consisted of Judge Thomas Tang, Judge Anthony Kennedy and Judge Robert Belloni, United States District Judge for the District of Oregon filling in as a Ninth Circuit judge on a temporary basis.

Judge Kennedy had been appointed to the Ninth Circuit bench by President Gerald Ford in 1975. Eight years after hearing our appeal, President Reagan nominated Judge Kennedy to the Supreme Court of the United States. Before Judge Kennedy's nomination, Reagan had struck out nominating Robert Bork, who was rejected by the U.S.

Senate, and then Douglas Ginsburg, who withdrew his name from consideration after admitting to using marijuana. Judge Kennedy was subjected to an unprecedentedly thorough background check, which he easily passed, being unanimously confirmed by the Senate. He served as the 93rd Associate Justice of the U.S. Supreme Court from 1988 until his retirement in 2018, the last two years of which he was the Senior Associate Justice. It was a great honor to appear in San Francisco in front of a judge who later ascended to be a judge on the highest court in our land.

Unfortunately Judge Kennedy did us no favors. During the time that our case was pending in the Ninth Circuit, the Fifth Circuit Court of Appeals found in a case out of Florida that a stateless vessel is subject to the jurisdiction of the United States at least for the limited purpose of determining her true identity. Though not bound by a ruling in another circuit, our three-judge panel was persuaded to follow the Fifth Circuit's lead and rejected our appeal on September 10, 1979. Judge Belloni, who wrote the Opinion, stated:

> The Coast Guard had the necessary cause to board and every action taken with respect to the boarding and subsequent search and seizure was entirely reasonable. No search warrant was required. Even if we fail to consider the difficulty in obtaining a warrant to search a vessel that is beyond the territorial waters of the United States, there nevertheless was sufficient cause to believe the Helena Star was stateless and the attempted flight through the night without running lights created the necessary exigent circumstances. The oceans are vast and a vessel can often easily avoid initial detection or escape afterwards.

By this time, the first mate had served out his two-year sentence, less good time, and was deported back to Colombia. His passport had been stamped with an indication that he had been convicted of a serious drug charge in the United States. He had been put on a flight to

Bogota, with the pilot of the commercial airplane having possession of his passport. On arrival in Bogota, the pilot gave Colombian immigration authorities Pedro Vera's passport. After reviewing his passport, Pedro was immediately arrested and jailed until someone paid the necessary "mordida" (bribe) to obtain his release from custody.

Later in September 1979, Dan Smith and I filed a Petition for Rehearing and Suggestion of Appropriateness of Rehearing En Banc, which is basically a request to have the full court of twenty Ninth Circuit judges rehear our appeal rather than just the original three judge panel. Before deciding our petition, the Court also denied the appeals of David Victorson and Eric Hale. It was about this time that I began hearing rumors about the possibility that two lawyers involved in our case were under investigation and might be indicted. I was not one of them, nor were any of the other Seattle lawyers involved in the case.

Roman wanted to meet with me in person to discuss among other things the possible filing of a motion with Judge Voorhees to reduce his sentence. I had already met with him at the prison in Texarkana, Texas, on January 14, 1979. On November 13, 1979, I flew again to Dallas, rented a car and drove 175 miles east to the Federal Correctional Institution in Texarkana. It was a dismal place—the prison and the town.

Texarkana is best known for its favorite son, Ross Perot, a self-made Texas billionaire, whose 19 per cent of the vote in 1992 in the presidential race between President George H.W. Bush and challenger Bill Clinton was the largest percentage of votes for a third party candidate since former president Teddy Roosevelt's 1912 bid. As a boy in Texarkana, Perot delivered newspapers from the back of a horse. (This reminds me of a favorite quote of mine by President Reagan: "There's nothing better for the inside of a man than the outside of a horse.") Perot went on to graduate from the U.S. Naval Academy, worked for IBM and then started the incredibly successful Electronic Data Systems Corporation. Probably the most famous event in his business career, however, occurred a few days after I first visited Roman in Texarkana in January 1979. Perot financed a private commando raid to free two EDS executives from a prison in Iran, shortly after the Shah had to flee his country. Perot's team sneaked the executives out of the country and into Turkey, with the caper being written about in Ken Follett's bestselling book, *On Wings of Eagles*, later made into a movie.

On November 23, 1979, the Ninth Circuit, after filing a Revised Opinion, denied our request for a rehearing of our appeals. Six days later, on November 29, 1978, I filed a lengthy Motion for Modification of Sentence with Judge Voorhees. In an effort to differentiate Roman from the American kingpins—David Victorson and Eric Hale—I reminded the Judge that at their sentencing he had said that "a lot of people have been dragged down by these two", referring to Victorson and Hale. I stated that Roman's Case Manager and Unit Manager at the prison verified that he had had no disciplinary problems and was considered a responsible inmate. Based on his educational endeavors at Texarkana, Roman had been assigned to work on the refrigeration crew at the powerhouse, which was located outside the main compound of the prison (in spite of the Immigration and Naturalization Service detainer on him). The captain had in fact completed 1080 hours of a Refrigeration and Air Conditioning Program through Texarkana Community College and also completed a Residential, Commercial and Industrial Electrical Blueprint Reading course.

I also pointed out to the Judge that, because of the Immigration and Naturalization detainer, Roman was not eligible for furloughs, work release or time in a halfway house. Foreign prisoners were treated differently than the general population in regard to those benefits due to a greater risk of flight from the United States.

Unfortunately, on December 7, 1979, Judge Voorhees denied my motion. I was not to be deterred just yet. Our last resort was to attempt to get the U.S. Supreme Court to reverse the decision of the Ninth Circuit Court of Appeals. Mr. Smith and I collaborated in filing what is called a Petition for Writ of Certiorari, which is a fancy way of saying that we wanted the Supreme Court to take a fresh look at our case. In the conclusion to our brief we stated:

> Resolution of the issues involved in this case will have a great impact on thousands of mariners and yachtsmen that daily ply the high seas. It will determine to what extent if any the United States is bound by the multilateral treaties that it enters into and how much priority the United States places on the concept of freedom of the seas. The blatant violations of international law and the Fourth Amendment enumerated above must be rectified by dismissal of the charges or suppression of the evidence.

The Supreme Court grants less than one percent of the Petitions for Writs of Certiorari filed—long odds.

Continuing the saga, on March 11, 1980, Robert Moran, David Victorson's flamboyant attorney, and Dean Bowen became the latest defendants to be charged in connection with the ill-fated voyage of the Helena Star. Judge William Newsom of the Californian Court of Appeals had written a letter on Court of Appeals stationary attesting to Moran's good character in 1979 when it was first believed that Moran might be indicted in Seattle in the wake of the seizure of the Helena Star. Moran had given the letter to Assistant U.S. Attorney Steve Schroeder to review. It obviously hadn't dissuaded Mr. Schroeder from his mission to indict Moran.

Mr. Moran was 39 years old, the product of an Irish-Catholic family. He graduated from John Carroll University in Cleveland, Ohio, a Jesuit institution, followed by law school at the University of Maryland, graduating in 1964. In his final year of law school, he was elected President of the Student Body. I guess being elected President of your law school student body doesn't guarantee that at some later time you won't fall off the rails. Moran then enlisted in the United States Army, subsequently becoming a first lieutenant. During this time, he was active as defense counsel in court martials at Fort Ord in California. Thereafter, he was sent to Viet Nam for eight months, where he was selected by his superior officers to act as a prosecutor for the Army in court martials. While in Viet Nam, he was promoted to Captain and ultimately honorably discharged in 1967. Moran moved to Marin County and passed the bar in 1968. For the last few years, the primary focus of his legal work was in the area of domestic relations handling divorces. His only prior criminal record was for a DUI charge in Marin County, to which he pleaded guilty.

Mr. Moran was charged in United States District Court in Seattle with providing advice to the drug smugglers and making financial arrangements for the smuggling ring. The Indictment referred to David Victorson paying Moran $200,000 in November of 1977 and Moran transferring $128,000 from San Francisco to Seattle on April 20, 1978, to make the final payment for the Knik Wind tugboat and Chignik barge, which had been expected to be used to offload the final 37 tons of marijuana from the Helena Star. Moran was also charged with eight counts of perjury in connection with his testimony before a federal grand jury in Seattle when he testified that he didn't know what the Helena Star was going to be used for; that he didn't know the ship had been seized until he read about it in newspapers; that he didn't know Victorson was in Washington State to aid in the smuggling; and that he didn't know about the role of Colombian firms involved in the smuggling effort that he represented.

Mr. Moran hired Charles Morgan, a well-known attorney from San Francisco, not to be confused with the captain of the Coast Guard Cutter Yocona, with the same name. Attorney Morgan was a workaholic and always a formidable adversary. He kept two secretaries busy working 12-hour shifts, six days a week. He played football at UCLA on a team that included future baseball pioneer, the great Jackie Robinson. As an Air Force navigator in World War II, he flew 63 missions in the European Theatre. He was awarded the Distinguished Flying Cross when the B-24 he was on returned to its home field successfully despite receiving 220 flak holes. His client, Robert Moran, was released on $500,000 bond, using his hilltop Corte Madera home as collateral to secure the bond. When attorney Morgan filed his request for admission to practice in the U.S. District Court in Seattle to represent Moran, he failed to advise the Court that on May 5, 1977, the Supreme Court of California had suspended him from the practice of law in California for one year because he "misappropriated and commingled funds of clients entrusted to him." The execution of the suspension was stayed for one year, during which Morgan was placed on probation after serving one month of the original one-year suspension.

Prior to his indictment, Robert Moran had admitted that he had transferred the remaining balance on the purchase by Mike Lund of the Knik Wind and Chignik tug and barge from a San Francisco bank to Seattle, but that he had no knowledge of its purpose. "I thought it was a little odd at first. What did they need this boat for? But it's not my job to make judgments on people. My friends were suspicious and I was too. But what do I care where the money comes from? If IBM brought $10 million to the Bank of America for deposit, would the bank ask if they made the money violating antitrust laws?"

Dean Bowen, charged along with Moran, was accused of taking part in the smuggling conspiracy by flying from Seattle to Port Angeles, meeting the Chignik 105 barge in Port Angeles and agreeing to help unload the marijuana. Bowen was represented by Marcus Topel, another well-known lawyer from San Francisco. Mike Lund and James Turner remained fugitives.

Finally, on May 12, 1980, the U.S. Supreme Court denied our request for a Writ of Certiorari. Not prone to give up, I filed a Petition for Rehearing in the Supreme Court, which was denied on August 11, 1980. Just like the Helena Star, we were dead in the water, becalmed and out of alternatives. We had given it the good fight but lost in the end. My work for the captain, however, was not finished.

14

ALLIED BANK OF TEXAS

T HE CORPORATE HEADQUARTERS OF ALLIED BANKS WAS IN Houston, Texas. Allied was one of the largest banks in Texas. One of their customers was a slick operator named Barry Wilson. He had moved to Houston in 1978, sometime after the seizure of the Helena Star. He became the consummate money launderer, helping to solve the eternal problem faced by successful, high end criminals—hiding the fruits of their crimes. The trick was to take bundles of $100 bills received in exchange for illegal drugs like marijuana or cocaine and turn them into what appear to be legitimate investments. Wilson told an investigative reporter for Texas Monthly, "The way you begin is that you look for the bank that is young and hungry. Never the biggest bank—the one that wants to be the biggest. In Houston, Allied fit the bill." Vice President Samuel Hughes was hungry for new business.

Major league drug smuggler, David Victorson, became a client of Barry Wilson. Victorson provided Wilson with a steady stream of cash to be invested—as much as $100,000 at a time. Wilson developed a friendship with Samuel Hughes at Allied Bank and talked him into an unconventional system for loaning money. Victorson's money would end up in Hughes hands via Wilson in the form of cash, wire transfer or certified check. Investigative reporter John Bloom described how it worked:

> When Hughes received the money, he would call Wilson and ask him to come to the office. There the money would be used to purchase a certificate of deposit in Wilson's name and the CD would in turn be used as collateral for a loan to Wilson for the same amount. Wilson would use the loan money to buy expensive exotic cars, which sometimes appreciate at rates of 20 to 30 per cent per year. Then he would drive the cars to California, "sell" them to Victorson in a purely paper transaction. At the end of 30 days, the original CD would be used to pay off Wilson's loan. "There is one reason and one reason only for that kind of transaction," said Wilson. "It effectively hides the money. It converts dirty money into clean cars. And they are always cars that can instantly be sold for cash. All exotic car dealers deal in cash, because they all want to falsify the purchase price in order to avoid the exorbitant taxes."

By 1980, Victorson, out of custody waiting for his appeal to be decided, still had a showroom with a few high-end vehicles for sale. For some reason, none of them had been seized by the government, which gave him the confidence to keep buying expensive, exotic cars. He contacted his money launderer, Barry Wilson, to purchase some more inventory—four Ferraris. In early May 1980, Victorson flew from San Francisco to New York to meet Wilson. Victorson was carrying a suitcase full of cash and a stash of China White heroin. There was no airport security line in those days. No one went through carry-on bags or checked bags and Victorson had become a voracious consumer of China White. He checked into a suite in the Plaza Hotel, met Wilson and turned $280,000 over to him. According to Victorson, Wilson flew to Zurich, Switzerland, to purchase the Ferraris. Victorson was to wait in his suite at the Plaza till Wilson returned within two weeks.

On the night of May 9, 1980, Barry Wilson was driving a Ferrari that he had just purchased for Victorson, from Milan to Zurich. An oncoming car crossed over the center line into his lane near the town of Gallarate, Italy, by Lake Maggiore. Wilson ended up in a ditch. The Ferrari was destroyed and Wilson suffered a severe laceration to his head. Before an ambulance drove him to the nearest hospital, he was able to snatch his briefcase containing $75,000 in $100 bills. He stayed in the hospital overnight, prematurely leaving the next day to catch the next flight back to New York. When he arrived at JFK Airport, he was not thinking clearly and did not declare the $75,000 in his briefcase when going through U.S. Customs. In 1980, the law required travelers arriving in the United States from a foreign country to declare currency in any amount exceeding $5,000. Agents searched his briefcase, discovered the substantial amount of cash and seized it.

Wilson returned from Europe having spent most of the $280,000 on two Ferraris. He went to meet Victorson in his suite at the Plaza Hotel and told him that the $75,000 remaining after the purchase of the two Ferraris had been confiscated by U.S. Customs. They were holding the cash pending further investigation and documentation. Wilson said he would have to return to the airport in the morning to work things out with Customs. Wilson had told Customs that the cash belonged to Victorson. After their meeting, Wilson went down to the lobby of the Plaza Hotel under the pretense of getting his own room but rabbited.

According to Victorson, Ivan Fisher, who by now was representing both Victorson and his buddy, Eric Hale, eventually obtained the release of the cash from Customs, but Victorson said Fisher kept it to offset future legal fees.

Two weeks later, on May 24, 1980, Barry Wilson obtained another loan from Allied Bank in the amount of $70,000, secured by Victorson's money. A few days later, Victorson called Sam Hughes at the bank to return the money he had sent to the bank. Hughes was out of the office. Victorson raised hell on the phone with multiple officers of the bank, who had no idea what he was talking about.

What followed were a series of meetings between officers of the bank to figure out the relationship between Victorson and their Vice President, Sam Hughes. Even after Hughes explained the situation to bank President Walter Johnson, the President still did not understand what was taking place and called the bank's attorney, Joe Peck. Peck met with Hughes and then called Victorson in California. He had a very unsatisfying conversation with Victorson, in large part because Victorson was probably high on heroin.

Attorney Peck decided to switch gears and try to collect the $70,000 outstanding loan that the bank had made to Barry Wilson just one week earlier. Peck tracked down Wilson, who happened to be in Houston, and told him the bank was calling in the loan and it needed to be paid off immediately. Wilson was on a short stopover on one of his many buying trips between California and Europe. He was leaving for Houston International Airport to catch a flight and did not understand why the bank was calling the loan but figured that he could work it out with Vice President Hughes. Wilson told Peck that he didn't have $70,000. "All I have is $40,000 or so here in my briefcase, but I'm leaving for the airport right now." Peck told him even that much would help and that bank officials would meet him at the airport.

About one hour later, Wilson met up with two employees of the bank in a bar at the airport. Investigative reporter, Bloom, recounted Wilson's version of the meeting:

> Then, as curious passersby stared quizzically, Wilson pulled stacks of $100 bills out of his briefcase, patiently counting them out, and turned them over to the bankers. He kept $5,000 for his traveling expenses and gave them about $35,000 as partial payment on the loan. "I barely made the plane," said Wilson. "I couldn't get over it, these two guys from an enormous bank sitting in a dark bar and counting money with me. When I got up to leave, I said, 'And next time the drugs better be good or I'm not going to pay you.' I couldn't resist."

Back to Victorson's demand for money from the same bank. After lengthy interviews with Vice President Sam Hughes, Barry Wilson's go to guy, Allied Bank decided it might owe Victorson some money. Two bank employees flew to San Francisco in the dead of night to pay him off. The meeting with Victorson occurred on June 28, 1980, at the offices of Diversified Investment Portfolios, Inc. (DIPI), one of Victorson's companies. It was late at night, since Victorson preferred to do business after dark. Victorson was still out on bail pending the determination of his appeal. One of the topics discussed was the ownership of the $75,000 confiscated by U.S. Customs agents at JFK Airport from Barry Wilson when he reentered the United States. The Bank believed that it was their money that it had loaned to Barry Wilson to purchase exotic automobiles. Wilson, however, had told Customs that the money belonged to David Victorson, which muddied the waters.

In any event, the bankers ended up paying the big-time drug trafficker almost $18,000 in return for his agreement not to sue the bank. In the signed agreement Victorson disclaimed any right to the $75,000 seized by Customs, agreed that the money belonged to the Bank and, if paid the money by Customs, would deliver it over to the Allied Bank of Texas. Little did the bankers know that the $75,000 had already been obtained from Customs by Ivan Fisher, Victorson's attorney, and was used to pay Victorson's attorney fees. Victorson later bragged that he had brought a "bunch of Texas bankers to their knees." He had embarrassed one of the largest banks in Texas. A few days later, Vice President Sam Hughes left the bank and virtually disappeared. Efforts to locate Victorson by the Bank, when it found out that the $75,000 had already been returned by Customs, were utterly unsuccessful.

In late June of 1980, Victorson asked Barry Wilson to meet him in his office in San Francisco. Victorson was very worried about the seizure of $75,000 by U.S. Customs agents at JFK Airport in New York and wanted to distance himself from Wilson. To achieve that end, he asked Wilson to sign a three-page legal document. "David was very careful to let me see that his friends had guns while I was out there," said Wilson, "and his friends were very careful to let me know that I had screwed up and they weren't going to let me do anything to harm David. He scared me. He can be very mean when he wants to be. I signed the papers and left. That was the last time I ever saw David." Wilson did appear for a hearing on August 22, 1980, regarding the seizure of the $75,000 in cash from his briefcase at JFK Airport. He was fined $7,500 due to his failure to declare the currency when he returned to the United States.

Allied Bank of Houston had seen Barry Wilson for the last time. After his frightful meeting with David Victorson, Wilson moved to Milan, Italy, and on to Beirut, Lebanon. The bank had gotten back $35,000 of the $70,000 loaned to Wilson, but had no success reaching him again to recoup the remaining $35,000 owed.

In its September 1980, issue, Texas Monthly Magazine, a 300,000-circulation regional magazine, did a feature article on Barry Wilson and his involvement with stolen Picasso paintings and relationship with David Victorson. The point of the article was to shed some light on the murky European underworld—the purchase and sale of stolen paintings, cars and jewels from South Africa and the part that drug smuggling, including Turkish heroin, played in the world of international crime. "The cars were a kind of underworld currency. Barry (Wilson) had witnessed trades of cars for drugs, drugs for jewels, art for cash, and a dozen other variations on the theme." The reporter, John Bloom, interviewed Wilson prior to publication of the article, which included a description of the ever stylishly dressed and handsome David Victorson:

One man in particular, a notorious San Francisco dealer by the name of David Victorson, had Barry (Wilson) scared half out of his wits. Barry changed hotels three times during his week in Dallas, and all our meetings were held in crowded public places. One reason Barry was scared was that he owed Victorson a whale of a lot of money. But the more important one was that he had quit the business without an acceptable explanation. He knew enough to put Victorson and several others in prison, and Victorson apparently believed that Barry might do it. Victorson was right. Barry would never go directly to the police—he hates all law-enforcement agencies with a passion, but especially the "jokers" of the Drug Enforcement Administration. But he hoped that an expose would result in a long sentence for Victorson.

15

BOLIVIA

Attorney Robert Moran's trial was scheduled for September 8, 1980. His case would be handled by a different set of Assistant U.S. Attorneys, Steve Schroeder and Jose Gaitan, because Ron Sim was leaving the U.S. Attorney's office to go into private practice after a brilliant stint with the government. Schroeder had transferred to the U.S. Attorney's office in Seattle in 1979 from the U.S. Department of Justice in Washington, D.C., where he had been an attorney for five years. His first three years at the Department of Justice were spent with the Organized Crime and Racketeering Section in Washington, D.C. and New Orleans, followed by two years prosecuting public corruption cases with the Public Integrity Section in Washington, D.C. On August 14, 1980, I received a letter from Mr. Schroeder wanting to interview Captain Rubies for purposes of possibly using him as a witness for the government. In return, he would guarantee that Roman would be sent to the country of his choice upon his release from prison. We respectfully declined Schroeder's invitation and offer. Schroeder, nonetheless, was expecting to use David Victorson and Eric Hale as witnesses against Robert Moran. Their petition to the United States Supreme Court to accept their case for hearing still had not been decided and they were both still out on bail pending the appeal. According to Victorson, their lead attorney from New York kept saying, "This is a sure bang winner on appeal," referring to the questionable seizure of the Helena Star on the high seas of the North Pacific.

While Victorson and Hale's appeal was still pending, Victorson decided he wanted out of Marin County. He sold his home in San Anselmo in May of 1980 and bought a 125-acre ranch about 25 miles north of Santa Barbara, California, from a judge. It was a small part of a 14,500-acre development of ranches with 8 ½ miles of ocean front named Hollister Ranch. The Ranch had been subdivided in the early 1970s and is located west of Gaviota State Park. The ocean front was owned in common by the owners of the parcels. It had been a surfers' mecca until the owners of the Ranch closed off access to the public. Victorson bought the ranch in the name of one of his companies, Diversified Investment Portfolios, Inc. (DIPI), the same company that attorney Moran used to pay Bob Morton on April 20, 1978, the balance owed on Morton's sale of the Knik Wind and Chignik tug and barge to Mike Lund. Shortly after Victorson moved to the ranch, Eric Hale's and his convictions were upheld. They were ordered to report within two weeks to the McNeil Island Federal Penitentiary in Washington State where the first mate from the Helena Star had served his sentence. Meanwhile, Robert Moran's trial set for September 8, 1980 was fast approaching.

On August 19, subpoenas were issued at the request of both the government and defense for Susan Kessler and Dr. Mark Steven Becker to testify at Moran's upcoming trial. Victorson had met Susan in Costa Rica and Dr. Becker had treated him at times. Ms. Kessler had said that she knew Victorson better than anyone, as she had lived at his home for a while, taking care of it with her husband. Robert Moran's attorney, Charles Morgan, said that Ms. Kessler wanted to help Moran because she recognized that Victorson was dangerous, possibly because of his utilization of narcotics. She had been told by Mr. Victorson that Ivan Fisher, Victorson's attorney, had convinced him that it was Robert Moran's fault that Victorson was convicted. Clear back on June 16, 1978, the government had interviewed

Moran, and on June 20, 1978, before Victorson was indicted, Moran testified before the Grand Jury in Seattle. Victorson speculated that Moran had incriminated him when he testified. According to attorney Morgan, Ms. Kessler said that Victorson was paying his attorney, Ivan Fisher, in excess of $700,000, a part of which was to be utilized for seeing that Robert Moran in some way got indicted.

Attempts to serve Ms. Kessler and Dr. Becker with subpoenas at their addresses in California were unsuccessful. On September 27, 1980, according to her death certificate, Susan Kessler of Mill Valley, California, age 38, was found dead of an overdose (Multiple Drug Intoxication) in unit A-6 of the seedy Vagabond Hotel located at 7301 Biscayne Boulevard in Miami, Florida. Five days later on October 2, according to his death certificate, Dr. Becker of Lake Worth, Palm Beach County, Florida, age 31, was found dead of an overdose (Insulin) in unit 29 of the equally seedy Frolics Motel located at 3530 Biscayne Boulevard in Miami, Florida.

That is to say both Ms. Kessler and Dr. Becker overdosed in sleazy motels located on the same boulevard in Miami within five days of each other. Because they had died, it is difficult to assess to what extent they would have helped or hurt Mr. Moran if they had testified. Unfortunately, they had become silent witnesses—their lips sealed by death. Clearly, by this time a rift had occurred between Moran and his money machine—David Victorson. According to Victorson, Dr. Becker "had become addicted to shooting heroin. I was glad I was in prison when they died, as I am sure there would be suspicion that I was involved." Actually, by the time that Kessler and Dr. Becker were found dead, Victorson and Hale had fled the United States to avoid serving their sentences and presumably were on the run.

Found in Dr. Becker's room at the Frolics Motel was a suicide note expressing his love for his deceased girlfriend, Susan Kessler, as well as a syringe, needle, and insulin. Chief Medical Examiner, District 17, Broward County, Florida, Ronald Wright said:

Both were heavy users of drugs of abuse. Kessler's death was an accidental death from a combination of recreational drugs taken to get high—cocaine, Quaaludes, valium, and Darvon. Dr. Becker's death was clearly a suicide due to remorse and probably from a fear that his drug abuse would become known by the licensing authorities and that he could be prosecuted under Florida law for supplying drugs causing the death of Ms. Kessler. Becker overdosed on insulin he obtained for killing himself as he was not diabetic.

This conclusion by Dr. Wright debunked Assistant U.S. Attorney Jose Gaitan's suggestion that Dr. Becker's death was a homicide. Gaitan had been informed that one of the detectives investigating the deaths in Broward County, Florida, thought that the two deaths were highly suspicious and did not believe Becker's death was a suicide. The detective planned to investigate the deaths as murders. According to Gaitan, Dr. Becker had become involved in the conspiracy to import and distribute the marijuana from the Helena Star. Due to Becker's addiction to heroin and its concomitant financial pressures, Becker had driven one truckload of marijuana from Sequim Bay to the Chicago area. Motel and airplane flight records confirmed that he was in the Sequim area during the offloading of the thirteen tons of marijuana from the Helena Star.

In addition, Victorson and Hale were expected to testify at Moran's trial about Dr. Becker's role. Becker had indicated to other government witnesses and to Robert Moran that his paramount concern was to keep his medical license and that he would do whatever was necessary to keep his license, including testifying against other participants in the conspiracy. Consequently, Assistant U.S. Attorney Gaitan said, "The apparent homicide of Dr. Becker so shortly after efforts to subpoena him remains a matter of grave concern."

Meanwhile, Victorson and Hale made a plan to flee the United States in late August. Victorson said:

I made a call and arranged for two fake passports. I called Eric and told him to meet me at the Chateau Marmont in Hollywood in two days. We would go to New Orleans and then on to Costa Rica. After a few months of hanging out on the beaches of Costa Rica, we took a cab to the airport and headed to Bolivia. My Colombian family had strong ties with some Bolivian coca growers. I thought I might be able to find a safe place to live through these contacts. We arrived in La Paz and took a connecting flight to Santa Cruz, Bolivia. We met with one of those contacts and were driven to a mango farm that was kept as a safe house for fugitives and smugglers. There was a three-bedroom hacienda along with four outbuildings. This was a violent time in Bolivia. Bolivia was the largest grower of coca plants in the world. The leaves were shipped to Colombia for processing into cocaine for the North American market. Being a landlocked country, Bolivia had no seaport, so all exports, legal and illegal, had to be transported by truck or plane. The truck routes were dangerous, winding mountain roads with plenty of opportunity for ambush and hijacking. A new breed of violent bandits had emerged, going after growers and smugglers.

While in Costa Rica, Eric Hale had purchased a pound of pot. The hotel where they were staying was raided and both David Victorson and he were arrested and taken to jail. Within a few days, they were visited by a DEA agent. Victorson said they told the agent that, if he got them released from jail, they would lead him to the person who sold Hale the pound of marijuana. That person had a barn in the mountains loaded with tons of pot, they said. The agent obviously had no idea with whom he was dealing. According to Victorson, the agent took the bait and off they went, two fugitives convicted of one of the largest marijuana busts in U.S. history now working with the DEA in Costa Rica on a made-up story. Victorson recounted: "We got drunk with this guy and when he passed out, we took a cab to the airport and headed to Bolivia."

On August 25, 1980, a Santa Barbara County Deputy Sheriff had gone to the gate at the private Hollister ranch development where Victorson's ranch was located to serve him with a subpoena to testify against Moran. A private security guard denied him entry and would not answer questions regarding either Victorson or Hale. Two days later, on August 27, material witness warrants were issued for the purposes of holding them in custody if necessary, to make sure they would be present to testify against attorney Moran at his upcoming trial scheduled for September 8. On that same day, a DEA agent entered the development and found both at home. They indicated that their phone was out of order and were unaware of efforts to reach them. They were served with subpoenas to testify at Moran's trial but not arrested due to their explanation regarding their faulty phone. Once the agent left, Victorson and Hale hit the road and fled the United States for Costa Rica.

On August 28, in preparation for the upcoming trial, the government filed documents requiring the U.S. Marshal's office to return prospective witnesses Guillermo Cooke from San Quentin Penitentiary in California and Homero Ospina from the Allegheny County Jail in Pittsburgh to Seattle to testify at Moran's trial. Cooke had been convicted of sale and possession of 69 balloons of heroin in 1977 and had appealed his conviction. He was allowed to remain free during part of 1977 and 1978 while his appeal was pending. Bill Urich, an attorney in Robert Moran's office, was responsible for handling Cooke's appeal. Urich in turn hired a third-year law student from Hastings School of Law in San Francisco to do research for the appeal. The student's name was William Hodgman. Cooke came to their office to meet with his attorney regarding the appeal and said to law student Hodgman: "If you screw up my appeal, I will kill you." Serious or not, it was obvious to Urich that Cooke was psychotic.

Law student Bill Hodgman graduated from Hastings School of Law in 1978 and in November joined the Los Angeles County District

Attorney's Office. In 1994, he was assigned, along with Marcia Clark and later Christopher Darden, to be one of the lead attorneys in the double homicide prosecution of O.J. Simpson. Shortly after he and Marcia Clark had shared duties selecting the jury, Hodgman complained of chest pains and disorientation during a trial strategy session after court and was taken by paramedics to California Medical Center. He was kept for observation overnight; no definitive signs of a heart attack were found. Johnnie Cochran, O.J.'s lead defense attorney, said he would support a delay in the trial if Hodgman was seriously ill, recognizing that Hodgman was an integral part of the prosecution team. Cochran, a former high-ranking member of the district attorney's office, had hired Hodgman as a prosecutor and had publicly praised his former subordinate's formidable skills. *The Los Angeles Times* said that the two men were the case's most experienced trial lawyers. After Hodgman recovered from his untimely medical scare, he took a much more limited role in the trial.

Following the O.J. Simpson trial, Hodgman handled a protracted probation violation proceeding against Death Row Records rap mogul Marion "Suge" Knight. Knight was alleged to have beaten a Long Beach gang member and drug dealer in the lobby of the Law Vegas MGM Grand Hotel, an incident which occurred several hours before rapper Tupac Shakur was shot to death in Knight's car. Knight was sentenced to nine years in state prison. In January 2019, Hodgman retired from the Los Angeles County District Attorney's office after a sterling career. Guillermo Cooke had lost the appeal of his 1977 drug conviction and began serving his sentence at San Quentin about the same time that Hodgman became employed in the DA's office. Cooke never carried out his threat in 1978 to kill Hodgman if he lost his appeal.

Efforts to reach Victorson and Hale by Assistant U.S. Attorney Schroeder and their attorney, Ivan Fisher, on September 2 and 4, 1980, to testify at Robert Moran's trial scheduled for September 8 were unsuccessful. Schroeder had never met either Victorson or Hale, so he was unable to prepare for Moran's trial because he had never interviewed them. On September 4, Assistant U.S. Attorney Jose Gaitan working with Mr. Schroeder filed a motion on behalf of the government to continue Moran's trial date of September 8 due to the unavailability of Victorson and Hale.

Neither Victorson nor Hale showed up to testify for the government or turned themselves in to begin serving their five-year prison sentences. After Judge Voorhees denied the government's request to continue the trial, Assistant U.S. Attorney Schroeder decided to dismiss the charges against Moran and turn him loose, at least for the time being. Schroeder told the Judge, "The testimony of Victorson and Hale is material in that they identify Robert Moran as the individual who laundered monies used in the scheme to import marijuana." Arrest warrants were issued for Victorson and Hale on September 10, 1980.

In sum, the disappearance of Victorson and Hale, the deaths of Susan Kessler and Dr. Becker from overdoses in Miami, and the whereabouts of Michael Lund being unknown brought to five the number of defendants or potentially important government witnesses who were now either dead or missing in this case.

Bill Urich, the attorney in Robert Moran's office in San Francisco who was responsible for Guillermo Cooke's appeal, had flown to Seattle in mid-September 1980 to meet with Guillermo Cooke at Cooke's request. Cooke had been transferred to Seattle from San Quentin by the Marshal's office to testify at Moran's trial. Urich met with Cooke in the King County Jail. Cooke had just finished serving his California state sentence for sale and possession of heroin. He was still in custody because of an Immigration and Naturalization Service deportation hold on him, due to his lack of U.S. citizenship. The government had also obtained a material witness warrant with bail set at $1,000,000 to ensure Cooke's continued presence to testify against Mr. Moran. Material witness warrants are commonly used to ensure the presence of a witness to testify in situations where a witness may not want to testify and may be inclined to leave town to avoid testifying.

To justify setting a $1,000,000 bail on the material witness warrant for Guillermo Cooke and to satisfy the materiality of Cooke's expected testimony, Assistant U.S. Attorney Dick Tallman filed a sworn statement, part of which stated:

> The two conspirators, Victorson and Hale, have stated that one Guillermo Cooke is the individual who received forty thousand dollars ($40,000.00) in cash from Robert Leo Moran in May of 1978 for the purpose of posting bail for the captain and first mate of the Helena Star. It was contemplated that once their release was secured the captain and first mate would then be smuggled out of the United States.
>
> In his testimony before the Grand Jury, Robert Leo Moran falsely claimed that the money had come from an unidentified person. The evidence, however, showed that the money had in fact been possessed by Moran and that he gave it to Guillermo Cooke as the intermediary to give to the bail bondsman.

Prior to his stint as an Assistant U.S. Attorney, Tallman had served as a law clerk for Judge Morell Sharp of the United States District Court in Seattle and as a trial attorney for the Department of Justice. Despite being a Republican, he was later nominated by President Bill Clinton and confirmed by the United States Senate in 2000 to his current seat on the United States Court of Appeals for the Ninth Circuit. In 2014, Tallman was appointed by U.S. Supreme Court Chief Justice John Roberts to a six-year term on the United States Foreign Intelligence Surveillance Court of Review, which considers appeals under the Foreign Intelligence Surveillance Act (FISA).

A short time after Guillermo Cooke's bond was set at $1,000,000, the government interceded with INS and got Cooke's deportation hold dropped. Cooke was then hauled back to San Francisco and Charles Breyer was appointed to represent him. On September 26, 1980, he appeared before a United States Magistrate. The government was represented by Assistant U.S. Attorney Robert Ward of the San Francisco office. Mr. Ward advised the Magistrate that Cooke's attorney and the Assistant U.S. Attorneys in Seattle had reached an agreement whereby Mr. Cooke was to be released immediately from Federal custody and that the material witness warrant with bail set at $1,000,000 would be dismissed in Seattle. As a result, Mr. Cooke was released from custody. Presumably, Cooke had begun cooperating with the government.

Shortly after being released from custody, Cooke showed up at Urich and Moran's office in San Francisco driving a new Ford pickup. Cooke broke down the door to Moran's office, picked up Moran, and tried to throw him out the third-floor window resulting in flying glass. Moran's office mates interceded, so the possibility of Moran's death was avoided. Cooke wanted to remove all his legal records from the office. Urich complied with his request and helped put them in Cooke's truck. Before he departed the scene, Cooke said it would take $100,000 delivered to his home in Millbrae by midnight the following day to keep him from testifying against Moran. The next day Urich called the Seattle U.S. Attorney's office to make sure that they were aware of how dangerous Cooke was. Urich said he had met with Cooke and told the Assistant U.S. Attorney that Cooke had the ability to kill people. Urich knew that Cooke was a sociopath and had seen him in a rage. Cooke also held a black belt in karate.

Several months later, on January 22, 1981, at 8:00 a.m., my client, Captain Rubies, was released from the Federal Correctional Institution in Texarkana, Texas, with $39.43 in his pocket. He had been given credit for 451 days of good time deductions from the four-year prison term imposed by Judge Voorhees. Rubies had, therefore, served slightly more than 33 months of his 48-month sentence. Because an immigration detainer had been lodged against him, he was turned over to the U.S. Immigration and Naturalization Service and transported from Texarkana to Dallas for a deportation hearing the following afternoon.

The day before, I had flown to Dallas to represent the captain. The next morning, I arrived at the Federal Building in Dallas for the captain's deportation hearing. I was armed with a nonrefundable airplane ticket in my client's name for a flight later in the day from Dallas to Panama City, Panama. I was aware that the captain's first mate had been deported from the United States after serving his sentence, arrested at the airport in Bogota, Colombia, and taken straight to jail. It took quite some time until someone paid a bribe and eventually got him out. I was determined to ensure that a similar misfortune would not befall my client. Serving two sentences for the same offense would be unfair. I argued to Immigration and Naturalization officials that, because Roman had been arrested on the high seas of the North Pacific Ocean and was essentially forcibly taken into the United States, he could not be legally deported. He had not come into the United States illegally. I also argued that, as a result, they could not put a notation in his passport that he was deported due to a conviction for a serious drug offense. After much discussion and after I handed them the nonrefundable one-way ticket to Panama City, they bought my argument and caved in.

Shortly thereafter, INS agents physically put Roman on a plane leaving the United States for Panama. I bid him a safe journey—he seemed happy, grateful, and confident and said he would let me know when he reached Cartagena and his family. He was a free man the minute the plane took off and would work his way safely back into Colombia from Panama, which is contiguous to Colombia. Because Panama City is on the west coast of Panama, however, I couldn't help but wonder how he would make his way home—by boat or land—given the difficult terrain between the Panamanian border and Cartagena and his desire to avoid going through a border crossing and ensuing customs inspection. Not to mention the jungles of Colombia are home to jaguars.

16

ROBERT MORAN

A ROUND ABOUT THE SAME TIME THAT ROMAN WAS FLYING
over the Gulf of Mexico and the Caribbean Sea to Panama
City enjoying his newfound freedom, David Victorson and
Eric Hale were asleep in a hotel room in La Paz, Bolivia, when the
Bolivian Special Forces broke down the door and took them to a military prison.

Victorson would later say:

"They knew who we were and were tipped off as to our location. The U.S. Marshal Service (in charge of tracking down
fugitives) had found out we were in the country and pressured the Bolivian government to arrest us. I was chained
to my bunk most of the day and all night. I did not know
where Eric was as we were kept away from each other. I
thought about who had the most to gain by my death or
imprisonment. My strong suspicion was Robert Moran,
my lawyer in San Francisco. Over a ten-year period leading
up to my arrest I had earned around thirty million dollars.
All this money came from transporting and selling marijuana and hashish from Nepal and Colombia. If I died or
was imprisoned, Moran could have the ability to steal that

money. After all, it was his job to set up domestic and foreign bank accounts, stock and real estate portfolios, and cash businesses for me. He had all the connections in banks and investment houses to allow suitcases of cash to be deposited with no questions asked. He seemed to have an insatiable desire for money and power. He was a dangerous man with no loyalty or compassion for others."

After almost four months chained up in a Bolivian prison, Victorson and Hale were deported from Bolivia, put on a plane with two U.S. Marshals, and flown from La Paz to Miami. They appeared before a United States magistrate there who ordered them to be transported to Seattle. On May 1, 1981, they were charged again in the United States District Court for the Western District of Washington—this time with contempt of court and failure to turn themselves in to serve their earlier sentences. The authorities in Seattle were silent as to how the fugitives were discovered in La Paz. An informant, with whom Victorson was in communication, had ratted them out. Captain Rubies, on the other hand, contacted me to let me know he had made it back safely to Cartagena without fanfare or problems. Our strategy to avoid what had happened to his first mate, when he was jailed after getting off the plane in Bogota, had worked. Roman invited my wife and me to visit him sometime in Cartagena, indicating that he and his wife had room for us in their seventeenth floor condominium on the Bocagrande Peninsula.

Coincidentally, in early February 1981, shortly after Roman had been released from prison, I picked up another resident of Cartagena as a client. In the early 1970s while working for French entrepreneurs, Miguel was accosted by Colombian Indians, who attempted to extort money from him. A fight broke out and he was shot in the left bicep and right eye. When I first met him, he had a glass eye, covered by a black patch. He looked like a pirate. Miguel was arrested by U.S. drug agents along with an American and Frenchman in Anacortes, Washington, after having unloaded over one ton of marijuana from a

41-foot sailboat moored at Sekiu, Washington, on the Strait of Juan de Fuca. Or was it a coincidence? Miguel had hired the American and Frenchman crew members in Panama. They boarded the vessel at Taboga Island off the coast of Panama. After picking up the marijuana in Colombia, they sailed the load all the way from the west coast of Colombia north to the Strait of Juan de Fuca, much like the voyage of the Helena Star. It was an astonishingly, perilous voyage as the vessel's batteries died early off the coast of Central America. After receiving a relatively short sentence under the circumstances, Miguel told me that, if I ever visited Cartagena, he would be able to provide me with the keys to the city. Unfortunately, he did not take my advice to switch occupations. About seven years later, I received a letter from him on May 19, 1989. He had been arrested by DEA and Chilean narcotics agents on board the sailing yacht, Marco Polo, in the port of Talcahuano, Chile, south of Santiago. Drilling into the steel hull of the vessel, the agents uncovered 262 kilos of cocaine, by far at the time, the "biggest drug case ever in Chile."

Miguel needed my assistance. Though I eventually became admitted to practice law in three international criminal tribunals, two in The Hague in the Netherlands and one in Arusha, Tanzania, I had not been admitted to practice law in Chile. Miguel had run out of luck and ended up receiving a ten-year sentence.

I told the captain of the Helena Star that I had decided to take Spanish classes to better serve my Colombian clients. I went one step further. The following year, 1982, my wife and I bought a modest, one-bedroom condominium in the first condominium development in Cabo San Lucas, Mexico, at the southern tip of Baja California. Construction was in progress, but not finished yet. At that time, Cabo was a sleepy and unspoiled, little fishing village, even somewhat primitive. We could not get milk for our two young children, having to settle for a soy-based product that required no refrigeration. Most of the few Americans there came for the world-class marlin fishing. When the fishing was good, they all got drunk. When the fishing was poor, they all got drunk. I could tell this remote place was going to be discovered soon. All my friends thought my judgment had been impaired by tequila, when told that I had purchased a condominium in a third-world country. It turned out to be one of the best decisions I had ever made, and I did work on learning Spanish.

After their forced return to the United States from the confines of their Bolivian prison cells, Victorson and Hale began serving their five-year prison sentences. Presumably because the government agreed to drop the contempt charge and the failure to turn themselves in to McNeil Island Federal Penitentiary charge, they returned to their status as witnesses for the government against Robert Moran. Two other witnesses in the case, Susan Kessler and Dr. Mark Becker, had died of drug overdoses in Florida a few days apart. Concerned about this development, the government would move Victorson and Hale from one local jail to another for fear that they would be murdered while in custody.

The government's investigation of Moran expanded, going through two more grand juries, because the maximum length of any grand jury is eighteen months. The DEA, FBI, and U.S. Attorneys interviewed over 70 potential witnesses. According to an article in the *San Francisco Examiner* at the time, the "list includes Moran's bankers, accountants, and keepers of his financial records. At least two other convicted drug dealers and former clients of Moran, John Emery, and Guillermo Cooke have become government witnesses against Moran. Both were also employed by Moran at his office or home. Hired by Moran as a houseboy and bodyguard after serving a sentence for drug dealing, Cooke has been spared deportation because of his witness status." David Victorson had earlier paid Robert Moran to represent John Emery in connection with trying to gain an early release from his prison sentence. Moran had gotten former Bay Area congressman John Burton to intercede with federal authorities on behalf of Emery.

According to Moran, he met with Emery at a Sausalito restaurant in 1979 or 1980. "He suggested I come up with 50 grand to kill Victorson. So, they have a tape of me sounding like I wanted Victorson polished off. If someone listened to that tape it would sound like I was implicated. No question about it. But in the end, I waved it all off and offered Emery a job in Nigeria. The bottom line is he didn't kill Victorson and I didn't give him any money." Moran believed Emery was working for the government and was wired for sound to record the meeting. He was right. The government attempted to enter that tape recording into evidence at Moran's eventual trial, but Judge Voorhees denied the request.

Guillermo Cooke, who had earlier been convicted of sale and possession of heroin in California state court and spent time at San Quentin, said that Moran had friends associated with the San Francisco Police Department, including a retired former Police Captain, who he identified as Walter Martinovich. Cooke was concerned that he would be the subject of a "hit" by these people. Cooke, who Assistant U.S. Attorney Steve Schroeder described as a thug, turned into a goldmine of information for Schroeder.

Mr. Moran needed to launder a whole lot of cash. Guillermo Cooke advised the government that Patricia McGowen, Mr. Moran's housekeeper, had flown to London to request a favor from an old classmate of hers with whom she had gone to school in England. According to Cooke, she met her former classmate, Hargreaves Rawstrom, a humble textile worker, and told him a phony story that she was getting a divorce in California from a very abusive husband and needed a way to hide some major assets from him. She then talked Mr. Rawstrom into traveling to the Cayman Islands and open-ing an account at Barclays Bank there in his name, as the Caymans were known for their bank secrecy laws and tax haven status. Cooke said that he had personally met Rawstrom. Cooke went on to tell the government that, at Mr. Moran's request, Patricia McGowen, retired Police Captain Marinovich, and he had all flown to the Cayman Islands at different times with suitcases full of cash and deposited the cash in the bank account opened by Mr. Rawstrom. Robert Moran and former police captain Martinovich denied these outlandish accu-sations. Based on Cook's information, however, the government was able to locate Mr. Rawstrom and his wife, Veronica, in a village out-side of London. They confirmed Cooke's incredible story.

Guillermo Cooke's goldmine of information still had some gold to be mined. Cooke told the government that Moran had a neighbor, Charles Jones, who was a businessman and had a safe deposit box in a bank in Oakland, California, just across the bay from San Francisco. Cooke said he had received a letter signed by Jones giving Cooke access to the safe deposit box. Cooke had gone to the bank at Moran's direction, gotten into the box, and emptied it of several hundred thousand dollars, which he delivered to Moran. Jones was contacted by the government and said Cooke was lying and that there was no such safe deposit box. The government then served a subpoena on Reneirio Borromeo, the Operations Officer of the bank, requiring him to produce bank records relating to Jones' safe deposit box. Borromeo said he could find no letter in their records giving Guillermo Cooke authorization to get into Moran's neighbor's safe deposit box.

Borromeo was asked to go back to the bank and search through its archives. The result of that additional search produced the letter from Charles Jones giving Cooke access to Jones' safe deposit box. Borromeo even took measurements of the safe deposit box to show that the huge amount of cash taken out of the box by Cooke was capable of fitting into the box. The government next subpoenaed Jones to testify before the federal grand jury investigating Robert Moran. He showed up for his grand jury appearance in Seattle accompanied by a very well-regarded Seattle civil attorney, John Coughenour. Though Coughenour was not particularly versed in criminal law, he apparently quickly figured out that his client had rather blatantly lied to the government and had to come clean. Score another one for Cooke. The normally unscrupulous Cooke had suddenly told a lot of truth.

Shortly thereafter, Jones' attorney, John Coughenour, was nominated by President Ronald Reagan to a seat on the United States District Court in Seattle and confirmed by the United States Senate on September 25, 1981.

While Captain Rubies was trying to put his life back together in Cartagena, Assistant U.S. Attorney Schroeder's investigation of

Robert Moran progressed. Moran continued to publicly proclaim his innocence, saying he was the victim of a witch hunt by the U.S. Attorney's office in Seattle. His attorney, Charles Morgan of San Francisco, indicated that prosecutors were "abusing their powers" by pursuing Moran and "harassing the daylights out of Bob." The expanding investigation included federal agent contact with about a dozen Bay Area attorneys, bankers, and accountants because of their association with Moran.

Charles Morgan told the *San Francisco Examiner* that he expected Moran to be indicted again. He said, "I don't see how they can spend all this time and money and not indict him." Morgan said that his "best educated guess" was that Moran would be indicted on a RICO (Racketeering Influenced and Corrupt Organization) charge. RICO, a federal charge, is used to prosecute alleged criminal organizations through which two or more related crimes are committed. RICO charges are generally reserved for extremely serious criminal cases. The investigation of Moran touched on his million-dollar real estate deals, boxes full of cash kept for drug dealer clients, and bank accounts that he established in offshore tax havens for wealthy South American clients. Of course, Moran claimed the transactions were all legitimate, all part of the legal maneuvering of an attorney/investor. "They're clearly investigating money laundering. They think I'm the financial muscle behind major drug transactions and the legitimizing of drug money—laundry city." Investigators looked at the source of money for such Moran investments as his plan to erect portable, collapsible schoolhouses in Nigeria and the purchase of valuable Texas land, with a mysterious Colombian corporation as a co-investor.

Moran insisted that his extravagant lifestyle was a product of hard work and smart investments, not illicit acts. "Sure, I'm rich. I worked hard for it. There is an aura, the way I live, my place in life, a flat in London, that, oh yeah, Moran's money is dope money. That no one at my age could have made that much. I represent the kind of people who can afford me. I have wealthy people around me. Having the right connections is important in this city. Knowing the right people.

It's important to get things done." Moran thought of himself as the "cock of the walk."

Moran admitted he had lost some friends because of the Seattle investigation, friends who were unwittingly dragged into the case, such as San Francisco lawyer William O'Brien. Prior to Moran's indictment, Moran called O'Brien and told him that both of them were going to be indicted. O'Brien hired Anthony Savage, a legendary criminal defense attorney in Seattle. Savage, along with Bill Kinzel, who was instrumental in my getting a job in the King County Prosecutor's Office; Irwin Schwartz, the Federal Public Defender who represented one of the deported crew members of the Helena Star; and Larry Finegold, who represented David Victorson, were all selected and profiled in the December, 1976, issue of *View Northwest Magazine* as among the best criminal defense attorneys in Seattle. I felt I was in great company.

Mr. O'Brien had attempted to arrange bail for my client, the captain of the Helena Star, without success because the government had persuaded Judge Voorhees at the last minute to raise his bail from $25,000 to $250,000 cash or bail bond. O'Brien told *The Examiner*: "I had known Bob (Moran) for years. I was just doing him a favor." I had worked with O'Brien off and on during my representation of the captain. He had been helpful and professional in all his dealings with me. Clear back on November 17, 1978, he had written me a letter indicating that he had "discovered things I had no idea were going on, and, frankly, since this matter is concluded, I may share with you that I was used to a fare-thee-well." I held him in such high regard that later I got him involved in representing a codefendant of one of my clients charged in a case on the island of Maui. I never had any reason to believe that Bill had engaged in any unethical, illegal, or dishonorable activity.

O'Brien told me that he had no objection to me providing any documentary or other evidence of his relationship with me if the government asked for it. As it turned out, Bill O'Brien was not indicted. *The San Francisco Examiner* reported that O'Brien said he was told that he would have been indicted along with Mr. Moran if he had not personally visited the Assistant U.S. Attorney in Seattle to explain his association with Moran. Said Moran, "My friends won't talk to me and I don't blame them."

Since Victorson and Hale were returned to Seattle from Bolivia in April 1981, the government had continued its investigation of Robert Moran for another two years. *The Examiner* reported: "Brash and aggressive, Moran is still operating at maximum warp in his Battery Street office. One day recently he was making ski plans and waiting for a check for $1,000,000, profit from the sale of his Texas land that authorities are investigating. He bought the land, he said, for $60,000." According to Moran, rumors had been increasing that further indictments in the case were imminent. His attorney, Charles Morgan, said, "We're both waiting for the phone to ring."

On June 18, 1982, Judge Voorhees sentenced Dean Bowen after his plea of guilty to one count charging him with "possession of more than one ton of marijuana with intent to distribute." Bowen was the young man from California who had met and paid Al Wolover in Port Angeles for bringing the Chignik barge purchased by Mike Lund from Seattle to Port Angeles. Wolover had had some difficulty identifying Bowen from a photo montage displayed to him by DEA agents. As a result, Judge Voorhees had suppressed the compromised identification of Bowen. Because Wolover's pretrial identification of Bowen could not be used against Bowen at trial, the case against Bowen got a lot weaker from the government's standpoint. That is a roundabout way of saying that his lawyer had a lot of leverage to work out a favorable plea bargain for his client. Bowen got a great deal. He was given a suspended sentence on condition of five years of probation and a requirement that he do 300 hours of community service—not bad for someone who was involved in offloading many tons of marijuana.

Bowen, however, did not learn his lesson. Less than a year after he was sentenced by Judge Voorhees, he was arrested on June 10, 1983, in southern California by the DEA and indicted on June 22 for (1) conspiracy to import approximately 4000 pounds of marijuana, (2) aiding and abetting the importation, (3) conspiracy to possess with intent to distribute over 1000 pounds, and (4) possession of 1100 pounds of marijuana with intent to distribute it. While in custody in the San Diego Metropolitan Corrections Center awaiting trial, he was also charged on June 29, 1983, with violating probation imposed by Judge Voorhees in Seattle. On September 25, 1984, Judge Voorhees revoked Bowen's probation on the basis of his new conviction in San Diego and imposed a new sentence of eighteen months in prison to run consecutively with the sentence previously imposed in the United States District Court in the Southern District of California on February 13, 1984.

On September 17, 1982, it was James Turner, represented by the very competent Seattle lawyer Dave Shorett, who appeared before Judge Voorhees for sentencing after failing to appear for his change of plea hearing over three years earlier. Turner, like Dean Bowen before him, also pleaded guilty to one count of possession of more than one ton of marijuana with intent to distribute it. Turner met David Victorson when Victorson brought a vehicle to Turner's car repair shop for some work. He also met Mike Lund through work on his vehicle and Lund's professional skiing. Turner introduced Lund to Victorson because he was aware of Lund's sailing ability and familiarity with the Strait of Juan de Fuca. Turner acted as a middleman in connection with the provision of cash for Lund to purchase the Joli and the house on Sequim Bay. It was Turner's part in the conspiracy to see that the marijuana was offloaded from the Joli in Sequim Bay and loaded into trucks for transport out of state.

In exchange for his assistance to the conspiracy, according to Mr. Shorett, Turner

"Was to receive some substantial assistance with his automobile racing career, which was only beginning at this time. He had been to a racing school in Europe. He received very little financial assistance. In fact, Jim was only up in the State of Washington on two occasions, the second time arriving late and flying out over the coast to locate the Joli with the result that the Helena Star was located. Jim did participate in offloading the Joli, did rent a U-Haul truck, which he drove with a substantial amount of marijuana to California where it was picked up by another individual to be driven to the East."

Turner eventually chose to cooperate with the government. At the time of his sentencing, he was already serving time on sentences imposed in the Northern District of California in a different case. Judge Voorhees imposed three years of imprisonment to run concurrently (at the same time) with the sentences he was currently serving on the California case.

17

REINDICTMENT

ON FRIDAY, APRIL 15, 1983, ROBERT MORAN WAS RE-INDICTED by a federal grand jury in Seattle on charges that he helped launder profits for the Helena Star drug running ring, which was dismantled with the seizure of the freighter on April 17, 1978, five years earlier. The seventeen-count indictment, similar to the one dismissed in 1980 as a result of the disappearance of David Victorson and Eric Hale, alleged that Moran conspired to defraud the IRS by concealing income from drug smuggling, helped "wash" large sums of money through dummy foreign corporations to finance drug running between 1976 and 1978, and that in testimony before the grand jury, he made false declarations (eight counts) and produced a false document (one count).

Assistant U.S. Attorneys kept the grand jury working late on a Friday to obtain the 39-page indictment against Moran before the five-year statute of limitations ran out on the drug charges. Victorson, Hale, and Lyle Sawicki were named in the indictment as coconspirators, rather than defendants. Sawicki, a distributor for Victorson in the Bay Area, avoided being charged with a crime because of his cooperation. At the time of Moran's trial, Sawicki lived in Los Angeles and was pursuing a music career. If convicted, Moran faced a maximum of five years in prison and a maximum fine of $10,000.

The Overt Acts section of the new indictment against Moran provided some interesting facts alleged by the Government. A corporation, Diversified Investment Portfolio, Inc. (DIPI), was formed in Panama, listing Alvaro Azuero, an associate of Victorson's, as its President. Victorson was the agent for DIPI, the same corporation used by Moran to pay off Bob Morton for the sale of the Knik Wind and Chignik tug and barge and the same corporation used to buy Victorson's ranch near Santa Barbara, from which he had fled with Hale to Costa Rica and then on to Bolivia. Moran had said that Victorson was like one of Azuero's family members. In a letter to the International Bank Officer of Security Pacific National Bank in San Francisco dated August 25, 1976, Moran informed the Bank Officer of background information on Mr. Azuero provided by David Victorson:

> Mr. Azuero is a practicing attorney in Bogota as well as the President of one of the largest insurance companies in South America. Mr. Azuero has substantial holdings in real estate. He holds a unique position in that he maintains petroleum rights which are not often granted by the Colombian government to its citizens. Mr. Azuero has been active in politics and he held the position of Commissioner of the El Dorado Airport, the largest airport in Colombia. He is also a patron of the arts, has underwritten many young artists, and contributes to schools and other worthy institutions in Colombia.

Bank accounts in the name of DIPI were opened in San Francisco through Security Pacific National Bank and in Panama through Security Pacific Inter-American Bank. In June of 1976, Moran and Victorson traveled to Colombia to meet with Alvaro Azuero, the President of DIPI, and about two months later in August traveled to Panama for the same purpose. On April 14, 1977, Victorson transported $600,000 in cash to Panama, concealed in a Ming vase, and deposited it in the bank. Two weeks later, $335,000 was wired from the DIPI bank account in Panama to the DIPI bank account in San Francisco. In mid-1976, the conspirators began using an existing, inactive corporation in the Netherlands Antilles. This is the same Netherlands Antilles in the Caribbean where on January 30, 1978, the Helena Star was given a Deratting Certificate indicating it had no rats scurrying about the vessel. I doubt if there was such a certificate available for the absence of scorpions. If available, however, the Helena Star would not have been eligible.

The indictment of Moran went on to allege that Eric Hale had travelled to Bogota to meet with Alvaro Azuero to obtain his signature on various documents relating to the corporation in the Netherlands Antilles. Hale signed a signature card for a bank account for the corporation in Panama and deposited $45,000 in cash into the account. The following year he deposited $200,000 received from Victorson into the same bank account at Security Pacific Inter-American Bank in Panama. In November of 1977, another bank account was opened in the Cayman Islands at Barclays Bank by Hargreaves Rawstrom at the request of his former classmate in England, Patricia McGowan, Moran's housekeeper. $65,000 transported from the United States was deposited in that account at that time. The following month Moran caused an additional $200,000 received from Lyle Sawicki and $175,000 received from Victorson (in return for Moran's services to the conspiracy) to be transported to the Cayman Islands for deposit in Rawstrom's account. Then in April 1981, Moran caused others to transport another $120,000 to the Caymans. These other deposits were all made at Moran's request by Patricia McGowan, Guillermo Cooke, and retired police captain, Walter Martinovich

Lastly, of significance and one month after the seizure of the Helena Star, on May 22, 1978, Moran directed Eric Hale to purchase a typewriter and prepare a phony letter in which Alvero Azuero requested Moran to purchase the tug and barge, that were to be used to offload the remaining 37 tons from the freighter. Azuero's signature was forged. Moran was obviously trying to cover his tracks.

To summarize, the conspirators with Robert Moran's assistance had established foreign corporations in Panama, the Cayman Islands, and the Netherlands Antilles, and bank accounts in Panama and the Cayman Islands for purposes of washing the never-ending stream of cash emanating from the importation of Colombian Gold into the United States. The stream did not necessarily stop with the seizure of the Helena Star because a number of truckloads containing thirteen tons of marijuana had already left for the Midwest to be sold and distributed.

Attorney Moran was arrested on the new charges and released on his own recognizance without the necessity of having to post a bond. A trial date for Moran was set for September 6, 1983. Prior to trial, Judge Voorhees dismissed sixteen of the seventeen felony charges against Moran on the basis that the government waited too long to file the charges. The only charge not dismissed was that Moran had conspired to defraud the Internal Revenue Service by concealing income from drug smuggling. One of the dismissed charges had accused Moran of conspiring with others to import approximately 50 tons of marijuana aboard the Helena Star. Judge Voorhees ruled that the government's two and a half-year delay in refiling sixteen of the charges prejudiced Moran's ability to defend himself and deprived him of his due process rights under the United States Constitution. The tax fraud conspiracy charge was not dismissed because it wasn't part of the original indictment of Moran brought in 1980. The primary reason that it took the government over two years to re-indict Moran was the addition of the tax fraud charge relating to money laundering which opened up a whole new area for investigation beyond the drug smuggling allegations.

Charles Morgan, Moran's defense attorney, also convinced Judge Voorhees on August 3, 1983, to move the trial to San Francisco, in part because so many of the witnesses lived and worked in the Bay Area and because Moran was trying to keep his law office afloat, which would have been more difficult to do from Seattle given that the trial was expected to last over one month.

The government was represented at trial by Assistant U.S. Attorneys Steve Schroeder and Bill Hogan, who had replaced Jose Gaitan, who had left government service for the private sector. Schroeder was very experienced—a career prosecutor. Before trial, the government made a motion to allow for the deposition of six potential witnesses located in three different foreign countries. Four of the witnesses lived in London. Colin Peters, a British citizen, acted at defendant Moran's request as a shareholder nominee of a corporation established for the benefit of Eric Hale on Grand Cayman Island. Hargreaves Rawstrom, also a British citizen, similarly acted at the behest of Moran's housekeeper, Patricia McGowen, for another Grand Cayman corporation established on behalf of Hale and Lyle Sawicki, who was a big distributor for David Victorson. Rawstrom's wife, Veronica, was present at a meeting between her husband and his old classmate, Patricia McGowan. James Leech, an American attorney residing in London, had done some work for Moran. Leech was not willing to testify at a trial in the United States.

Another potential government witness, Alvaro Azuero, the Colombian national, who acted as President of David Victorson's Panamanian corporation, DIPI, also was not willing to testify at a trial in the United States. No surprise! The government was working through the U.S. State Department to arrange his deposition. The last witness that the government wanted to depose was the Custodian of Records of Barclays Bank International, Limited, in Georgetown, Grand Cayman Island, who would authenticate certain business records.

Judge Voorhees allowed the depositions to be taken and allowed defendant Moran to travel to London for the depositions to be held at the U.S. Embassy. His attorney, Charles Morgan, had the right to appear at the depositions and cross-examine the witnesses that were deposed.

The trial lasted about one month. The government called over 40 witnesses. The Rawstroms travelled from London to San Francisco to testify. During the trial, an investigator for defendant Moran was trying to contact Mr. Rawstrom at his hotel in San Francisco. This information was provided to Assistant U.S. Attorney Steve Schroeder. The very savvy Mr. Schroeder began to wonder why an investigator for Mr. Moran would be sniffing around a witness for the government. It dawned on him that Mr. Rawstrom was probably still the owner of record of the Barclays Bank account in the Cayman Islands that he had opened years before at the request of his former classmate and now housekeeper for Robert Moran, Patricia McGowen. At least the account was still probably in Rawstrom's name, even though he had opened it up for his old friend, Patricia McGowen, so she could hide the money for Mr. Moran.

Mr. Schroeder called the lawyer for the international department of Barclays Bank in New York (a former assistant U.S. Attorney himself) to see about getting records from their bank in the Caymans documenting Rawstrom's account there. The lawyer told Schroeder he would check and get back to him. The lawyer called back and verified the existence of the account in Rawstrom's name. Still in the middle of trial in San Francisco, Schroeder said he wanted to send Rawstrom to the Caymans accompanied by an agent to obtain the bank's records pertaining to Rawstrom's account. The New York lawyer for Barclays said he would meet them in Georgetown, Grand Cayman. Another Assistant U.S. Attorney, Jim Frush, and Mr. Rawstrom then flew to Georgetown, were met by the Barclays attorney, and obtained records from the Bank verifying deposits in the 100s of thousands of dollars into the account. Among those records was the coup de grace—a letter signed by defendant Moran requesting the bank to accept cash deposits from his agent, former Police Captain, Walter Martinovich.

Colin Peters and James Leach were deposed in London and their depositions were entered into evidence at trial. The government was never able to depose Alvaro Azuero, but they were able to have both former fugitives David Victorson and Eric Hale present to testify at trial. U.S. Marshals brought Victorson from Federal Correctional Institution Terminal Island in California and Eric Hale from the Metropolitan Correctional Center in Tucson, Arizona, to Seattle for

Moran's trial. At the trial, David Victorson testified that the marijuana on the Helena Star was expected to bring in $8 million and that Moran's share would have been $1 million. Government investigators showed the jury how Moran had laundered at a minimum $845,000 in Panama and $565,000 in the Cayman Islands. Other important witnesses who testified for the government included Lyle Sawicki, Patricia McGowan, John Emery, Bill Niemi, Bill O'Brien, and Bob Morton, who sold the Knik Wind and Chignik tug and barge to Mike Lund. The Judge would not allow Moran's lawyer to ask Eric Hale about his arrest for possession of one pound of pot while on the lam in Costa Rica.

One especially important witness the government put on the stand was Moran's neighbor, businessman Charles Jones, who had the safe deposit box in a bank in Oakland. He admitted that he had originally lied to the government when he said that Guillermo Cooke never had access to his safe deposit box and never took any money out of his box. Jones stated that Moran would give him a lot of cash to put in his safe deposit box and, sometime later, Cook would come by the bank and pick up the money in the box for Moran. It was obvious to Jones that he and Cook were somehow helping Moran launder the money. He also stated that Moran asked him to lie to the authorities. Surprisingly, Jones never admitted that he had made any money for helping Moran. Super thug, Guillermo Cooke, of course, also added to the wealth of evidence against Robert Moran.

The defense called about twenty witnesses, including Bill Urich, who had worked in Moran's office. He testified to seeing Guillermo Cooke break into Moran's office and attempt to throw Moran out of his third floor office window and Cooke's parting words that, to insure he would not testify against Moran, he would expect $100,000 to be delivered to his home by midnight the following day. When Moran took the witness stand, he denied any connection to the foreign accounts. Assistant U.S. Attorney Steve Schroeder eloquently argued to the jury that Moran had conspired to cover up the proceeds of illicit drug smuggling and sales by "counseling and assisting"

Victorson, Hale, and Sawicki in "mischaracterizing the illegal origins" of the drug trafficking money and the identities of its true owners.

The jury in San Francisco deliberated for two days. At 3:50 p.m. on October 7, 1983, the jury found Robert Moran guilty of Count 1—conspiring to defraud the government, the only remaining count left after the Judge had dismissed the sixteen other counts. The UPI characterized the jury's verdict as "High Flying Attorney Gets Wings Clipped." Sentencing was scheduled for November 18.

On November 18, 1983, Judge Voorhees sentenced Moran to eighteen months in prison and fined him $10,000. He was allowed to remain free pending the outcome of an appeal of the single-count conviction to the Ninth Circuit Court of Appeals. Not only did Moran appeal his conviction, but the government also appealed Judge Voorhees decision before trial to dismiss the sixteen other counts filed against Moran. Moran hired an appellate lawyer, Bernie, to handle his appeal. In return for handling the appeal, Moran allowed Bernie to move into Moran's "castle" high in the hills of Marin County.

In May of 1985, Moran got a double dose of bad news from the Ninth Circuit Court of Appeals. It affirmed his one count conviction and reinstated the sixteen felony counts that Judge Voorhees had thrown out, concluding that the Judge had erred in tossing those counts. "The district court characterized the government's delay in this case as 'unjustified,' but it never expressly found any fault on the part of the government," the appeals court ruled. The United States Attorney now had to decide whether to try Moran on the reinstated counts, which accused him of conspiring to import 50 tons of marijuana aboard the Helena Star.

On May 31, 1985, Assistant U.S. Attorney William Hogan asked Judge Voorhees to revoke Moran's appeal bond and have him taken into custody to start serving his eighteen-month sentence because the Ninth Circuit had denied his appeal. Charles Morgan, Moran's attorney, said he planned to file a petition for rehearing before the Ninth Circuit and, if unsuccessful, would attempt to get the United States Supreme Court to hear the case. Judge Voorhees allowed Moran to remain free upon posting $300,000 and executing a deed of trust in the amount of $200,000 on his home for a total bond of $500,000. The Ninth Circuit denied Moran's petition for rehearing and revoked his bail on July 15, 1985. The following day, Judge Voorhees allowed Moran to self-surrender to Federal Correctional Institution Lompoc, California, to begin serving his previously imposed eighteen-month prison sentence. Within a week, he was transferred to the adjacent minimum-security prison camp due primarily to the reasonably short length of his sentence and his lack of any serious criminal record.

By the time that Robert Moran began to serve his eighteen-month sentence and was waiting to see if the government would try him on the formerly dismissed counts, David Victorson and Eric Hale had finished serving their five-year prison sentences. Victorson said, "My old crew from Marin got together and put on a party for me as a free man. The party featured coke, pot, booze, and about twelve hookers in lingerie. By the time I got out of prison all my houses and cars had been seized and most of my cash was gone. However, I did have more than a hundred thousand in cash and gold stashed away in the U.S. and more in Colombia."

The government decided to retry Mr. Moran on the sixteen criminal charges that had been reinstated by the Ninth Circuit Court of Appeals. A trial date was scheduled for April 7, 1986. By this time, Moran was incarcerated at the prison camp in Southern California and owed his attorney, Charles Morgan, over $215,000. He decided it was time to deal. His attorney worked out a plea bargain with the government whereby the government agreed to recommend a sentence that would run concurrently with the sentence Moran was currently serving and Moran would agree to resign from the practice of law. Neither side really gave up or got much from the plea bargain as the government was still free to recommend up to five years in prison and the California Bar Association was already working on disbarring Moran.

On May 16, 1986, Mr. Moran, now age 46, pleaded guilty to one of the sixteen counts that had originally been dismissed by Judge

Voorhees, but reinstated by the Ninth Circuit. The Judge imposed a three-year sentence to run concurrently with the eighteen-month sentence that Moran was currently serving. He was released from prison in 1988. About the same time, Guillermo Cooke, the felon who had greatly assisted the government in the prosecution of Moran, was convicted again of a drug-related offense and eventually deported back to his home country after serving out his sentence. Charles Morgan, Moran's defense attorney, eventually passed away having been stiffed by Robert Moran to the tune of $240,000.

Not long after Mr. Moran's release from federal prison, Assistant U.S. Attorney Steve Schroeder received a phone call from a counterpart in the United States Attorney's Office in San Francisco, First Assistant U.S. Attorney Bob Ward, indicating that Moran had become involved again with Colombians and the cocaine trade. Moran had also sold his "castle" on the hill and failed to pay capital gains tax. Ward asked Schroeder if he thought that Moran was worth going after again. Schroeder said, "Yes."

18

STEVEN "LANCE" MCCAIN

CCORDING TO THE MAY 18, 2001, ISSUE OF *The Seattle Times*, Steven "Lance" McCain had been a lot of things in the last 23 years. "He's been a ski bum who dazzled friends with stories of past adventures, a quiet family man, an unassuming motel clerk and handyman who impressed his neighbors with his devotion to his young sons, and he taught himself to fly planes. And lost his family to divorce." McCain had lived a relatively normal life for 23 years, from California to Wyoming to Colorado and Nevada—"only to be tripped up because in the end, he apparently was so stubborn in his refusals to pay child support that a judge in Colorado had him arrested." McCain, who had used different dates of birth over the years, but believed to be 65, was initially arrested by the Arapahoe County Sheriff's office on May 11, 2001, for contempt of court. He was fingerprinted and released on May 14, 2001, after serving three days in jail. After his release, the authorities matched his fingerprints to Michael Lund, back from the dead, and found there was a 23-year-old arrest warrant for him out of the U.S. District Court for the Western District of Washington in Seattle in connection with the largest marijuana bust on the west coast of the United States.

Mike Lund had been on the run as a federal fugitive living as Steven McCain for 23 years. After the seizure of the Helena Star and his lightning fast disappearance, a fugitive investigation ensued. Lund had been the marijuana conspiracy's principal Washington State connection but could not be found. The U.S. Marshals Service and other law enforcement agencies had expended substantial manpower, resources, and time over a period of many years trying to track him down, including attending his mother's funeral in 1986. He had severed all ties with his mother, four children from his first two wives, and friends.

One day after his release from jail, U.S. Marshals tracked down Mike Lund to a cut-rate hotel near Denver. Deputy U.S. Marshal Angel "Tito" Del Valle of the Seattle office flew to Colorado to coordinate Lund's re-arrest on May 15, 2001. Tito was known for his love of tracking fugitives. However, it was nonpayment of child support, not Tito, which led to Lund's downfall. Lund was located, arrested, and locked up to await transfer to Seattle to face the charges that he fled from in 1978.

During a post-arrest interview conducted by Marshal Del Valle in Colorado, Lund stated that he knew law enforcement agencies were looking for him, so he "kept his mouth shut." He said he stopped calling his mother after the seizure of the Helena Star because he thought "her phone was being tapped." Lund commented to Marshal Del Valle that he "knew from his time spent as a San Diego Deputy Sheriff for four years that the way fugitives got picked up was because they could not stop contacting people from their past." It appeared to the government that Lund's primary motivation for becoming involved in the scheme to import marijuana and taking the many steps and actions, which he took to accomplish that end, was his own self-interest. As compensation for his efforts, Lund was expecting to retain ownership of the $255,000 ocean racing sailboat Joli and the waterfront house and lot on Sequim Bay worth $80,000, both of which were to be fully paid for through the scheme. As stated by Lund to Marshal Del Valle following his arrest, "I saw an opportunity to have a lot of nice things," like an incredible ocean racing sailboat that he would never have been able to afford.

On May 16, 2001, Lund waived his right to have his real identity established and did not fight his transfer to Seattle. A U.S. Marshal Supervisor said, "He's been in the wind for 23 years. We had no information on his new ID or his new life or any of that stuff. We knew where he was in '78. We know where he is in 2001." Where he spent the intervening years was a mystery. DEA spokesman Tom O'Brien said, "We're looking at a gathering of retired agents for the trial."

Sports Illustrated reporter, Kostya Kennedy, wrote:

Lund's fellow freestylers dubbed him the Gull, after Jonathan Livingston Seagull, the hero of Richard Bach's best-selling novel about a bird that, by dint of discipline and perseverance, learns to fly more swiftly and gracefully than any gull before him. "We gave him that nickname because when you were around Mike, you felt anything was possible," says Stan Larson. "He also had a lot of mystique and intrigue about him, partly because he was older. His name always came up at our freestyle reunions. Everyone figured he'd sailed off into the sunset with a lot of money or weed or both. Then a few months ago an e-mail started circulating around our group. It said: 'They caught the Gull!'"

McCain was wondering about his old life, too. For all the happiness of his life in Santa Barbara, the loss of his identity and of the children he'd left behind at last began to weigh heavily upon him. In early 2000, approaching his 64th birthday, McCain contacted the county recorder in Beloit, Wisconsin, the town where he had been born, and obtained his original birth certificate. "I was thinking about becoming Mike Lund again."

19

BACK FROM THE DEAD

AFTER MIKE LUND AND PATRICIA KARNIK DITCHED THE Knik Wind tug and Chignik barge on April 18, 1978, in a remote area of western British Columbia and fled south back into the State of Washington, Patricia Karnik "dumped Lund off somewhere in Oregon." On May 3, 1978, Karnik was stopped by the DEA in Lund's pickup at Ray's Boathouse Restaurant on Shilshole Bay in Seattle. She was questioned and the pickup was searched. According to Lund, Karnik told him that the DEA said then that "two Colombian hitmen were looking for Mike." "I was in Portland, Oregon, at the time, and I changed my name then and there to Lance Hill, never again using the name Mike Lund, as I feared for my safety and the safety of my family. That had a lot to do with why I fled."

Lund went to Santa Barbara, California, where he met Wendy Starcher, a 27-year-old Pennsylvania woman. He began searching graveyards and eventually found the tombstone of a Steven McCain, born in Pomona, California, around the same time as Lund. McCain had died before he was one year old. Lund went to a Pomona city office and claimed to be McCain. According to Lund, with Wendy's help, "I obtained a birth certificate and changed my name to Lance Steven McCain." He assumed a new identity and Wendy became his third wife in 1980. In 1982, they had a son and named him Michael, his father's real name, but couldn't call him Junior. A couple of years later, they moved to Jackson, Wyoming, and had another son, Hans, in 1987. By the time Lund became Steven McCain, he had already fathered four children, two each from prior marriages in his 20s, both ending in divorce.

In the mid-80s, Tom Robbins hired McCain as a clerk and handyman at the Parkway Inn in Jackson. He would take Robbins' hotel guests on ski trips to Jackson Hole. David Gonzales, a Jackson author writing a book about the town and its ski-bum culture, said, "He didn't ski down the regular runs; he went straight down through the trees. People used to come back and say, 'I've never seen anyone ski like that.'" Gonzales went on to say, "It's easy for people to blend in here in Jackson Hole. People do not question each other here. If you're a good skier, and you don't mind buying a few beers at the Mangy Moose, nobody asks any questions." McCain spent his time in Jackson playing guitar and teaching himself to fly gliders and other planes. He taught his boys to ski almost as soon as they could walk.

In 1989, however, Wendy filed for divorce, citing "irreconcilable differences." She got the kids, the new Saab, the furniture and the charge cards. Mike got an order to pay $380 a month in child support. "That kind of destroyed him," Robbins said. McCain packed up and moved back to California, taking a job at a small airport in Northern California. In the early 90s, he moved back to Santa Barbara and filed for bankruptcy in 1993. He got a job in construction, became a superintendent and fell in love with Gayle Sandell, an elementary school administrator. She loved him, but said his arrest was a shock. He had told her that his mother died when he was two. Mike's former wife, Wendy McCain, remarried. According to her new husband, Mike Ayler, the boys visited their dad often in California. Ayler described McCain: "He was a good father, and a good person, I guess, except at paying child support."

That is apparently what ended his life as Steven McCain. Colorado court records show that in September 2000, Wendy filed suit in Arapaho County District Court claiming that McCain had not been paying the $380 a month child support ordered for his teenage boys. Mike Ayler said, "He just fought it so hard, and he'd been getting off so cheap for so long." A hearing was set in Colorado for May 11, 2001.

Steven McCain drove to Colorado from Santa Barbara and appeared in court without legal counsel for the hearing relating to his obligation to pay child support. As part of the divorce decree, he was also required to provide his former wife with copies of his tax returns. At the hearing Judge James Macrum found that, while Lund had provided some of the required materials, he was not in compliance with the divorce decree. The judge found McCain in contempt of court for this and failure to pay back child support. McCain was ordered to jail. He served three days before being released on May 14, 2001. *Sports Illustrated* reported:

> "Rather than return to his home in Santa Barbara, he stayed in Colorado to spend a few days with his boys, who lived with their mother in Aurora. They went fishing that afternoon and then checked into a Motel 6 outside Denver. The next day McCain was standing in the motel parking lot with his sons when two U.S. marshals approached him and told him to put his hands behind his back. 'Are you Michael Lund?' one of the marshals asked. 'Yes, I am,' he said. Michael and Hans looked at their father, bewildered."

Jailers had taken Lund's fingerprints, sent them to a computer database and got the results back just after Lund had been released from jail. They got a hit and he was rearrested on the federal warrant out of Seattle the following day without incident. Michael Lund was reborn and his past began to unravel. The moral of this story is, if you have something big to hide, keep your nose clean and make sure you make your child support payments.

Assistant U.S. Attorney Jerry Diskin, who was assigned to this new development, said, "He's been right here in our fugitive file. I'm going to have to gather my retired (Drug Enforcement Agency) agents to go over the file." In actuality, the files were still all in existence 23 years after the seizure of the Helena Star. Patricia Karnik, Lund's girlfriend at the time of the Helena Star's seizure, testified for the government at Robert Moran's trial in 1983. After her testimony, she had an off-the-cuff conversation with Assistant U.S. Attorney Steve Schroeder, who was directing Moran's prosecution. Karnik said to Schroeder, something to the effect that Lund is safe now since the five-year statute of limitations has run. Schroeder responded that the statute of limitations had not run out because Lund had already been charged and was a fugitive from the beginning. He was not out of the woods. The look on Karnik's face was one of surprise and shock. This made Schroeder realize that Lund was probably still alive, contrary to popular opinion. Every time the DEA wanted to destroy the voluminous files due to their age and unlikelihood of further usage, Schroeder squashed the idea. As a result, Jerry Diskin was in great shape to jump in and put the screws to Lund. A real bulldog of a prosecutor, Diskin was not inclined to give Lund a break because he had been an effective fugitive for 23 years.

Lund had been charged in 1978 with four counts relating to the aborted attempt to smuggle 50 tons of marijuana into the United States. If convicted in 2001, he would face the same maximum five-year penalties in effect in 1978, rather than the much more severe penalties for the same crimes in existence in 2001. In the interim, Congress had substantially increased the penalties on each count. Federal Sentencing Guidelines were also enacted, which for Mike Lund's crime, would have been 24 to 30 years in prison if his crime had been committed in 2001 instead of 1978.

When Michael Lund slipped into the night after the Helena Star was seized on April 17, 1978, he left behind more than just an empty seat in the United States Courthouse in Seattle. He left behind two ex-wives, a son, three daughters, and his mother, Dorothy. According to Lund, he did speak with his mother on rare occasions for about a year until he worried that her phone was tapped. Lund met his mother one final time in the spring of 1979 at a park in San Diego. They hugged and said goodbye. Being a fugitive can be very stressful and lonely—always watching your back, fearing the inevitable knock on the door and never knowing if you will be recognized on the street. Imagine abandoning four children from two prior marriages and not having any contact with any of them—no letters, no telephone conversations, and no physical contact with them during their formative years.

For the next 23 years as Lund lived as Steven McCain, marrying again and having two more sons, his first two families lived with the assumption that they would never see him again. His four children from his first two wives grew up and bore him grandchildren. In all those years he was only recognized once—by someone, who vowed to keep his mouth shut.

Meanwhile federal agents continued to search for Lund. In 1992, U.S. Marshal Todd Kupferer, a former California ski bum who had followed Lund as a youngster, took a keen interest in the case. Lund's four children from his first two wives were contacted and monitored without success. Kupferer staked out the nursing home where Lund's mother, Dorothy, lived and was there the night she died in 1996. Lund was a no-show. Kupferer attended her funeral. Again, Lund was a no-show. Dorothy had died, convinced her son was dead. In an interview of Lund by *Sports Illustrated* reporter, Kostya Kennedy, at the Federal Detention Center in Seattle while waiting to be sentenced, Lund said, "I didn't know Mom had died until I got caught." The reporter continued: "Lund speaks of his life with an almost surreal detachment. There is no remorse, but rather a stony aloofness when he talks of his decision to obliterate one life and embrace another." After Lund's arrest, one of his daughters, Heidi Grady, 36, of San Diego, said, "It's like a dream come true. I get to tell my children their grandpa isn't dead." She is the daughter of Mike's second wife, Linda Lund, also of San Diego, and had not seen her father since she was 13.

Before their divorce, Linda and Mike had two daughters, Heidi and Kastle. He had a son and another daughter with his first wife, whom he divorced in San Diego in the early 1960s. His oldest child was 40 years old at the time of his arrest in Colorado. The kids remember that, when he vanished, they were told that he had been murdered by drug dealers. According to Kastle, 34, of Joshua Tree, California, Lund's mother "would always say to me, 'I know he's dead because he's such a good son, he would have sent me something.'" Over the years, federal agents came looking for Mike at all their homes. After Lund's arrest on May 15, 2001, his first two families were anxiously waiting for a reunion. His girlfriend, Gayle Sandell, was shocked when she found out about his past and couldn't understand how Lund could not have seen four of his children and mother for 23 years.

In late May 2001, Michael Lund, back from the dead with his past unraveling fast, was transferred from a federal detention center in Littleton, Colorado, to Seattle and made his first court appearance on June 1. On June 5, he filled out a financial affidavit showing him to be unemployed with only $300 to his name. The very savvy Rick Troberman of Seattle was confirmed as his attorney. Lund pleaded not guilty and a trial date was scheduled for September 10, 2001. Because of his history of flight, Lund would remain incarcerated till his case was resolved.

On September 7, 2001, three days before his trial was scheduled to begin, Michael Lund with the assistance of his attorney entered into a plea agreement with the government, commonly referred to as a plea bargain, whereby he pleaded guilty to Count Three of the Indictment (conspiracy to distribute marijuana). He was now 65 years old, graying, balding, and using reading glasses to read the court documents. The government agreed to recommend that he serve three years in prison. By this time, Judge Voorhees, after a wonderful judicial career, had died and the case was reassigned to Chief Judge John Coughenour, a no-nonsense and equally courageous Judge—the same John Coughenour who had represented Charles Jones, Robert Moran's neighbor, at his grand jury appearance in early 1981. Jones was the neighbor that allowed Moran to stash hundreds of thousands of dollars in his safe deposit box.

Judge Coughenour had been appointed to this lifetime position by President Reagan in late 1981 to the seat vacated by Judge Morell "Mo" Sharp, a highly respected Judge, whose untimely death in 1980 opened up a new vacancy on the federal bench. Judge Coughenour was Chief Judge of the United States District Court in the Western District of Washington from 1997 to 2004. He would frequently visit individuals in prison to better understand the system and effects of mandatory minimum sentences, many of which he came to oppose. He was probably best known for his sentencing of Ahmed Ressam, named the "millennium bomber," who planned to blow up the Los Angeles International Airport on New Year's Eve, 1999. I remember Judge Coughenour for his sentencing day, often referred to as the "rocket docket," due to the speed and efficiency that he handled sentencing hearings and imposed sentences.

Immediately after Judge Coughenour came out from his chambers to sentence Mike Lund on November 16, 2001, he advised the lawyers of a potential minor conflict of interest that he might have. Before ascending to the federal bench, he had represented a client in a lawsuit involving a freestyle ski organization and some prominent freestyle skiers, including "Airborne" Eddie Ferguson. Airborne Eddie was the World Freestyle champion in 1973. *Skiing* magazine named him "Hotdogger of the Year." Both lawyers quickly agreed that this potential conflict should not prevent the Judge from imposing sentence in this case.

Present at Lund's sentencing were his oldest son, Eric, from his first marriage, and daughter, Heidi, from his second marriage, as well as a lot of other people in support of him, including Gayle Sandell, Mike's significant other, and Tom Robbins, who had employed Mike at the Parkway Inn in Jackson, Wyoming, who hadn't seen Lund in 15 years. It was the first time that Eric and Heidi had seen their father in over 23 years.

Ms. Sandell, the Head of Lower School for an independent school in Santa Barbara, California, where she had worked for 15 years, wrote a particularly compelling letter to Judge Coughenour. In part, she wrote:

I can only talk about the man I know, Lance McCain. I first met Lance back in 1981 when he lived in Santa Barbara with his wife, Wendy. It was not until he returned to Santa Barbara from Jackson, Wyoming, around 1991 that I came to know him on a more personal level. Lance lived in a trailer that was parked in the driveway behind our house. Somehow, he found time to take my son and his friends surfing, skateboarding, and golfing. His two sons came to visit in the summer each year, and I was always amazed that the three of them found comfort and happiness living in that tiny trailer space. He taught them the wonder of nature through surfing, sailing, skiing, and skateboarding. Volunteering his time and energy, he has worked with Direct Relief International building disaster shelters at the local schools. He also helped to build a playground for the city. He has given of his time freely to design and build stage sets for productions at my school.

I have lived with Lance for the past seven years. I do not know Michael Lund. I only know Lance McCain, and, while I will learn to call him Michael, I will continue to see those qualities that have made him Lance in my heart and mind.

Mike's attorney, Rick Troberman, advised the Court that, at the time of his recruitment into the conspiracy, Mr. Lund had been down on his luck. Lund had lived the first 42 years of his life without committing a crime, served as a deputy sheriff in San Diego, lived in the fast lane during his freestyle skiing years, but fell on hard times working as a yacht salesmen with not much success. He had just sold his prized Porsche 914 to James Turner, a skiing companion of his and the so-called offloading expert for the drug conspiracy, because Lund could no longer make his car payments. Troberman tried to distance Lund from Turner, who received a three-year sentence, indicating that Turner had rented U-Haul trucks, driven one across country, and had supplied all the cash via David Victorson and Eric Hale to Lund to buy the Joli and the house on Sequim Bay. Troberman said, "Mike Lund has lived far better a life as Steven McCain, average citizen, than he ever did as Mike Lund, ski celebrity. Mr. Lund is now 65 years old. He has grandchildren he has never seen before. I understand that the Court has to send a message, but I think the message Mr. Lund has sent over the past 23 years is he has paid a price for this." Lund had apparently not been charged or convicted of anything during his status as a fugitive for 23 years, except being found in contempt of court in connection with divorce proceedings in Arapahoe County, where his downfall occurred.

Assistant U.S. Attorney Ron Friedman, representing the government at the sentencing, admitted that he "was a senior in high school when this event occurred and was probably hoping the boat would succeed at that time." He countered Mr. Troberman's arguments by stating that Mr. Lund had not exactly led a crime-free life the last 23 years, in that he had acquired a false and fraudulent passport, used social security numbers belonging to others (both federal felonies), and used a false identity to further his anonymity. He could not be charged with these crimes, because the Statute of Limitations for charging him had run out. Friedman argued that Lund only sought to withdraw from the conspiracy when he was heading towards the Helena Star with the Knik Wind tug pulling the Chignik barge and saw the Coast Guard already escorting the freighter back toward the Strait of Juan de Fuca. Of seemingly great importance, Friedman emphasized that Lund only admitted to offloading between one or two tons of marijuana from the Helena Star. This statement by Lund was clearly false in that other witnesses including David Victorson stated or testified to their own detriment that thirteen tons were offloaded from the freighter before its seizure. In his Sentencing Memorandum to Judge Coughenour, Friedman wrote:

> Making a sentencing recommendation in a case like this is not an easy task, due largely to the passage of time and the truism that if Lund was to be sentenced today for the offense

as if it had been committed today, he would be looking at a guideline sentence of between 24 to 30 years imprisonment. However, it is clear the sentencing structure in effect at the time the offense was committed governs. Accordingly, in making its recommendation, the government is guided by the sentencing structure then in effect, the sentences meted out to others, and the role and participation by this defendant. In considering these factors, the government recommends a sentence of 36 months imprisonment.

Mike Lund wrote a three-page letter to Judge Coughenour substantially minimizing his involvement in the conspiracy. He said, "Of course, no one ever told me that the Joli was going to be used to meet an ocean-going freighter. I helped to take the marijuana off of the Helena Star on only one occasion, refusing to destroy the Joli in order to make it more suitable (by removing the interior cabins and bulkheads). I also agreed to buy a barge and a tugboat and deliver them to Port Angeles, but I had decided by that time that that was going to be the end of my involvement with this group." Actually, Lund was at the helm of the Knik Wind tug with barge in tow when it headed out the Strait of Juan de Fuca to meet the Helena Star to offload the remaining 37 tons. When he observed the Helena Star being escorted by the Coast Guard in his direction, he split for Canadian waters. That was the precise time that he decided to withdraw from the conspiracy—when the conspiracy had already been shut down by the seizure of the mothership. To his credit, however, Lund did admit that he had allowed his "desire to have a beautiful high-tech sailboat at my command (with hopes of ultimately owning it) cloud my judgment to the point that I became involved in this smuggling scheme." This was to some extent confirmed by coconspirators. Before the tug and barge were purchased by Lund, he believed in the adequacy of the Joli and was in favor of making multiple trips to meet the Helena Star, versus getting something larger, because the Joli was something that he wanted to retain after the mission was accomplished.

Mike Lund's son by his third wife, Wendy Starcher, Michael, Jr., a 19-year old student at Colorado State University, wrote a particularly compelling letter to Judge Coughenour. The Judge said, "I read it, and it brought tears to my eyes." Michael, Jr., concluded his remarks by writing:

My father has taught me that no matter how hard and how much it hurts, one must be honest. He has shown me that a humble man is one that others can trust and respect, someone who is known for what he has done in his life and not how great he did it. I've learned modesty as more of a word, modesty as a trait that is inherent within us all, and when applied a great tool to achieve satisfaction in the world. It is with my father's guiding words that I embrace the hardships and obstacles of life as times to learn and grow. It is thanks to him that I do not fear mistakes, but rather know that through mistakes you can make miracles.

I write you this letter in hopes of perhaps sharing with you a glimpse of my father as all that he is and all that he will forever be. For his is a spirit that is something my words cannot possibly do justice. As I continue to take my baby steps into the world, I carry the words and thoughts of my father with me. I use them as a guide when I get lost and need his comforting counsel. And when I grow up, I wish to become a man like him.

Standing at the podium with his attorney waiting for his judgement to be pronounced was a 65-year-old, slight, gray-haired, bespectacled man—quite a contrast from the celebrated, dashing skier that Eric and Heidi remembered from their youth. Mr. Lund addressed the Judge before his sentence was imposed. Judge Coughenour then followed Mr. Troberman's recommendation and imposed a prison sentence of one year and one day, also recommending to the Bureau of Prisons that the sentence be served at the Federal Prison Camp in Lompoc, California. That prison camp was the same camp where Robert Moran had served his sentence. The difference in a sentence of one year and a sentence of one year and one day is that a sentence of one year and one day accrues good time and all but assures a defendant that he will get out in about ten months—perhaps just in time for spring skiing with his children, back in his life. Lund became the tenth and final person convicted regarding the conspiracy to import 50 tons of marijuana into the United States. Judge Coughenour's parting words to the defendant were: "You might tell your son, Michael, he saved you a couple years' time."

Michael Lund's case, however, would not be the last criminal case decided regarding the infamous M/V Helena Star.

20

THE DERELICT— A HORRIBLE WAY TO DIE

S INCE THE M/V HELENA STAR WAS SOLD AT AUCTION IN 1979, she had received little respect. At one point, she had been seen moored in the ship canal near the Chittenden locks with a tree growing out of its hold. She had gone through a series of owners before winding up moored in Tacoma, Washington, waiting to be scrapped. In January 2013, the old freighter, tied to a dock, began to sink in the Hylebos Waterway. By afternoon, gawkers could still see her stern sticking out of the water at Mason Marina. Chained up next to the 161-foot Helena Star, the 130-foot Golden West fishing boat was being pulled down by the freighter and barely above water also. Supposedly both vessels were owned by Mason Marine, but it had filed for bankruptcy in 2012.

Directives to take responsibility for both vessels to the supposed owners by state and federal agencies were ignored. A Department of Natural Resources (DNR) spokeswoman said that Mason may have recently sold the vessels and also said, "We're not sure really who the owner is. Finding out who that is, is going to be challenging." It was apparently later learned that the Helena Star had been acquired in 2010 by California investors who hired Stephen Mason of Mason

Marine to scrap the vessel on his property adjacent to the Hylebos Waterway. Mason did not finish the job, or hardly even started the job, instead leaving the vessel dormant on his property. She continued to deteriorate.

The old girl slid slowly into its temporary grave on January 25, 2013—an ignoble death by drowning—spilling 640 gallons of diesel fuel and oil into Tacoma waters. The Golden West fishing boat went down quietly with her. A spill-response team with Ballard Drilling put oil containment booms in place. Two months later, the Washington Department of Ecology ordered the ship to be removed from the Hylebos Waterway. Federal oil-spill money and funding approved by the Washington State Legislature after the spill was expected to pay for the removal of the abandoned freighter from the Waterway. DNR took custody of both vessels in August. The Golden West was moved out of the waterway on October 16. In December, contractor crews tried to raise the Helena Star using a 700-ton crane and barge but could not lift the hull with a single crane without causing further damage.

In January 2014, Stephen Mason, the owner of Mason Marine Services, was charged in Washington state court with the gross misdemeanors of causing the Helena Star to become abandoned or derelict and discharging polluting matters into state waters. Those charges carried maximum penalties of up to one year in jail and a maximum fine of $10,000. Restitution could also be imposed. Any restitution paid would go to the state's Derelict Vessel Removal Account. Mason eventually accepted responsibility and was sentenced to twenty days of confinement, which he was allowed to serve on electronic home detention, and two years of probation. He was also ordered to pay $300,000 to the State toward the total cost of $1.25 million for the cleanup and removal of the sunken vessel. He has been making monthly modest payments toward his restitution obligation, but he did file for bankruptcy in 2012 and did have to close his business down, so the remaining amount owing is substantial. As part of his plea bargain, he also agreed to help get restitution from other Helena Star investors from California. None, however, have stepped up to the plate. Mason was the last of eleven defendants to be charged criminally in connection with the saga of the MV Helena Star.

The United States Department of Justice also got into the legal fray. It eventually filed a civil lawsuit in the United States District Court in Tacoma, Washington, naming six different owners as defendants, including Stephen Mason, and claiming unpaid damages sustained by the United States exceeding $633,898.06. As of early 2020, that case was still awaiting trial.

Plans were drawn up by the State for another attempt to raise the Helena Star from the dead but had to be timed to minimize impacts to fish and wildlife habitat in the Hylebos Waterway. According to a press release from the Washington State Attorney General's Office, on July 22, 2014, a new contractor, Global Diving and Salvage, engaged two floating cranes to raise the sunken freighter and pump the water out of it. Their efforts were successful. The Helena Star was destined for the inevitable oblivion of the scrapheap. The coordinated response team also included the Washington State Department of Natural

Resources, Washington State Department of Ecology, U.S. Coast Guard, and Tacoma Fire Department. The sinking of the freighter wasn't all bad as the press release went on to say, "The sinking of the Helena Star shines a light on the continuing problem of derelict and abandoned vessels in Washington State. We commend the federal, state, local, public, and private partners that successfully brought an end to this unfortunate and environmentally destructive incident."

Escorted by the 62-foot landing craft Prudhoe Bay, the tugboat Red Bluff towed the rusty Helena Star out of the Hylebos Waterway in Tacoma, up Puget Sound, through the Hiram Chittenden locks and into Lake Union to the Stabbert Yacht and Ship Drydock for scrapping. The old girl was returned to the same lake in Seattle where she had been auctioned off in 1979. Throughout the journey, a four-person crew remained onboard the disrespected freighter to monitor leaks and to assist with mooring lines. The amount of money recovered by Stabbert for the scrap metal—though not nearly enough to pay for the anticipated $2 million salvage and cleanup process—would go back to the state Derelict Vessel Removal Program.

The ill-fated voyage of the Helena Star started when it went through the enormous locks of the Panama Canal in 1978 and ended unceremoniously in 2014 when she was towed through the Chittenden locks in Seattle to be scrapped. The last voyage of the M/V Helena Star was over.

EPILOGUE

ABOUT THREE YEARS AFTER SAN FRANCISCO ATTORNEY Robert Moran was released from prison, but probably still under investigation by the U.S. Attorney's Office in San Francisco, the former attorney's dead body was found on a beach in Marin County, dead of a "probable suicide" on his birthday in 1991. He had been shot in the head and bled to death with a firearm close to his body. Bill Urich, an attorney who had worked in Moran's law office, was on the phone with a mutual friend of his and Moran's, George Mattusch. Urich, who had little contact with Moran since he had been released from prison, inquired about Moran, because no one had seen him for some time. Mattusch responded that Moran was lying next to him on a slab in the Marin County morgue. He had gone to identify the body. A wake was held for Mr. Moran a few days later at the San Francisco Yacht Club.

Guillermo Cooke, the thug who turned into the government's most valuable witness against Robert Moran, was later convicted of another drug offense, did time, and was deported.

Shortly after hearing the news of Moran's death, Assistant U.S. Attorney Steve Schroeder, who had prosecuted Moran, was in Judge Voorhees courtroom, the same Judge who had sentenced Moran. Before the Judge came out on the bench, Mr. Schroeder had an offhand conversation with Elva McGregor, the Judge's in-court Deputy Clerk. She was well-loved in the United States Courthouse in Seattle and known for her direct approach to attorneys. Schroeder told her about Moran's apparent suicide. She responded, "Steve, you ruined his life." Questions still persist as to whether Moran's demise was a result of suicide or an elimination by other members or non-members of the drug conspiracy, known or unknown, American or foreign born—cartel hit men known as sicarios.

Sometime after Robert Moran died, Mr. Schroeder received a phone call from Eric Hale, David Victorson's good friend, gofer, and coconspirator. He had received five years in prison, fled to Bolivia with Victorson, was captured, testified against Moran at his trial in 1983, served his time, and was on the equivalent of parole. He was married to a schoolteacher, working as a carpenter, had a daughter, and was trying to buy a house—pursuing the American dream. Besides having to serve prison time, Hale and Victorson were both fined $30,000. Victorson had paid his fine, but Hale did not have the resources at his disposal like Victorson to pay off his entire fine. Hale had an outstanding lien as a result, which was preventing him from obtaining a loan to buy a house. He asked Mr. Schroeder if there was any way that his fine could be dissolved so he could buy a house. Schroeder called Hale's parole officer and obtained glowing reports on Hale's "rehabilitation." By this time Judge Voorhees had died, so Schroeder went to U.S. District Court Judge Barbara Rothstein requesting that Hale's fine be forgiven. Judge Rothstein granted his motion. Hale called Schroeder and expressed his deep appreciation for what he had done. A couple years later, Schroeder received a phone call from Hale's wife indicating that her husband had just passed away from colon cancer.

On March 14, 2013, the grievance committee of the United States District Court in Manhattan suspended Eric Hale's flamboyant former attorney, Ivan Fisher, from practicing law in that court. This Court had been the site of many of his celebrated trials. The committee found that Fisher had improperly kept money belonging to one of his clients.

Starting In 1996, Ivan Fisher had been a tenant of Jeffrey Epstein, the disgraced financier and pedophile, who in 2019 was charged with sex trafficking, accused of sexually abusing young girls, and allegedly committed suicide while in custody awaiting trial. It was because of Prince Andrew's close friendship with Epstein that the Queen of England gave the Prince permission to "step back from his public duties for the foreseeable future." Beginning in 1992, Epstein rented the former mansion of the deputy consul of Iran on the Upper East Side of Manhattan for $15,000 a month. It had been taken over by the U.S. State Department during the revolution in Iran. Epstein was sued by his landlord, the U.S. government, in United States District Court in 1996, for failing to pay rent on time and later subletting the palatial residence without the State Department's permission to Ivan Fisher for $20,000 a month. Once the State Department terminated Epstein's lease, Fisher stopped paying rent. *The New York Daily News* described the mansion's ostentatiousness: "carved oak doors, a white marble foyer, three kitchens, three bedrooms, a library with floor-to-ceiling bookcases, a steam room, 19th-century chandeliers, brass sconces, and a white marble central staircase." The government also sued Fisher and several other lawyers, who were subletting office space in the opulent mansion from Fisher. The tenants, including Fisher, were eventually evicted and all moved out in July 1998.

Robert Moran and Ivan Fisher weren't the only lawyers involved in the Helena Star case who had problems with their continuing ability to practice law. Sometime after assisting Assistant U.S. Attorney Steve Schroeder in prosecuting Moran, Assistant U.S. Attorney Bill Hogan moved from Seattle to the United States Attorney's Office in Chicago, where he had grown up. He became responsible for a wave—actually more like a tsunami—of prosecutions that started in 1989 of the El Rukn gang. One judge called it "the most infamous gang of organized criminals that Chicago has seen since the days of Al Capone." One man finally brought them down—Assistant U.S. Attorney Bill Hogan. By late 1992, Hogan had netted 54 convictions, with many defendants facing decades or life in prison. In 1986, El Rukn generals

Nathson Fields and Earl Hawkins were convicted in a nonjury trial before then Cook County Circuit Judge Thomas Maloney of murdering two men. They were sentenced to death. Fields sought a new trial, alleging that Judge Maloney accepted a $10,000 bribe to acquit Hawkins and him, but then returned the money and convicted both after becoming suspicious that the FBI was investigating him. Judge Maloney was charged with accepting bribes to fix five cases, including three murder cases.

Many El Rukn gang convictions were set aside, as Jeffrey Toobin reported in the *New Yorker* magazine, "because of one of the most significant cases of prosecutorial misconduct in the history of the Justice Department—prosecutorial misconduct by Bill Hogan. The convictions have evaporated because of accusations that Hogan's cooperating witnesses (coconspirators) were given drugs and alcohol and allowed to have sex in prison and sex in the prosecutors' offices, and that the prosecutors condoned these practices and then covered them up." A memo prepared by an agent of the Bureau of Alcohol, Tobacco and Firearms (ATF) indicated that Hogan's office suite in a building separate from the main U.S. Attorney's Office in Chicago functioned like a frat house. El Rukn witnesses, who were supposedly in custody, even answered the phones saying, "ATF."

Bill Hogan had been a rising Justice Department star since his transfer from Seattle to Chicago. With the possibility of losing his job and license to practice law in the background, Hogan was assigned to the prosecution of Judge Maloney for accepting bribes during his thirteen-year career as a judge. On April 16, 1993, Maloney became the first judge in Illinois history to be convicted of fixing murder cases (three), and El Rukn general Nathson Fields, whom Judge Maloney had sentenced to death, won a new trial. Three months after his successful prosecution of Judge Maloney, Hogan was placed on paid administrative leave while the subject of an investigation by the Justice Department's Office of Professional Responsibility. He was eventually fired but fought to clear his name. Two years later, he was ordered reinstated to his job at the United States Attorney's Office in Chicago by an administrative law judge who found no convincing evidence of wrongdoing by Hogan. He continued to work in the United States Attorney's Office well into his 60s.

After being released from prison, American drug kingpin, David Victorson, went into an intensive drug treatment program and became a drug counselor for young people. He was offered a marketing position in a new hospital program in Orange County, California, that had a wing set up for drug and alcohol treatment with beds for both adults and adolescents. He was elevated to Vice President of marketing for the parent company and got married in 1989. He and his wife, Claudia, had one child. Victorson soon became addicted to high-stakes gambling, but somehow he had time to coach his son's soccer team. After his son's graduation from high school, Victorson and Claudia moved to Washington, D.C. According to Victorson, during his career in the drug treatment field, he ended up developing, owning, and operating inpatient and outpatient healthcare programs in California, Delaware, Florida, and Ohio for both adult and adolescent patients suffering from addiction and underlying psychiatric problems. Victorson would speak at various twelve-step meetings, halfway houses, and homeless shelters throughout the District of Columbia.

As for other conspirators, Mike Lund is now in his 80s and resides on a sailboat in Ventura Bay, California. His old girlfriend, Patricia Karnik, has resided for many years in the Jackson Hole area and currently publishes a magazine catering to the real estate industry. She continues to attend yearly champion freestyle skier reunions.

Americans now have an insatiable appetite for avocados. Between 2001 and 2018, average annual consumption of avocados in the United States increased from two pounds to almost seven and a half pounds per person. The Mexican drug cartels have diversified. Mexico's huge avocado industry, located largely in the state of Michoacán, has grabbed the attention of the drug cartels located there, leading to forcible takeover of land and much attendant violence. Homicides reached an all-time high in Mexico in 2019. The city of Tijuana closed out the year with 2,185 murders—a reduction of 321 homicides from the record breaking 2018, which earned it the title of most violent city in the world by a Mexican nonprofit advocacy group. Part of the problem in Mexico is that only one in ten homicides are solved and the conviction rate is less than six percent. In October 2019, Sinaloa Cartel gunmen virtually took control of the city of Culiacan on Mexico's west coast to free the son of Sinaloa cartel drug lord Joaquin "El Chapo" Guzman. The cartel's operation was a success with Ovidio Guzman, the son, being released to the streets. Luck ran out for his father. After at least two highly publicized escapes from Mexican prisons, "El Chapo," meaning "Shorty" in Spanish, remains salted away in a prison in the United States for the rest of his life.

Americans' monumental appetite for marijuana has increased unabated. The legal sale of recreational cannabis began January 1, 2020, in Illinois, with customers spending about $3.2 million on the first day and more than $10 million over the first five days.

After hearing my client, Captain Rubies, talk in glowing terms about the city where he lived, I became enchanted with the idea of visiting Colombia and the walled city of Cartagena. It is generally considered today to be the most beautiful Spanish colonial city in the Americas. I had written the captain a couple of letters, the first in 2008 and the second several years later, to see if he was still in Cartagena, so that I could visit him and possibly take him and his wife out to dinner. I had his address from 1978 but had no idea if he was still there or even if he was still alive. After all, he was 47 years old when I met him in 1978, which would make him 77 in 2008. I received no response from my letters to him, but neither letter was returned to me. I was not surprised in the least as people frequently move and perhaps, I thought, mail delivery in Colombia was not predictable as in the United States.

I eventually made plans for a two-week vacation to Colombia with my wife in early 2015, planning to stay primarily in Bogota and Cartagena. I booked two hotels in Cartagena, one on the Bocagrande Peninsula, where Roman had had a condominium, and one in the historic walled city. The hotel in Bocagrande was the historic Hotel

Caribe, already well known before some members of the U.S. Secret Service made it even more famous during President Obama's trip there—by cavorting with a select number of eye-popping prostitutes. I selected the Hotel Caribe because of its proximity to the extremely old address that I had for Roman and its access to the beach.

Cartagena appeared to be prosperous and safe. It was clearly as beautiful a city as my three Colombian clients over the years had told me. It met my expectations in spades. Colombia was clearly in the process of putting behind it the outrageously negative aspects of Americans' insatiable appetite for marijuana and cocaine. Marijuana was becoming legalized in several states and was being home grown in the United States under ideal conditions, so there was no longer any great necessity to import marijuana from the Far East, Mexico, or South America. Our only brush with uncertainty as to Colombia's safety occurred when we walked into a splendid restaurant in Cartagena to check it out to see if it might be a good place to have lunch or dinner. A Toyota Land Cruiser with heavily tinted windows, the cartel's vehicle of choice, pulled up to the curb in front of the restaurant. Two gentlemen, armed with AK 47s, got out of the vehicle and ambled into the same restaurant, apparently to check it out as well—for its safety for their passenger still in the back seat of the Land Cruiser. We decided to come back later.

On about the third day at the Hotel Caribe, I told my wife that I was going to take a walk while she had a siesta and that I would be back soon. Armed with an address 35 years old that I had for the captain in the El Laguito area of Bocagrande, I set out on a mission to find his condominium to see if there was any chance he would still be living there. I felt my odds were extremely slim. I knew the condominium was on the seventeenth floor of a high-rise building, of which there were many, most of which were probably built with the proceeds of smuggling Colombian Gold and cocaine. I went less than two blocks from the Hotel Caribe before approaching a Colombian gentleman, who pointed out the building I was looking for and directed me to its entrance just a short walk away.

I entered a nicely appointed lobby and contacted a man working at the front desk. He spoke no English. The lobby was at the base of an open-air atrium that reached for the sky. By this time, we had sold our condominium in Cabo San Lucas, Mexico, after eighteen years, and I had lost most of the limited amount of Spanish that I had learned many years earlier but had not retained. After going back and forth and many hand gestures, somehow, I was able to glean that Captain Rubies no longer lived there—he had died. The gentleman manning the desk, however, said that Roman's son still lived in the same condominium and he would ring him and let him know I was in the lobby. He rang Roman's son, spoke to him, and directed me toward a sitting area.

Shortly thereafter, an enormous man exited the elevator and approached me with a serious look on his face. About age 40 at the time, he obviously had no idea who I was or what business I might have with a dead man. As he lumbered toward me, I began to have second thoughts about embarking on this adventure, but I would rather regret the things I've done than the things I haven't done. I introduced myself to him in English and was happy to find that he spoke perfect English and worked in a local hotel. We sat down and I told him that I had represented his father beginning in 1978.

Domingo was only two years old when his father was captured on the high seas of the North Pacific and five years old when his father returned to Cartagena from captivity in the United States. He knew that his father had gotten into some serious trouble, but the captain and his wife never wanted to talk about it. It was a black mark on an otherwise well-lived life. He invited me up to his condominium on the seventeenth floor and introduced me to his wife, who spoke no English. He took me out on the veranda to show me the extraordinary view. I could see the vast swimming pool and terrace of the Hotel Caribe below, where earlier in the morning we encountered sensationally, beautiful toucans trying to steal our breakfast. Domingo's condominium was neat and tidy. His father had died in 1997 from cirrhosis of the liver and his mother, whom

I had met in Dallas, had died in a car accident two years before his father. He showed me photographs of his parents and of a tugboat that his father had purchased in Spain after his release from prison and sailed to Cartagena to work it in the Caribbean.

We parted amicably after a compelling and pleasant conversation. He was clearly proud of his father's accomplishments during his life—with one exception—and obviously shocked at my appearance in the lobby, but glad that I had filled in some blanks. My trip to the astonishing and only walled city in South America brought a fascinating closure to my involvement in the case of the M/V Helena Star.

ABOUT THE AUTHOR

S TEWART RILEY lives in Seattle with his wife and Nova Scotia Duck Tolling Retriever. After graduating from the University of Washington Law School in 1969, he began practicing law in Seattle as a Senior Deputy Prosecutor in the King County Prosecutor's Office for three years before embarking on a lifetime career as a criminal defense attorney, specializing in cases having international aspects and implications. During his career he has represented individuals from over

Author photograph by Jessica Cantlin

40 countries. Mr. Riley has been admitted to practice law before the United States Supreme Court as well as three international criminal tribunals, including the International Criminal Court in The Hague, located in the Netherlands, and is well known for his successful defense of a Blackwater security contractor investigated for the shooting and killing of a bodyguard for the Vice President of Iraq in 2006. He is an avid outdoorsman and tennis player.

www.stewriley.com